GRAPPLER

Memoirs of a Masked Madman

Lynn Denton and Joe Vithayathil

Grappler: Memoirs of a Masked Madman

Authors: Lynn Denton and Joe Vithayathil

Photographs courtesy Edward Lynn Denton

Cover Art: David Sherman

Printed in the United States of America

First Printing, 2014

ISBN-13: 978-0692246085
ISBN-10: 0692246088

Throwback Press
Beaverton, OR USA
grapplerbook@gmail.com
Grapplerbook.com

DEDICATION

I dedicate this book to the memory of my father, Edward Howard Denton.

FOREWORD

To whom it may concern… and to my brother, Lynn Denton:
Lynn Denton is the epitome of a man who has the right to say "I paved that highway"… but never would.

The truth… and business of wrestling: There is a whole clan of men who most people have no idea of their contribution to the sport of professional wrestling. I remember "Lenny" Denton as a skinny ass little kid in North Carolina driving Ric Flair's car because Flair lost his license… and Flair's car does not go below 80… sweat running down his face like beads… breath still smelling like baby formula as he passes Flair a beer, while trying to haul ass to the next town….Baby Jesus.
While I was sneaking late into an arena one night, I stopped and hid behind the curtain to see who had a riot going on. I love riots, so I stopped to watch. Lenny was having a blast, blood from head to toe, taking brains--not names. Whose? We still don't know… I watched him struggling like a cock rooster, yellin' the Rebel Yell and it dawned on me that "The Grappler's" got some talent.

A friendship of thirty-eight years began, which I'd like to stop now.

I'm not gonna tell you all the stories of "The Grappler" because they're in the book…and yes, he is guilty as charged. But for you people who don't know, when you wrestle with a mask, no one sees your facial expressions. No one notices if you're in pain. And you can't sell as easy. The Grappler had to use his arms, legs, and body to sell. If the audience can't see a face, it's harder to sell, but Lenny was the best at it.

That's how you know Lynn Denton is the real deal.

"The Grappler" and his generation who worked on top and booked different territories received an education that was second to none. Lenny was hired and trained by Harley Race and Bill Watts. Two bad men. Harley being the good kind of bad. Bill? You figure it out. But still, hell of an education.

I will make this story short, but you're gonna love it. So now... The Grappler is booking Portland Wrestling, and I was brought in to help. Lenny was booking and I was running the ship. Literally.

My agent called me. Said, "Wanna do the Love Boat Anniversary show? It's six weeks on the Love Boat in the Atlantic." Rod has a decision to make.

It seemed to me that if Hot Rod and "The Grappler" divided forces, we could conquer. Since Lenny had the Pacific covered... figured I would take care of the Atlantic.

So, I'm on the Love Boat and it's Portland Wrestling time. I pointed to the Captain's phone sitting next to the lobster and said, "Hand me that phone. I gotta call Lenny. I hope they bring out that ice cream with fire on it again."

PROBLEM in the Pacific, Lenny tells me. Billy Jack Haynes decides to grow a dick. Now credit where credit is due... Billy Jack is one big, strong, tough boy. If his cup was filled with pencils you could slam your hand down and never get pierced. But anyways, Billy Jack was being an ass and Lenny tells me that he is bucking like a bull in the dressing room. After I listened to the problem, I slowly rose up out of my chair on the deck of "The Love Boat" to make one hundred percent sure that I was still in the Atlantic Ocean.

I made the business decision: "LENNY! GO FIRE THE BASTARD, AND TELL HIM I SAID SO!"

And as always, "The Grappler", Lenny, my brother... got the job done.

Lenny, thank you for the honor of allowing me to express in your book what I've wanted to express to you for as long as I've known you:

I love you with all my heart.

Ever Forward,
Roddy Piper

PROLOGUE

April 18, 1981
New Orleans, Louisiana

"You're going over."

"WHAT?"

The Cowboy glared at me- halfway pissed and halfway amused. It was the happiest I'd ever seen him.

"Do I really have to spell this out?" he asked. "You're beating Andre the Giant and Dusty Rhodes."

Holy Fuck.

In a daze, I staggered out of the office, in search of my tag-team partner. When I shared the news, Scott Irwin was equally stunned.

"Do you think Watts was joking?" he asked.

"Have you ever heard that sumbitch joke about anything?" I grabbed my silver and black mask, loosening the strings in the back. "Where's Frank? We have to go over the finish."

The Louisiana Superdome had hosted Super Bowls, Sugar Bowls- even The Rolling Stones. But tonight 22,000 pro wrestling fans were on hand to see the hottest promotion in the United States. "Cowboy" Bill Watts' Mid-South Wrestling was the talk of the wrestling world. And I was despised in every quarter of the Crescent City.

"Eat shit Grappler!"

As I walked towards the ring, the insults bounced right off me, alongside the occasional wad of toilet paper or empty beer cup. None of that stuff could break my concentration; I was fixing to slay a giant and crush the American Dream.

Andre the Giant and Dusty Rhodes were a pro wrestling dream team-perhaps the two biggest stars in the world. Andre was already an international icon and the sport's top attraction. Dusty was America's most beloved professional wrestler: a blue-collar champion who captivated fans with his soulful interviews and "bionic" elbow.

The two superstars had come to New Orleans for a wrestling extravaganza: a one-night tournament to crown Mid-South tag-team champions. The tournament bracket read like a future Hall-of-Fame ballot. Participants included the Wild Samoans, Fabulous Freebirds, Jake Roberts, Ernie Ladd, and NOLA's favorite son, the Junkyard Dog. But even with this field of heavy hitters, most fans had no doubt: Andre and Dusty were the favorites.

But I hadn't come to play favorites.

My family knew me as Lynn Denton, but the wrestling world called me "The Grappler". I was just 22 and already the promotion's top singles champion, holding the North American Heavyweight title. I was a barrel-chested 240 pounds in long black tights and a monochromatic mask. I had won the title seven months prior, and since then I had beaten every top star by hook or by crook (usually by crook).

My partner Scott also wore a mask and was called "The Super Destroyer". An agile mountain of muscle, he was the first wrestler that I ever saw perform a top-rope suplex. Our manager Frank Dusek was a former wrestler who now annoyed fans with his condescending promos and outside interference. The people hated us and they let us know it:

"Kill him Dream!"

"Fuck You Grappler!"

The bell rang and Dusty and I locked up. I tossed him to the ropes and he dropped me with a shoulder tackle. I popped right back up and sent him to the ropes again. This time, Dusty grabbed the ropes, stopped, and shook his ample rear in my direction. The fans went nuts. Hell, back in 1981 Dusty Rhodes could blow his nose and bring a crowd to its feet.

We locked up again.

"Here comes the elbow baby."

When Dusty whispered his cue, I shot him back to the ropes and this time he dropped me with his trademark spot. As soon as I hit the mat- WHAM!- another elbow across the chest. The Superdome came unglued as Dusty tagged in the big man.

"ANDRE! ANDRE!"

The crowd was hungry for blood, but they didn't know the ugly truth- Andre and I were friends. Whenever he was in Mid-South we rode together, and I spent many a late night watching the Giant consume ungodly amounts of alcohol. He was a lovely man and a big teddy bear.

He also scared the shit out of me.

"Backdrop boss." Andre called everyone boss. It was somewhat ironic because he was always the one calling the shots.

I came off the ropes and Andre dropped his head. As I approached, he reared up and tossed me into the air for the longest backdrop of my life. Seriously, it felt like I was in the air for twenty seconds. I just kept going up, up, up… until gravity found me.

WHAM!

In wrestling the term "sell" means to convince an audience that you were really hurt by a wrestling move. Well, I didn't have to "sell" that backdrop.

"Jesus Andre," I would have said more but

a) I just had the wind knocked out of me and

b) Andre was grabbing my tights with a hand that resembled a catcher's mitt.

"UP!"

I swear to God, that man pressed me overhead with one hand and then dropped me across his knee. I didn't jump or do anything to lighten the load. He just tossed me around New Orleans like some old Mardi Gras beads.

"ANDRE! ANDRE!"

9

The fans knew I was done. Andre lumbered methodically towards my limp carcass. He bent over, grabbed my mask and lifted me to my feet.

And here's where things got interesting.

If he wanted to, Andre could have pummeled me all over the Superdome, thrown me down Bourbon Street and dumped me in the Gulf of Mexico. And if he didn't like somebody, that's exactly what he would do.

But Andre liked me. What's more- he respected me. I was one of wrestling's bright, young stars. I was a champion who had paid his dues and gone about business the right way. And that's why Andre the Giant let me rake my fingers across his eyes and kick the ever-loving shit out of him.

"Get him! Get him!"

Frank howled encouragement from ringside as Scott and I took turns stomping and abusing the fallen Frenchman. But of course, you can't keep a good Giant down forever.

"BOOM!"

Andre ran my head into Scott's and we both went down. He tagged in Dusty, and the American Dream was ready to roll.

Elbow. Elbow. Right hand. Elbow.

Dusty cleaned house as Andre came to his senses. The furious giant grabbed all 290 pounds of the Super Destroyer and dragged him to the arena floor. The referee tried in vain to separate the behemoths, leaving Dusty and I alone in the ring. With the Dream temporarily distracted by the melee I nailed him in the ribs with a high knee. Down he went.

"Here it comes!"

I began kicking the mat with my right boot. The Superdome responded with a chorus of boos. All Mid-South fans knew about The Grappler's "loaded boot". As it was explained on television, my kicking the mat loaded the front of the boot with some sort of illegal object. After that, one kick was always an instant knockout. The boot had helped me win the Heavyweight Title, and now it was ready to drop the Dream.

"No way daddy!"

Dusty caught my foot just before the kick landed. He wagged his finger at me as the crowd roared its approval. Finally, The American Dream was going to put an end to The Grappler's evil ways. Until…

"Hey Dusty!"

Frank leapt on to the ring apron and waved his hands at the Dream. Now, every long-time wrestling fan knows that, in these situations, a "babyface" is legally required to drop everything and slap around the loudmouth manager that dared to distract him (I'm pretty sure that's in the first chapter of the pro wrestling rulebook). And so, Dusty stunned me with one punch, grabbed Frank by his lapels and prepared to fulfill his heroic duty. But before Big Dust could unload another right hand, the devious Dusek tossed a cloud of white powder in his face. Dusty staggered back. As far as the crowd was concerned, he was temporarily blind.

But I could see just fine.

WHAM!

One shot from the boot and the Dream was on his back. In another example of pro wrestling's perfect timing, the referee was right back in the ring to count the 1…. 2…. 3.

22,000 jaws hit the floor. Unlike today, there was no music or pyrotechnics for the winners. Just stunned silence.

"Your winners… Super Destroyer and The Grappler!"

I dropped to my knees and looked up at the domed ceiling in amazement. *I did it. I did it!* Yes, this was pro wrestling and I knew going in to the match that I was going to pin Dusty, but the moment still felt incredibly surreal. After all, I had defeated two wrestling deities in one match and by the end of the night I would own every major title in Mid-South Wrestling. This was my crowning achievement; what I had suffered, bled and nearly died for the past five years. I *knew* that this victory would be a giant step towards pro wrestling immortality… soon every fan in America would know my name.

At least that's what I thought back then.

Now, the year is 2014 and most current wrestling fans have never heard of The Grappler and even fewer have heard of Lynn Denton. Can you blame them? After all, I never fought at Starrcade or Wrestlemania. I never became an action figure. I never worked for Vince McMahon at all.

So just who the hell am I?

Well, I'm the villain that helped Jake Roberts invent the DDT. I'm also the greenhorn that drove Ric Flair across the Carolinas and the monster that choked Bret Hart with a chicken. I'm the champion that set records in legendary promotions and the also-ran that taught the Ultimate Warrior how to perform a press slam. I was Harley Race's booker, Roddy Piper's right hand man and Muhammad Ali's favorite white supremacist.

In short, I'm proof that not every legend wears a Hall of Fame ring.

This is my story, a journey through a bygone era when icons wrestled five-star matches in one-horse towns and a foolish kid could chase his dreams from Texas to Germany to the Great Northwest. These were the days when you could be murdered for attacking your opponent (almost happened), disfigured with a single slap (happened) or stalked in a locker room by a lunatic in pink underwear (trying to forget that happened). If you somehow survived those obstacles, you could become a widely-admired professional wrestler whose work continues to inspire star athletes to this very day. Yes, that also happened and if you don't believe me, just keep on reading.

For years I had a saying:

"They've got a name for you when you're the greatest wrestler in wrestling today! They don't call you a great wrestler... they call you THE GRAPPLER!"

Now it's time to show you why.

CHAPTER ONE

A HUMBLE KID

I spent years telling wrestling fans how great I was, but I was born Humble with a capital H. Humble, Texas is the Houston suburb where I grew up. The H is silent so it's pronounced "Umble". A Texas thing I guess.

Back in the early 70s it was a lower-middle class neighborhood, or upper-lower class- whichever one is poorer. My dad worked construction, but we were still on welfare and our diet included a healthy dose of government cheese. Of course, if my parents didn't have six kids maybe we wouldn't have been so damn broke.

"Man, you should have seen that Jose Lothario!" My uncle John had stopped by to tell us about a wrestling show that he had seen the previous weekend. "He knocked that guy right out of the ring! You guys have to go next week!"

I was 13 and had never cared about professional wrestling. I certainly saw my share of fights- Humble was a rough place to grow up. But I was more interested in being the next Johnny Bench than the next Harley Race.

"I haven't seen that stuff in years," my dad said. "Man, I used to hate that Bull Ramos."

In those days I was convinced that my father was the biggest man in the world. Edward Denton towered over everyone he met. He was a stern son of a gun with a handlebar mustache, broad chest and even broader shoulders.

"It might be fun to check out a match," he told my uncle, "How much are tickets?"

"We can get some for pretty cheap," John replied. "It's a blast. Hell, bring Lynn."

I was named after my father- Edward Lynn Denton. There could only be one Edward in our family, so I was Lynn or Lynny from the start (as a wrestler I was also billed as "Len"). I shared Dad's name, but not his stature. While he could have passed for a pro wrestler, with my skinny frame and brown mop top I looked more like a member of the Partridge Family.

I had two brothers, and when it came to his sons, Dad was old school in every way. He never hugged us, not even when we were little kids. From an early age we were expected to be "real men", and what could be more "real" and "manly" than watching some sweaty giants beat the hell out of each other? I'm guessing that's what was going through the old man's head when he turned to me and said:

"Lynn- it's time you saw some rasslin'."

In 1972 the Houston Astros finished ten games out of first place and the Oilers were the worst team in the NFL. If Houstonians wanted to see champions, there was only one place to go: Paul Boesch's Houston Wrestling.

A veteran announcer, Boesch was one of Houston's best-known television personalities. He was also a very successful promoter, and Friday nights he brought the nation's top wrestlers to the Sam Houston Coliseum.

"This is it?" I asked my dad as we walked through the coliseum doors. "I thought it would be bigger."

The Sam Houston was constructed in the 1930s. It was dark, dank and showed every bit of its age. We took our seats next to a couple of old ladies who had gotten all dressed up for the occasion. I had no idea what to expect when the house lights went down, but brother, I was hooked from the opening bell.

Lothario, Red Bastien, Bruiser Brody... these could *not* be normal, mortal men. As far as my 13-year-old brain was concerned, Superman and King Kong were real and they were having a fistfight right in front of me! Their brawls were damn sure better than anything I'd seen on the streets of Humble- these fellas *really* knew how to beat the crap out of each other!

From then on, I watched Houston Wrestling every Saturday night on channel 39. When dad could scrape together some extra cash we'd see a live show at the Coliseum and I would cheer until I was hoarse.

Rocky Johnson was one of my favorites. The guy looked like he was carved out of granite, and as far as I was concerned he did a better Ali Shuffle than Ali himself. Speedy, strong, smooth- Rocky was the handsome badass every young boy longed to be.

But the wrestler that really captured my imagination was The Sheik.

We didn't have a lot of Arab royalty in Humble, so as far as I was concerned Ed Farhat really was a murderous lunatic from the deserts of Syria. Like any rambunctious kid, I loved carnage and chaos, and when The Sheik wrestled you *knew* there would be blood.

He'd hit his opponent with any weapon he could get his hands on: pencils, forks, even fire. I'd say everything but the kitchen sink, but I'm pretty sure he cracked one of those fuckers across Bobo Brazil's head. From the Coliseum cheap seats I watched with sadistic glee. I had no idea that one day I would also make a living as a weapon-wielding villain.

"Damn Denton- is that your kid?"

It was my junior year of high school, and this Saturday (like most Saturdays) I was working for my old man. We were building a new carport for a gentleman who owned a local fencing company. He also happened to be a pro wrestling pioneer.

Tiger Conway was one of the first black wrestling stars in the state of Texas. When he broke in, back in the 1950s, the sport was segregated. Tiger was crowned the "Texas Negro Wrestling Champion" if you can believe that. When the '60s rolled around, he finally battled the top white stars of the day.

"That boy's in shape!" Tiger continued. "You know, he could be a wrestler."

Until then, the thought had never occurred to me. I was a wrestling fan, but my main focus had always been baseball. I was pretty good, and had attracted the attention of some pro scouts and a few small colleges. But that was before a football injury sidelined me for a year.

"A wrestler?" My dad was intrigued. "You really think he could do it?"

"Maybe," Mr. Conway answered. "Would need to bulk up some. And learn how to take a whuppin'."

I chuckled a bit and Tiger gave me a look that said *I ain't joking boy.* I cleared my throat and tried to look as serious as possible.

"There's schools for that sort of thing," he continued, "Gotta find a good one though."

"What about you?" my dad asked, "If he wanted to do it, could you train him?"

Tiger Conway crossed his arms and gave me a good look over. It was hard to read his expression. Maybe he was trying to decide if I was worth his time.

Maybe he was regretting bringing up the whole wrestling thing in the first place. Either way, his answer didn't take long.

"I don't think so," he said, "Maybe the kid can do it, and maybe he can't. Either way, I'm not the guy to do it."

With that the conversation ended and we went back to work. But the rest of the afternoon I was oblivious to building carports or whatever else we were doing. All I could think about was pro wrestling and the dream job that I had never dreamt of.

On the drive home that night, my dad and I discussed the idea some more. My senior year of high school was a month away and I had no concrete plans after that. I wasn't much of a student, so without a baseball scholarship I knew college was out. When school ended I could always work construction. But man, to be one of those tough bastards on Channel 39?

By the end of that drive, I knew what I wanted to do with my life.

"Three thousand dollars. All Cash."

The office was in the corner of an old warehouse- a shabby old space with a cheap desk and vinyl chair. Everything was nondescript... except for the walls. The walls were covered in history.

LIVE WRESTLING TONIGHT!

SPECIAL ATTRACTION: TWO OUT OF THREE FALLS- NO TELEVISION.

From floor to ceiling I saw nothing but yellowing wrestling posters and 8 X 10 photos. My dad was able to point out a few wrestlers he remembered watching as a kid. But most of the pictures featured a man that he had never seen before- a rather unremarkable man with a black crewcut and goatee. He was even less remarkable in person.

Dad had stumbled upon an ad for Joe Mercer's wrestling school in the local TV listings. Joe had wrestled for years as "Dropkick" Danny Mercer, "Joe Pizza" and most recently as "Karl Von Helm" (a rip-off of the famous Karl Von

17

Hess). He was an old-timer who never made the big time, but if you think about it, it's pretty impressive that he was able to play an Italian *and* a Nazi.

"I don't do payment plans," Mercer continued from his seat, "So that's three grand up front."

"Three thousand dollars?" Dad let out a low whistle. "That's just about everything he has. What's he get for all that money?"

"One year of training, five days a week… and no guarantees."

This guy may have been a wrestler but he wasn't much of a salesman.

"He'll still be going to high school. Seems like a lot of work."

"That's his problem, not mine," Joe shrugged, "And yeah, it's a lot of work."

I silently weighed my options. Wrestling school would mean no baseball for my senior year. In addition, my grades weren't great, and it was going to take some work just to get my diploma. Wrestling wouldn't make that any easier. And three thousand dollars was literally all I had. If I blew this, I could end up just another broke-ass high school dropout. Still- if this *did* work out… man, it was hard to imagine what that could mean. Money? Girls? I decided to speak up.

"I think I can do it."

Mercer finally trained his dark eyes on me. He was not physically imposing, but if you could maim a man with stares, this guy would have been heavyweight champion.

"You *think* you can do it?" He rose to his feet, old joints popping in the process. "Well, let me tell you one thing."

He got right in my face. Up close, you could tell he was an old wrestler-his scars blended into wrinkles and then back into scars. Joe Pizza looked me up and down like I was a rotten slice of pepperoni.

"Kid, wrestling is a big man's sport. I can make you wider and I can make you thicker. But I can't make you taller. I'll take your money and I'll train you. But you will *never* make a dime in this business."

18

He just stood there staring at me. I felt the blood rush to my face. I had saved money from all those summers and weekends of working for my dad, and this old fart was telling me I was fixing to flush it down the toilet. All because I was 5' 10".

"Well- what do you think?" Dad broke the silence.

What do I think? Well, first I think this old coot is calling me short when he ain't exactly Wilt Chamberlain. Second, I think that Tiger Conway said I could be a wrestler, and I've actually heard of him. And third, I'm thinking I'd like to smack that smug look off Dropkick Danny's face.

"Let's do it." I said, never breaking eye contact.

"OK," Joe's expression didn't change either. "Let's see the money".

I was one day away from the start of wrestling school when I asked my best friend to kick my ass.

"What the hell are you talking about?"

Tony Gonzales and I were in my bedroom when I made the request. We had hung out for years- playing ball in old sandlots and eating his mom's fresh tortillas.

"I have to toughen up for wrestling," I explained, "These are some big guys. I gotta show them I can take a beating and come back. So just beat the hell out of me. I won't fight back."

"You're serious?"

"Yeah, just watch the nuts."

Tony started slugging me in the arm and the chest.

"Harder man, come on!"

He complied: a left hook here, a right cross there.

"OK, tha…"

Before I could finish the sentence, Tony found his groove. Brother, he started laying it in like he was Bruiser fuckin' Brody. I fell to the ground and the kicks came.

"JESUS, TONY!" Right boot, left boot, "THAT'S ENOUGH MAN!!!"
He had broken out in a light sweat. Tony smiled and offered me a hand.
"That's what you wanted right?"

"Yeah," I replied as I wiped the blood from my lip, "Thanks a lot man."

Historical note: Tony would go on to join the Houston SWAT Team where he would inevitably beat the crap out of many poor unsuspecting perps. His older brother Alberto Gonzales would make history as the first Hispanic U.S. Attorney General. Looking back, Alberto should have probably charged his brother with "accessory to being an idiot".

The truth was, no beating- no matter how severe- could have prepared anyone for the hell that was Joe Mercer's wrestling school. About twelve of us hopefuls were packed into that old, dusty warehouse and for the first three months we didn't once get on our feet.

"Contrary to what you may hear, this ain't some show," Joe yelled at us, "This is a sport. You will respect it or get the fuck out!"

The ring looked (and felt) like a souvenir from the days of George Hackenschmidt. My face was constantly being rubbed into the mildewed mat as Joe taught us the basics of technical wrestling. Sit out, go behind, back down, sit out. Then it was a chicken wing, a hammer lock, or any other move that he could demonstrate while inflicting agony and suffering.

When we finally got off the mat, it wasn't much better. We had to learn how to "run the ropes". I quickly noticed that term was false advertising because these "ropes" were really steel cables. I had to keep bouncing off of them until I swore that I broke a rib.

Then it was time to take bumps. Joe was still "protecting the business" so he wasn't necessarily trying to "protect our bodies". He would slam us to the mat as hard as he could, and we had to land correctly in order to lessen the impact. It wasn't easy- if you landed on your heel the wrong way you'd be limping for a week. That old mat was harder than a slab of concrete.

After a couple months of this shit, the school's enrollment shrank considerably. That three thousand dollar entrance fee was non-refundable, but apparently several of my classmates thought that was a fair price for not getting their asses kicked any more.

"We're going to have our first card soon," Joe told us at the beginning of class one day, "You will not be paid. This is part of your training. You will hang up posters, you will set up the chairs, you will set up the ring. As a matter fact, you will build me a ring."

The old grump wasn't lying. The next day he brought in a bunch of lumber, cables and some metal posts and we built him a damn ring from scratch. The materials didn't come with any instructions, although Joe would damn sure yell at us if we did something wrong.

I should mention that at this time, I was also in the middle of my senior year of high school. School was definitely an afterthought (although I did graduate, don't ask me how). I had quit baseball and football. So now when the final bell rang, I'd hop in my car and drive 45 minutes to Joe Mercer's Warehouse of Pain.

You know how in the old comic books Peter Parker went to high school during the day, and then he would live a secret second life as Spider-Man where he would kick the shit out of Dr. Octopus? Well, my life was like that. Nobody at MacArthur High knew that I was going to wrestling school. The only difference between myself and Peter Parker was that my secret life involved getting abused and strangled by a man named Joe Pizza.

A few weeks after building the ring, we were ready for the big show. Well, most of us *weren't* ready, but screw it, we were going to do it anyway.

The cigarette smoke in the Silver Wings Ballroom was thick enough to choke a horse, or at least a ring full of wrestlers. Waitresses worked their way through the smog, handing out bottles of Lone Star beer and glass ashtrays (most of which would later be hurled at the villainous Karl Von Helm).

It was a packed house- maybe 250 people. Peeking through the black curtain, I made out my dad's substantial profile. He was next to my mother, brothers, sisters and a few aunts and uncles. They had all driven an hour to Brenham, Texas to watch my pro wrestling debut.

This was considered an "outlaw" show, in other words, one not affiliated with Paul Boesch's Houston Wrestling. The card was made up of the kids from the wrestling school, Joe (as the evil Nazi) and a couple of local journeymen. The opening bout was wrapping up and Match 2 was the masked wrestler Mr. Pro vs. Lynn Denton.

I wanted to puke but couldn't even muster the courage for that.

"Gary, I'm not sure I can do this man."

Gary Young was a fellow student in Joe Mercer's wrestling school. He would end up being the only Mercer graduate to make it in pro wrestling (besides me of course).

"Relax brother," he slapped me on the shoulder, "You've been kicking butt since we started. If you can't do this, we're all fucked."

He had a point. After the first couple months of training, Mercer had pegged me as one of his top students. Eventually I became his teaching assistant; showing my classmates how to properly take a bump or execute a hold.

It just came easy to me. With baseball and football, I had initially struggled. Yeah, I was good at baseball, but that was only after years of practice. For some reason, I was a solid wrestler right out of the gate. Lynn Denton was on his way to becoming a professional ass-kicker.

Then one day, we got "the talk".

"Look," Joe began, "I told you this was a sport, and that's exactly what this is."

By this time, the class had whittled down to six students. We were all gathered around the ring, most of us still recovering from the day's beatings.

"You have to be tough, you have to be aggressive. But, you also have to tell a story."

Story? I exchanged sideways glances with a couple of my classmates.

"You need to be able to protect yourself and even hurt a guy- if necessary. But that's not what's going to make you money... The money comes when you and your opponent can go out and have a great match night after night after night."

That's when Joe Mercer taught us how to "work" a match. He told us we weren't opponents so much as partners. It was in your interest to protect the other guy, and make him look good. If he didn't return the favor, then you could hand out an ass-whipping- but you didn't want it to come to that. The big payoffs came from great matches- and those came from cooperation.

I had always thought wrestling was a shoot (i.e. a legitimate fight) so it was a bit of a surprise. But when I thought back to the matches that I had watched and all the punches that did not result in broken noses or black eyes, it made sense.

Now, just because we were working together didn't mean that this was "fake". There was nothing fake about the pain. If someone used the "f-word" we were told to put that idiot in a submission hold and let them "fake" their way out of it. You had to be a tough S.O.B. to do this. I got hurt more while learning to work than I did when Joe was stretching me on his nasty old mat. But I listened and took my lumps until it was time for my first match in front of a live crowd.

And now it was here.

Mr. Pro was already in the ring. Sitting backstage at the Silver Wings I felt like I was getting thrown into the deep end of the pool and I never had swimming lessons. I'm not kidding you, they had to push me out of that curtain. It wasn't an arena or anything, so I had to walk through the fans to get to the ring. With the exception of my family members, the crowd really didn't pay me any mind. To them I was just some scrawny kid in a blue speedo.

"Who the hell is that supposed to be?"

Good question. For now, I was a petrified high school student quaking in his boots and gagging on second-hand smoke. All I could think was: *I paid three grand for this?*

The bell rang and Mr. Pro and I circled each other. We were getting ready to lock up, but my palms were so sweaty, I was afraid they would slip right off of him. Finally, I grabbed the back of his neck with my right hand and his elbow with my left.

From there it was smooth sailing.

I can't explain why, but once the match actually started, I felt a serious sense of Déjà vu. It was like I had done this before. We'd go from one spot to the next and it was seamless: I'd toss Pro to the ropes and drop to the mat, he'd jump over me, I'd pop up and drop him with a hip toss. I just instinctively knew what to do and when to do it.

"You got him Lynny!"

My family was loving it. Of course, my mom didn't like it when Mr. Pro put the boots to me, but my dad could see that I was doing well. Pro and I went back and forth in a fun match until he threw me to the ropes and put his head down for a backdrop. I jumped over and rolled him up with a sunset flip. It was over.

I was still glowing when I finally got to meet my family after the show. Mom showered me with kisses. My dad gave me a firm handshake and a pat on the back.

"Nice job," he said.

I almost teared up. For Edward Denton, Sr. those two words qualified as a heartfelt show of emotion.

I worked several more shows for Joe Mercer where every night I earned "experience" in lieu of actual cash. Joe said he would get me booked in a paying promotion once I passed my final exam. That day came just a few weeks after my high school graduation.

"I want you to give me ten good minutes," he told me. "You're wrestling that."

Joe pointed to a corner of the ring where a broom was propped up against the turnbuckle.

I waited for an explanation.

"When you get out in the world, you're going to have to face guys that you've never seen before. You won't know if they can work a lick or not. If you can have a match with that broom, you can have a match with anybody. And *then* you'll be a professional wrestler."

Now, I probably could have still had a wrestling career even if I didn't pass this test. But I came this far and figured I might as well finish it. So, I locked up with that broom and we put on a wrestling clinic.

I tripped the broom and jumped on top, attempting a quick pinfall. He (She? It?) kicked out and tried to roll me up with a cradle. Before I knew it, we were exchanging suplexes and it was on.

In later years, when I started training wrestlers, I would make my own students pass this test. Joe Mercer was right: a good wrestler must be prepared to face anyone, from an all-time-great to an absolute stiff. Frankly, some of my future opponents could have learned a few tricks from Joe's broom.

When it was all said and done we went well over ten minutes in a match that was by no means the worst of my career. I was feeling good about things until that damn broom caught me off-guard with a cross body block. 1- 2- 3.

I'm still waiting for the rematch.

CHAPTER TWO

MANHANDLED IN THE PANHANDLE

I didn't go to college, but I always imagined that after graduation most students worked on their resumes, applied for jobs and embarked on careers that could one day bring them wealth and security. Instead, I went to wrestling school, and my post-graduation schedule involved getting humiliated on television by some of the world's finest wrestlers.

Joe Mercer kept his word, and got Gary Young and I booked in a professional wrestling promotion where we would actually be paid. Amarillo, Texas wasn't the biggest territory in the world, but it featured two of the biggest stars of the 1970s. Terry Funk was the current World Heavyweight Champion and his brother Dory Jr. was one of the greatest World Champions of all time. Dory also ran the territory where I was about to make my professional debut.

"Greenhorns! Get your skinny asses over here!"

Art Nelson was yelling at Gary and me from the far end of an Amarillo television studio. They say everything is bigger in Texas, but nothing in the state was bigger than the giants sitting around that room. Swede Hanson was every bit of 300 pounds with hands the size of frying pans. Abdullah the Butcher was even bigger- at least 350. He might have hit 400 if he wasn't missing giant chunks of his forehead.

Nelson was a masked wrestler known as "The Super Destroyer" (not to be confused with my future partner Scott Irwin who would adopt the same name). In addition to his wrestling duties, Art was Amarillo's booker- the man who made matches and lorded over the locker room. He was a legendary hardass who was not impressed by my 18-year old frame.

"Seriously kid, what do you weigh?" he asked me.

"I'm almost 190 sir."

"Fuck. Skinny as a rail and green as gooseshit. You two sit down somewhere and try not to talk too much."

That wouldn't be a problem.

Just 24 hours prior I had been on my parents' front porch, saying my goodbyes. My mom was crying. Dad handed me a hundred bucks.

"This is for emergencies," he said as he shook my hand, "Be careful.... I love you."

What did he say?

I looked to my mother, and we both smiled in confusion. In 18 years I had never heard my dad say that phrase. Hell, I didn't even know the word "love" was in his vocabulary. I kept reliving that moment the entire nine hour drive from Houston to the Texas Panhandle.

"Alright, which one of you is Young?" Art Nelson had returned with his sheet of the day's matches. Gary raised his hand.

"You got Abdullah tonight."

"Alright."

Art didn't have to tell Gary who was winning that match. My buddy was about to get curbstomped by the Madman from the Sudan. Art turned to leave, but then spun back with one final detail.

"Oh, we want you to get some color too," he said, "Don't worry, he'll do it."

Jesus.

"Get some color" meant that Gary was going to bleed. And "He'll do it" meant Abdullah the Butcher would be slicing his forehead open with a small razor blade.

"You can't let him do that," I whispered when Nelson was out of earshot, "Joe always told us that if we're going to juice, we should cut ourselves."

"I don't see what the problem is," Gary replied.

"Look at that man's head!" I screamed/whispered, "He's got three giant canyons on his forehead from slashing himself the last twenty years. If that's how he treats his own head, what do you think he'll do to you?"

"I'll be alright," Gary said with resignation.

With that, he headed to the ring, where Abdullah worked his magic with a fork and blade. By the end of the match, Gary Young looked like the victim of a botched lobotomy.

My television debut would be less bloody but equally emasculating.

"You're working Dory," Nelson told me.

I tried to process his words. One week ago I was wrestling a bunch of nobodies for free. Now I was getting paid (albeit barely) to face a man who had held the NWA World title for an incredible four year reign. I was in awe of the man, but tried to seem matter-of-fact about it:

"Should I talk to him?" I asked, "You know, work out the finish?"

"Nope, he's busy," Art said dismissively, "Just meet him in the ring- you'll figure it out."

So an hour later I waited in the ring, completely ignored by the cameras and studio audience. Dory was at ringside, giving a pre-match interview. I can't remember who he was talking about, but I can assure you that it wasn't the scrawny teenager he was about to wrestle.

When Dory stepped in the ring, I played the heel and attacked him with a couple of cheap shots. The audience didn't even bother booing because they knew what was coming next.

Dory blocked a punch, grabbed me in a headlock and flipped me to the mat. After a couple quick stomps, he grabbed my right ankle and stepped over my leg. He began turning his body and stepping over my leg, over and over again. This was the famous Funk Spinning Toe Hold. I immediately submitted.

The match lasted *maybe* thirty seconds. Whatever the time, Dory didn't break a sweat. He just left the ring and I didn't see him again.

"Ha Ha! Serves you right, punk kid!"

The crowd let me have it and I savored the moment: I had just been manhandled in the panhandle by Dory F-ing Funk. Yeah, it was a butt-whuppin', but one that I happily accepted. Here I was a couple weeks out of high school and wrestling a legend on television? Brother, I was in heaven.

Art Nelson was not nearly as impressed. Right after my match, he was waiting for me in the dressing room.

"These are the dates for this week," he said while handing me a piece of paper.

The booking sheet listed the promotion's upcoming cards in the area. I scanned the page for my name. There were six shows coming up: I was wrestling on two of them, and in the other four I was supposed to work as a referee.

"Why does this say I'm a ref?" I asked.

"Because you are," he growled.

"I don't understand," I said, "I've never reffed before."

Nelson let loose a deeply annoyed sigh. His tone suggested that this would not be a long conversation:

"Look, I got a lot of shit to do, so let me make this clear: You are scrawny as a beanpole and don't look remotely like a wrestler. So if you want to work those shows, then you're working as a damn referee."

"But sir," I said, trying to sound as humble and appreciative as possible, "I didn't train a year to be a referee. I'm a wrestler- not a ref."

Art snickered for a second and then his expression became stone cold serious.

"So you're a wrestler are you?" he began, "Well, I tell you what Mr. Wrestler- do you see that sheet? You can take it and work those dates. Or you can take it and WIPE YOUR ASS WITH IT!!! I don't give a fuck what you do. Whatever happens, when the week is over, you're <u>done</u> here. Got it?"

It was obvious that Art Nelson was not waiting for my reply. He turned away, and in a matter of seconds was yukking it up with some other old-timer.

I just stood there: a scrawny, silent child in a roomful of monsters.

I swallowed whatever pride I had left and hit the road for those six shows. I had already sacrificed three thousand dollars and a year of my life to be a professional wrestler- I figured what was another week?

Besides, I still had two matches where I would actually wrestle. Maybe I could show Art and Dory *something* that would convince them to keep me on. Unfortunately, the locker room veterans had no interest in making me look good.

"You're fucking dead," The Super Destroyer told me before our match, and he wasn't exaggerating that much.

We were somewhere in New Mexico and Art Nelson had decided to book himself against the scrawny beanpole that looked nothing like a wrestler. So, for twenty minutes Art imitated a pit bull while I played the role of his favorite chew toy. He outweighed me by about 70 pounds and I can assure you there was nothing choreographed about our match. I was smothered, strangled and damn near swallowed whole.

That was almost as bad as my match with Swede Hanson. Before the bell rang, he decided to have a word with me in the middle of the ring.

"Hey kid.... Mumble mumble mumble..."

What did he say? I leaned in close, so Swede could repeat his instructions.

WHAM!!!!!!

That big monster slapped my ear with a force that would make Mike Tyson jealous. Earlier in this chapter I compared Swede's hands to frying pans, but now that I think about it, that's probably an unfair comparison.

Frying pans are a lot softer.

"Welcome to pro wrestling kid," Swede chuckled as he applied a side headlock. At least I think that's what he said- I was half-deaf at the time.

For about ten minutes the blonde giant squeezed my head like he was trying to pop a pimple. After that, he slapped me a few more times and began rubbing my bloody ear into the mat. Fortunately, by that time I had lost all feeling above my shoulders.

When the match was over, I received a special souvenir that I would wear for the rest of my life. Most wrestlers acquire cauliflowered ears after years of in-ring action; I received mine after one match.

My week of hell eventually ended and I drove back to Amarillo with a hungry psychopath in tow.

"Hey baby, make sure to stop in Tucumcari. They got a nice buffet there."

Abdullah the Butcher filled nearly every inch of the Ford Maverick's backseat. His eating exploits were almost as legendary as his wrestling exploits. Apparently, mutilating people can build quite the appetite.

It was common practice for the rookies to drive the veterans from show to show, and I was happy to be The Butcher's chauffeur. Despite his bloodthirsty reputation, Abby was one of the more approachable vets in the locker room.

"Sir, can I ask you something?" I asked, after assuring Abby that, yes, we would stop at that buffet in Tucumcari.

"What is it champ?"

I poured my heart out to Abdullah. I told him how I had gotten my ass kicked for nothing- Art Nelson refused to book me anymore. I was dead broke with no options and nowhere to go.

"What should I do?" I asked, glancing back in the rear-view mirror.

The Madman from the Sudan sighed.

"Just keep at it baby," he said as he closed his eyes for a nap, "Now, be sure to wake me up when we get to Tucumcari. Got a nice buffet there."

Eventually, we made it to the restaurant and Abby tore up the buffet like it was Gary Young's forehead. The damage done, we continued on to Amarillo. We were thirty miles out of town when my Maverick decided to speak up.

KER-THUNK! KER-THUNK!

I didn't know what that sound was, but I knew it wasn't good. The car jerked and convulsed the rest of the way- sputtering out just as we rolled into Abby's apartment complex.

"Damn it!"

A tow truck eventually arrived, along with a mechanic who told me the repairs would cost several hundred dollars that I did not have. The whole episode stung worse than Swede Hanson's right hand. I was stranded in Amarillo with no job, no money and no way to get home.

"I'm done," I told Abby, "My dad will have to send me some cash and then I'm going home and getting a real job. Fuck this wrestling shit."

There was no way I was going to cry in front of Abdullah the Butcher so I turned my back to him and sat on the curb. I clenched my fists and tried to forget all of my stupid dreams.

What the hell was I thinking? I'm just a poor little shit from Humble, Texas and that's all I'll ever be.

Unexpectedly, Abdullah the Butcher interrupted my pity party and saved my career.

"Baby, do you really want some advice?" he asked.

I looked up at him, surprised by the question. With his bald head, big belly and brown skin, Abby kind of looked like The Buddha- if he had gotten in to a fight with a biker gang.

"Sir," I said, "I'd appreciate any help you give me."

He grinned. Buddha the Butcher then offered this piece of enlightenment:

"Baby, this business is all about respect. Write a letter to Dory Funk. Thank him for the opportunity to wrestle in Amarillo. Tell him about everything you've been through- wrestling school, the car, everything. Tell him you will do anything to be a wrestler, and would appreciate any help or advice."

I chewed on his words for a bit. Until now, I had felt alone in that locker room. All the veterans seemed more interested in torturing me than teaching me. Now, I was getting some heartfelt advice from the man who had just disfigured my friend.

Man, this was a weird business.

"Sir," I finally said, "Do you really think writing a letter will work?"

Abdullah the Butcher just shrugged and lit a cigar. He responded between puffs.

"I don't know if it will work," he said, "But you got to admit, it's a lot better than your other plan."

It took a week to fix my car and a day to write my letter. I put it in a sealed envelope with Dory's name on it. He wasn't in his office when I stopped by, so I handed the letter to Art Nelson and hoped that it would reach its intended recipient.

For six days I didn't hear a thing.

The following Friday the repairs were done and it was time to pick up my car. I called my dad to tell him I was coming home. When he heard my voice, the old man flipped.

"Lynny, what the hell is going on?"

"What do you mean?"

"Dory Funk Jr. just called our house! He says you need to get to Louisiana- you're wrestling there next week!"

The scene was like some mutant offspring of High Noon and The Mary Tyler Moore Show. I was sitting with two other young wrestlers in a local television newsroom; typewriters sat on every desk and police scanners blared in the background. But instead of Ed Asner barking orders, Killer Karl Kox patrolled the room like an old gunslinger. He wore cowboy boots and had a .38 revolver stuffed into one side of his pink bikini briefs.

"Listen you motherfuckers," he said to our terrified group. "I'm working with one of you little shits tonight. If you hurt me at all- I WILL kill you."

Kox was a bald, paunchy old-timer with the eyes of a lunatic. I had no doubt that he really would kill us if given the opportunity. After all, this was the same guy who wore the initials "KKK" in front of crowds that were 90% black.

"D-d-don't worry sir," I stuttered. "It would be an honor just to work with you. And I'm sure…"

"SHUT THE FUCK UP!" Kox bellowed, "No one likes a kiss ass!"

And with that, thankfully, he moved on.

Two days prior I had arrived in Shreveport, Louisiana, the home of Tri-State Wrestling. Bill Watts had recently transitioned from wrestling to promoting and (with long-time promoter Leroy McGuirk) was running shows throughout Louisiana, Mississippi and Oklahoma. KTSB was the local TV station where they taped the studio wrestling show that aired throughout the territory. The newsroom was our de-facto dressing room, and it was filled with seasoned tough guys and scared-shitless greenhorns like me. When Kox stepped out of the room, my new buddies gave me grief.

"Next time Lynn, you may want to just shut the fuck up."

Jake Roberts punctuated his words with a raspy laugh. He was even skinnier than I was, but much taller. The son of a wrestler, Jake had already been working for several years, but was still looking for his big break.

"Aw, don't worry about that shit," Paul Orndorff said. "Once you prove you can take it in the ring, he'll respect you."

Paul had been wrestling just as long as me, but was already working main events. With his pro football background and incredible physique, the man was destined for stardom. That is, if he could work a match without killing somebody.

"I know," I replied, "I better get warmed up. Man, I hope I'm not working with that guy."

I dropped down and started cranking out push-ups.

While making the long drive from Amarillo to Shreveport, I had prepared myself for the worst. Shannon Powell, a fellow student from Joe Mercer's wrestling school, had gone straight to Tri-State following graduation. After one match with Karl Kox he ran out of the arena (while still wearing his tights) and never wrestled again.

I recognized a lot of the wrestlers from their various stints in Houston, but knew next to nothing about Tri-State Wrestling. That's how it was back then. Most people didn't have cable TV yet, so you only saw the promotions from your local markets. Yeah, it was next to Texas, but Louisiana might as well have been Libya.

Nonetheless, I was here to learn, get experience and then eventually… *hopefully*… make a crapload of money.

"WHAT THE FUCK IS THIS?"

I stopped my pushups and looked up to find the pink briefs and .38 directly overhead.

"Push ups? What kind of sport do you think this is?" KKK demanded, "If I ever see you doing this shit…"

"Leave the kid alone!"

It was the voice of our boss.

"Dammit Kox, we don't want to lose another one. Give him a break."

Bill Watts coming to my aid was a big surprise. A legitimate badass, "The Cowboy" demanded that all his wrestlers be badasses too. At 300 plus pounds, Watts was like a tank, only less cuddly. He had headlined everywhere, and was now applying his no-bullshit approach to promoting.

"Alright you jabronis," he bellowed after Kox went on his way, "Quit staring and get to fucking work!"

Thankfully, I didn't have to tangle with KKK- although that would come soon.

My Tri-State debut was with a guy named Larry Booker, who would one day achieve some fame as "Moondog Spot". The match went fine, but it became clear that my role in Tri-State would be similar to my brief run in Amarillo. The only difference was I didn't have to referee.

Occasionally I got to show what I could do in the ring with guys like Jake and Paul. But much of my tenure was dedicated to putting over veterans like Kox and the incredible Ernie Ladd.

In just about every way, Ladd was the exact opposite of Karl Kox. At 6'9" and 320 pounds, the former All-AFL lineman could have been the biggest bully in the locker room. Instead, "The Big Cat" was everybody's friend: it didn't matter if you were a headliner, a rookie or the guy sweeping up the arena. I could not get enough of Ernie's interviews:

"I am the Big Cat, number 99 Ernie Ladd. If I tell you something, you can take it to the bank. If I tell you the moon is made of cheese- get your crackers! If I tell you a mosquito can pull a plow- hook him up!"

Because Ernie was so enormous, he would often wrestle two or three undersized men at a time. I participated in more than my share of the Big Cat's handicap matches. He always won, and I never looked impressive.

Just paying my dues, I would tell myself, *Just paying my dues.*

Then one of those humiliation-fests aired on TV and my grandfather in Nacogdoches saw the damn thing.

"Boy, what the hell's wrong with you?" he asked, "Three of you and you couldn't do a damn thing to that man!"

"Sorry grandpa- I tried."

"You ain't much of a wrestler," he helpfully offered. "You should probably consider another line of work."

It was so nice to have the support of my family.

From the time Art Nelson called me a scrawny little shit (and other less-flattering names), I knew that I had to get bigger if I wanted to be a professional wrestler. Today, you see all these young, fit guys with shredded abs and stuff and that's fantastic. But in the late 1970s all of that took a backseat to just being a big, brawny son of a bitch. If you could look good at the same time, well, that was a bonus.

I needed a mentor, and so I approached the man with the biggest guns in the locker room.

"See this arm right here?" Porkchop Cash asked, "21 inches cold brother."

I didn't doubt it for a second; in fact that number may have been on the conservative side. Bobby Cash was *jacked*. His nickname came from the giant chop- sideburns that crawled down from his afro and onto his cheeks.

"Sir," I asked him, "Do you think you could maybe train me? I need to be big like you."

"Man, you'll never be big like *me,*" he correctly noted.

"Please sir," I begged. "Anything you can teach me."

I had no problem groveling. If I didn't bulk up soon, this whole wrestling thing was going to be a thing of the past. Promoters wanted Popeye, not Olive Oyl.

Porkchop looked me up and down, probably trying to figure what, if anything, he could do with this bony white boy.

"Meet me at the YMCA tomorrow. 8 AM sharp." he said.

"Yes sir, thank you sir."

37

"One more thing," Porkchop added, "If I hear you complain *one time...* it's over."

The following morning I showed up at the Y at 7:45. Porkchop was already warming up.

"Remember," he said. "No bitching."

And with that, my new teacher spent the next three hours trying to murder me with dumbbells.

"First, you're going to do these preacher curls and go right into push downs" he instructed, "After that, it's dumbbells and close grip bench. We're talking supersets. Got to do some hammer curls too."

I was told not to complain, and thankfully, I would never have the energy to do so. That man worked me like a mule- an hour straight of arms, then shoulders, then back. All in that godforsaken Louisiana humidity. We never worked on our legs. As Porkchop would say:

"Man, you ever seen a racehorse with big legs?"

The whole thing was one of the worst experiences of my life, but I was too dumb and desperate to quit. After a year of abusing my body in the gym and in the ring, I had added fifty pounds of muscle. It was all thanks to the Porkchop Program.

Well, that and the steroids.

You have to remember that in those days anabolic steroids were not yet "controlled substances". That classification wasn't put into place until 1990; in 1977, they were regulated like any other prescription drug. Yes, plenty of people sold steroids on the "black market", but the government did nothing to stop them.

Porkchop always said he was "natural." If that was true, good for him. But I didn't have the slightest reservation about using steroids because they weren't the evil taboo that they are today.

Now that we know some of the long-term effects of performance-enhancing drugs, I certainly would advise any young person not to take them. Not only are you breaking the law, you could be endangering your health.

But it's important to remember that in the late 70s and early 80s, every major sport tacitly allowed steroids (with the exception of The Olympics). And there's a reason so many people used them- because they worked.

I knew my physical transformation was complete when I went back to my hometown.

I had finally gotten booked in Houston, where my friends and family could see me under the not-so-bright lights of the Sam Houston Coliseum. I decided to make a surprise visit to my parents' house. When she walked into her home that afternoon, Maddie Denton found a bearded, 240-pound stranger sitting on her couch.

My mama screamed like a banshee.

"HELP! HELP!" she yelled, while whacking me with purse.

"Mama- stop!" I pleaded between shots to the head.

"THERE'S A BURGLAR- CALL THE POLICE!"

More purse shots. I'm telling you, my Mama worked stiffer than Wahoo McDaniel.

"MAMA!" *WHACK! WHACK!* "IT'S ME- LYNNY!"

She stopped and adjusted her glasses. Mama searched my face for her fresh-faced little boy. After catching her breath, she finally spoke:

"Lynny…. What happened to you?"

We hugged and laughed about it, and she gave me another well-deserved whack for scaring an old lady. I left my home that evening confident in two things:

1) If my own mother couldn't recognize me, I was doing something right. I finally looked like a wrestler.

2) If any burglar ever *did* break into my mama's house, they were probably in for an ass-whuppin'.

"You know for a stupid little fuck, you can at least work a bit."

Kox and I were in the backseat of the car, with one of my fellow greenhorns at the wheel. We were speeding our way through Nowheresville, Mississippi.

"Don't get cocky," he added, "You're still not going to make it in this business. But you ain't the worst piece of shit I've ever seen."

I tell you, if "Killer" Karl Kox wasn't a wrestler, he could have written greeting cards for Hallmark.

"Thanks." I replied, fighting away a giant yawn.

After ten months on the road, I was still trying to adjust to the daily grind of being a pro wrestler: Wake up, drive to the next town, try to hit a gym, get to the arena, get your ass kicked, have some beers, get a couple hours of sleep and do it again in the morning. I was constantly exhausted.

We were heading back to Baton Rouge, where some of the wrestlers lived (myself included). A lot of the other boys lived in Shreveport, but Baton Rouge was closer to New Orleans and the Mississippi towns. Living there would save you several hours on the road every week.

"Get me a Coke," KKK demanded. Karl didn't drink alcohol, and as far as I was concerned that was just more proof that he was nuts.

I reached into the cooler at my feet and handed Kox his drink. Then, leaning against the car door, I shut my eyes and prepared for a nap. It took a while to catch some winks- my brain was still working through all this wrestling shit.

Things had been going *O.K.* I guess. I wasn't making much money, and I certainly wasn't winning matches. But it seemed like I was at least earning some respect for my in-ring ability. Like Kox said, for a stupid little fuck, I could work a bit, and the word was spreading. My matches were no longer complete squashes- I got to show my skills from time to time. But it remained to be seen if any of this would translate into an actual *career*.

Sleep finally came. I was dreaming about Bo Derek when I received a rude awakening.

WHACK!!!

The slap was Swede Hanson-esque. Bo's lovely figure morphed into a scowling Karl Kox.

"What's your problem idiot?" he wanted to know.

"hmmm?" I mumbled.

With a smirk, he gestured to the endless pine trees lining the Interstate.

"Do you know how much money people pay to go on vacation and see scenery like this? We're driving past all this beautiful shit and you're missing it- wake your ass up!"

He giggled a bit as he took another swig of his Coke. I wiped my eyes, looked out the window and followed the orders of KKK.

Just three more hours to Baton Rouge.

A couple weeks later Kox went hunting in the newsroom.

It was another TV taping and he had upgraded to a new .306 rifle with a fancy scope on it. The pink bikini briefs were back- apparently they didn't come in camo.

"What do you boys think?" he asked while peering down the scope, "Who wants a permanent place on my wall?"

The barrel moved from greenhorn to greenhorn, and we all ducked. We didn't know if the rifle was loaded. It probably didn't matter- if it was empty he'd likely beat us to death with the doggone thing.

"I don't know who I've got tonight," the great white hunter added, "But you're going to wish I shot you!"

"Kox!"

Watts was standing outside the men's room (which doubled as his office). He was calling in the wrestlers to go over their matches for the taping. I looked nervously at the other young guys. We knew that one of us was going to be in the ring with KKK.

Please not me. Please not me.

"Denton!"

Fuck. My. Life.

My friends hummed a funeral march as I made the long walk to the restroom. The door shut and Watts told us the finish for our match (big surprise- it involved Kox whupping my ass). After receiving our instructions, Karl turned to me. His normal lunatic expression had disappeared and he was smiling from ear to ear. Not in a crazy way- it was just a plain old, normal smile.

"Those kids out there- your buddies- they think I'm insane don't they?"

Oh man. This better not be a trick.

"Um… yeah."

"You do too?"

I just shut my mouth, hoping it was a rhetorical question.

"Tell you what," Karl said, "We're going to get them good. I've already cued in the Oates brothers on this one. Here's what we do…"

KKK then gave me some very animated instructions. A few minutes later, we walked out of the bathroom together.

"Don't fuck it up you little shit eater!" Kox yelled at me in a voice that everyone would hear, "I'll kill your ass!"

I kept walking. After a few steps, Karl kicked me in the butt and I fell to the ground.

At first, no one in the newsroom batted an eyelash. Karl Kox was harassing a rookie: just another day at the office. But his kick was really my cue. Following the plan that Kox had laid out, I jumped to my feet and got right in his face.

"DON'T YOU KICK ME MOTHERFUCKER!" I yelled with all the fake rage I could muster, "I'LL BEAT YOUR FUCKING ASS!"

With that, I grabbed a rolling chair and threw it right at Karl. He knew it was coming and ducked just in time. Right on cue, Jerry and Ted Oates grabbed my arms and dragged me away as I kicked and screamed like a madman. They planted me in my chair as Kox walked off screaming profanities.

Man, if you could have seen the look on my buddies' faces. As far as they were concerned, I had just tugged on Superman's cape *and* spit into the wind.

"Are you insane?" Larry Booker asked me. "That man is going to kill you!!!"

It took everything I had not to laugh. The whole thing was a practical joke, but in a way, it was more than that. It was a rite of passage.

By including me in his rib, Killer Karl had given me his somewhat-twisted sign of approval. Turns out, the guy wasn't *completely* crazy. He just loved to scare greenhorns. The fact that I was his partner in this prank showed that he now considered me to be "one of the boys".

Later that night, we wrestled our match for the Tri-State television audience. Killer Karl Kox continued his show of respect by only kicking 95 percent of my ass.

I was convinced that I had arrived. The Cowboy disagreed.

"You're a good worker and have a good attitude, but you're just not there yet."

Watts and I were back in the men's room. It was a couple of weeks after Kox and I made the boys shit their collective pants.

"Here's the thing," he continued, "You're not ready to be a top guy. If I keep you here, you'll never make that next step. You need to go somewhere else, get some experience and learn how to cut a promo. If you do that, we may be able to do something bigger with you down the road."

I nodded in agreement. I knew Watts spoke the truth, and what's more, he did it without making me feel worthless. As break-ups went, this one wasn't so bad.

"I'll call around and get you booked somewhere," he offered, "Where do you want to go?"

Without missing a beat I knew the answer:

"Portland."

The Pacific Northwest promotion had a great reputation. According to the vets, promoter Don Owen was one of the best payout guys in the business. Also, it was a small territory so travel was minimal.

"Don't think I can make that happen," Watts informed me, "Lots of guys want to work there. But I'll see what I can do."

I thanked him for the opportunity. Bill Watts shook my hand and then asked me to kindly get the hell out of his office.

A week later, I packed up my car and headed out for the next phase of my career. No longer a rookie, it was time for me to hone my skills and transform into a true-blue main event talent. Reaching that goal would require a lot of assistance and insight from my wrestling brothers. Over the next few years my teachers would include a kid named Dynamite and a legend named Flair.

CHAPTER THREE

WORLD TRAVELER

I was in the wrestling business for 15 years before I bought my first house. Most guys in the old territory system didn't own homes because they were constantly moving. The cycle was simple: you arrived in a territory, worked for a year or less and then moved on to the next spot where you were a fresh new face. Wrestlers were renters, not buyers- our homes an endless parade of cheap apartments and seedy hotels.

When I left Tri-State, I embarked on a three year journey that took me from Texas to Tokyo and Germany to Georgia. I never put down roots, hopping from one spot to the next like a hobo (with only a slightly better paycheck).

Bill Watts had found me a spot in Eddie Graham's Tampa promotion. From there, I went to- in no particular order- Charlotte, Atlanta, Knoxville, Europe, Houston, Japan, Charlotte (again), Calgary and I'm probably forgetting a couple of stops. Brother, it's been thirty-five years and I've taken a lot of bumps.

If Joe Mercer's wrestling school was the equivalent of college, these three years would be my version of medical school. I'd either wind up an ass-kicking M.D. or a burnout bitching about what might have been.

"Just remember, there's a reason why you're a wrestler and I'm your boss. Just do what I say- don't try to think. I'm here because I am smart. You're here because you're a dumb ass hick."

Ole Anderson's motivational speeches really sucked. He just loved to be an asshole. Bill Watts was short-tempered and callous, but I don't think The Cowboy took any pleasure in berating wrestlers. *This* S.O.B. was a different matter.

"Go out there and give me a twenty minute draw," he instructed, "You can handle that right?"

Ole was the booker for Georgia Championship Wrestling. He had traveled to Columbia, South Carolina to watch me perform. I told him I would do my best, and walked through the curtain into the Township Auditorium.

I'd been working in Tampa for the past few months, making little-to-no impact as far as wins go, but getting some kudos for my in-ring work. Apparently, Ole saw a tape of one of my matches and wanted to evaluate me in person. Eddie Graham told him if he wanted me, he could have me right away (which illustrates how valuable I was to Championship Wrestling from Florida).

I knew that if I could impress Ole Anderson, I had a future in wrestling. For all of his personality deficiencies, the man knew how to draw money. My opponent was a French-Canadian veteran named Rudy Kay. We went the full twenty minutes and it must have been good, because Ole offered me five words when I got to the back:

"You start in two weeks."

I thanked him and Ole walked off without a "you're welcome" or even a "sure thing." When he was gone, I grabbed some change and called my dad with the good news:

Lynn Denton was about to go national.

In 1976, Ted Turner's WTCG became the first basic cable network in the United States. When I arrived in Atlanta three years later, the call letters had changed to WTBS and Georgia Championship Wrestling was airing in all fifty states.

"Welcome my boy," Jim Barnett said as he passed me in the television studio, "If you need anything, you know where to find me."

Actually, I had no idea where to find him and would almost never see the man. Barnett owned the promotion. He was a tiny bookworm in a three-piece suit, and also openly gay. That's not a big deal these days, but in 1979, you can imagine what the locker room gossip involved.

"In this corner- "Mr. USA" Tony Atlas!"

Barnett's national reach had lured the sport's biggest stars to Atlanta and I made my cable debut against a man with the most insane physique I'd ever seen. Tony Atlas was one of the top stars in the territory and if you think I won that match, you obviously have not been paying attention.

After my customary beating, I sat in the locker room, enjoying a dip of tobacco and contemplating the future. As I spit into a nearby trashcan, I thought back to what Watts had said a few months back. I finally had the size, and I was a good worker, but I still needed that extra "something" to make a main event. If only I could...

"WHAT THE FUCK?"

I looked up and experienced a total eclipse. The locker room lights were blacked out by 320 pounds of a seething Stan Hansen.

"Is this a rib you little shit?" he asked, pointing to the ground next to me.

I looked down and damn near shit my pants. Apparently, my tobacco spit never made it into the trashcan. Instead, streams of brown saliva trickled down a very expensive-looking pair of cowboy boots.

Guess who they belonged to?

With one hand around my neck, the bull from Borger, Texas lifted me to the heavens. Somehow, with little to no oxygen in my lungs I was able to choke out enough words to apologize, explain the situation, and swear that I would never do such a dumbass thing again. He dropped me on my ass and I got those boots clean ASAP. Yes, I was off to a great start in Atlanta.

Damn thing was, I had to wrestle that big son of a gun the next week. In front of a national television audience, I took my first Stan Hansen lariat.

As the song says: That's the night the lights went out in Georgia.

Mid-Atlantic had The Four Horsemen, Mid-South had Akbar's Army and Portland had The Clan. But in Georgia Championship Wrestling, no wrestling stable could hold a candle to The POOM Squad.

The Squad included myself, Rick McGraw, Carl Fergie, Steve Regal (the American, not the Brit), and any other young guy on the roster. It was our job to "do the job" (the pro wrestling term for losing).

Before every TV taping, a list of the day's matches would be put up in the locker room. There would be a main event, a semi-main, and other matches featuring marquee stars. At the bottom of the list it would say "Plus One More Match", which meant one of us losing to one of the roster's bigger names. We shortened "Plus One More Match" to POOM, and our backstage brotherhood was born. Before every taping we would put our hands together and recite the saddest credo in the history of sports:

"We'll sell popcorn!

We'll set up chairs!

We'll do jobs- ANYWHERE!"

And that's exactly what we did- losing to Ole, Tommy Rich, Rick Martel and basically every other star on the GCW roster. But unlike my previous stops, I would also get some opportunities to shine. Every now and then I would tangle with a fellow POOMer and put on a show. Eventually, my work left an impression on our beloved locker room leader.

"We need some more job guys, but these idiots don't know shit," Ole told me after one taping, "You're going to fix that."

Translation: I was going to be a trainer. Before shows, I would work with the really green guys and fine-tune what little skills they had. We might work on basics like locking up, or work our way through more advanced stuff. The extra assignment was proof that Ole at least trusted me as a worker, even if he didn't see a potential star.

Of course, Ole was still an asshole, and no matter how good I was, he would always find fault in *something.*

One, night I wrestled Rick Martel at an un-televised house show. We had a great match- brawling in and out of the ring, and selling the shit out of each other's moves. I was feeling pretty good about myself when I walked through the back curtain. I certainly didn't expect Ole to grab me by my throat and throw me up against the wall.

"You stupid shit!" he fumed. "I'm in the main event and have to follow that? What the fuck am I supposed to do now?"

"Well," I replied, "If you can't follow a guy who's been in the business for two years, that's your own problem."

No, I didn't actually say that. I certainly thought it. Instead I just apologized and said it wouldn't happen again.

To his credit, Ole went out for the main event and had a great match. The miserable crank really whipped the crowd into a frenzy. I was standing in the locker room entrance as he left the ring and walked back up the aisle. The fans were unglued, pelting Ole with all kinds of garbage. He looked up and our eyes met. At that very moment, an irate fan nailed him in the head with a motorcycle helmet- I mean this guy really swung for the fences. It was a clean shot. Ole the Grouch was knocked out cold.

At that point, I should have probably ran to my boss' aid, and beat that fan into a pulp. That was the pro wrestling code. Instead, I had a good laugh at Ole's misfortune, went to the back and cracked open a beer.

A moment like that deserved a little celebration.

Atlanta's wrestlers lived at "The Falcon's Rest", a run-down apartment complex out by the airport. Its nickname was "The Wrestler's Roost", because the lady who owned it loved wrestling and gave us the run of the joint. You can imagine what that place was like- it made Animal House look like Downton Abbey.

I don't know the exact circumstances of what happened, but one night at The Roost, Angelo Mosca got into a fight with Ivan Koloff (a little surprising since "The Russian Bear" was one of the nicest wrestlers I ever met). Alcohol was almost certainly involved, and probably a woman. Whatever the cause, Mosca wound up with a busted shoulder.

"I had that bastard main eventing all week," Ole grumbled. "Now, he can't even lock up, and all my other top guys are booked."

We were backstage at the TV studio. I saw where this conversation was going, and for once, I was thrilled to be talking to Ole Anderson.

"I need a guy who can work so you're in," he said, "Try not to fuck this up."

So, I replaced Mosca for a series of main events with Thunderbolt Patterson. This is what I had been waiting for the past two years! With Angelo in my corner, T-Bolt and I had some great matches up and down the circuit. The matches weren't televised, so they didn't really establish me as a top guy. But that week proved that, as a worker, I could hang in a marquee match.

"Well, I guess you earned this," Ole said as he handed me my paycheck the following week.

900 Dollars. My first main event money- I almost fainted.

"One more thing," he added, "Barnett wants to see you."

I carefully folded the check and placed it in my wallet. Jim Barnett beamed at me as I walked into his office.

"Well my boy," he said, "What did you think of your check?"

"It's great sir," I raved, "The biggest check I've ever seen."

Barnett adjusted his glasses and sat up with an expression that suggested he was very, very pleased with himself.

"My boy," he said with a smile, "I want you to enjoy that money. Then, I want you to tell everyone you know that the biggest check *you ever saw* was signed by James Barnett."

I thanked him, shook his hand and made my way to the office door. As I left, I assured my boss that I would tell many tales of his greatness and benevolence.

The next week, he went back to paying me peanuts.

I had endured Stan Hansen's lariat, Ole Anderson's fury and Swede Hanson's right hand. But none of those dreadful moments could equal the sheer terror of speaking in public.

"You know, it's not all about wrestling," my dad told me. "If you want to be a star you have to get out there and talk."

We were in my sad little apartment at The Falcon's Rest. Dad had driven out from Texas to spend a week with me in Atlanta.

The old man had never wrestled a day in his life, but he was absolutely right about needing to talk. The big names like Dusty and Ole packed arenas with their actions *and* their words.

"But, that's just not me," I informed my dad.

The few times I had tried to "cut promos" had been disasters. I stuttered and stammered and my hands shook so bad that I couldn't hold the microphone still. The veterans would watch all of this on the backstage monitors and have a laugh at my expense.

"To hell with those guys," Dad said. "They aren't the ones paying your rent. You get them out of your mind, grab that microphone and say what you want to say. Once you do that, none of those bastards will be able to stop you."

I assured him I would give it my best shot, and assumed that this topic was closed. I had no idea that my Dad would continue our lesson during an unexpected appearance on Georgia Championship Wrestling.

"That big guy, with the handlebar mustache- I hear that's your dad?" Ole asked me.

I answered in the affirmative. It was a couple days after our conversation at the Falcon's Rest. Dad was visiting the studio to see a TV taping in person.

"Do you think he would want to do something on the show?" Ole asked, "I think we could use a guy that looks like that."

When I answered that, yes, my father would love to do something on TV, Ole had me fetch my old man and Bugsy McGraw.

Bugsy was a fun-loving, bearded wrestler with a tendency to giggle during his interviews. He had recently adopted a truck-driver persona and Ole was planning an interview segment that would take his gimmick to another level. Edward Denton, Sr. would play an important role in getting Trucker McGraw "over".

When I returned with Dad and Bugsy, Ole outlined the plan (I wasn't part of the segment, and just watched their conversation with my mouth shut). An hour later, my father joined Bugsy and Gordon Solie on the interview set of Georgia Championship Wrestling. Dad had a fake name- I can't remember what it was- and was supposed to represent some sort of truckers union. I watched the segment on a backstage monitor; it went something like this:

Dad: Gordon, I'm here on behalf of the tens of thousands of members of the International Brotherhood of Truck Drivers. These are the men that drive the highways and byways of this great land. The people that keep America going: hard-working, blue-collar folk fighting the good fight.

The crowd (primarily made up of hard-working, blue-collar folk fighting the good fight) started to cheer.

Dad: "We've been watching this wrestling show, and have been so impressed by this man Bugsy McGraw. Bugsy is one of us- he's out there fighting to keep this country great with his hard work and courage."

At this point I heard one of the locker room vets ask where they "found this old man? He's pretty damn good."

Dad: "Bugsy, on behalf of the truck drivers of America I want to present you with this special plaque. It's our way of saying thank you for exemplifying the very best of the International Brotherhood of Truck Drivers.

The crowd applauded as my father and Bugsy shook hands. Before Gordon could throw it to commercial, Dad interjected with another presentation.

Dad: One more thing, Bugsy! When you're out there fighting the good fight, we want you to remember that you always have our support. So, please accept this as another token of our appreciation.

With that, my dad handed Bugsy McGraw an air horn- you know, one of those annoying things you always hear at football games. The big fella started tooting that horn, and the audience went nuts.

Dad: Folks, y'all give it up for Bugsy McGraw!

Bugsy kept on tooting and Dad walked off the set to more cheers than I had *ever* received in my life. I just stared at the monitor in amazement. I'd been wrestling for over two years and could hardly speak a sentence, my dad had been in wrestling for two minutes and all of a sudden he was Superstar Billy Graham.

When the old man found me backstage, he gave me a nod that punctuated the confidence and focus behind his A+ promo. Then, in an expression of fatherly love, he told his son:

"That's how you do that shit."

Dad was a pretty good teacher, but it wasn't long before I was assigned an incredible tutor. He was one of the greatest interviews in the world. Hell, he was one of the greatest *everythings* in the world.

I had moved on to Jim Crockett's Mid-Atlantic territory. I was still a greenhorn and spent most nights looking up at the lights while the ref counted to three. Then, one night in Raleigh, I was assigned a new job (in addition to my normal job of doing jobs).

"Flair needs a driver," the booker George Scott told me. "We told him to pick one of the young guys and he asked for you."

I was blown away. Ric Flair was the promotion's top star, and everybody knew he was going to be World Champion someday. Fortunately for me, he was also having some travel difficulties.

Ric's promos always mentioned his expensive cars; that was no wrestling angle. Flair owned a souped-up Lincoln Continental and a brand new Cadillac. He drove those cars *fast*. So fast that he eventually had his drivers license revoked, and could no longer drive from show to show.

So, for almost a year I drove Ric Flair through Virginia and the Carolinas, picking his brain all along the way. Any young wrestler would have killed for that opportunity. It was like getting private piano lessons from Mozart.

Ric was amazing. He could have easily brushed me off and we would have had a "Driving Miss Daisy" relationship. Instead, he took an interest in my career and ended up being one of the greatest teachers I ever had.

"When I came here, nobody knew who Ric Flair was," he told me one day. "So I had to tell them."

During our long drives, Ric took me to promo school. He would make me spit out a three-minute monologue and then critique it bit-by-bit.

"Read the papers," he advised me. "Mention current events- politics, sports, movies- whatever. Work all of that stuff into your promos. Make your words *relevant*."

Following Flair's advice, I would take notes while watching TV or listening to the radio. If a comedian or DJ had a good line, I would write it down and save it for a future interview.

My education continued with every road trip. During one of my car promos, I said something to the effect of:

"That guy is nothing but an old, washed up has been. I'm going to destroy him!"

Ric stopped me immediately.

"Don't bury your opponent- build him up," he said. "Your match needs to mean something. If you say a guy sucks and you beat him- no one will care. But if you say this guy is an amazing athlete- now you've accomplished something."

That same philosophy carried over into Ric's matches. He taught me how to "qualify" my opponent. Essentially, it was knowing what a wrestler did well, and then playing towards those strengths during a match.

For example, if you were wrestling Andre, that would mean going up for big bumps, working the eyes and trying to chop down his legs. If you were with a guy like Ricky Steamboat, it would be technical wrestling, high spots and false finishes. It was all about working the right match for the right opponent.

"Make that other guy look like the baddest motherfucker around," Flair said, "And the two of you will draw money every single time."

After several months with Professor Flair, I received an impromptu pop quiz at a T.V. taping. Somehow, I found myself in a room with George Scott and Jim Crockett himself.

"Flair says you're a good kid and deserve a break," Scott informed me. "So, we want you to go on T.V. and give us a generic 3-minute promo."

I was struck simultaneously with feelings of gratitude, exhiliration and dread. Those familiar butterflies started flapping in my stomach, but I just focused on Ric's advice and our conversations on the road.

Then I went on television and delivered the best promo of my young career.

Ric looked like a proud papa when I met him backstage.

"Nice work kid," he said with a wink.

"Thanks," I replied. "I had a great teacher."

Life on the road with Ric Flair was everything you could imagine and more. Every night began in a sold out arena and ended in a bar overflowing with beautiful women and Wild Turkey.

You know how he says he's "a limousine ridin', kiss-stealin' wheelin-dealin' son of a gun?" Well, outside of the limousine that was all true. Ric wouldn't let me touch his luxury cars, so I drove him around in my old Ford LTD. Other than that, he was Ric Flair- as advertised.

Except for this one time.

We had wrapped up a show on an army base. As usual, Ric had torn the house down with a promo about his beautiful women, Lincolns and Cadillacs. We were in the back of the exhibition hall and a group of soldiers watched as the Nature Boy packed his beautiful, sequined robe into the trunk of my old beater.

"Are you kidding me?" one of the soldiers said. "You're talking about Cadillacs and you're riding home in that piece of shit?"

Ric ignored them, and made his way to the passenger side door.

"I knew you were full of shit," the guy continued. "Cadillacs, women, money? You're the phoniest fucker of them all."

That was it. Flair spun around, wide-eyed. He spoke in the voice he usually saved for big money promos:

"Listen hot shot- you want to see who the phony is? You follow us off this base. We'll pull over and settle this shit."

"You got it," the soldier replied, and he got into a jeep with a couple of his buddies.

They followed us as we drove towards the exit gate.

"As soon as we get off this base, pull off at the first off-ramp," Flair instructed. "You with me on this?"

"I'm with you," I said.

My heart was pounding. We were out-numbered, but I was with the Nature Boy. No way we were losing this fight.

We reached the gate and the MPs let us through. Then, the second we were off the base, an explosion rocked the car.

BOOM!

The LTD started shaking and the driver's wheel jerked from side to side. We came to a scraping halt. I jumped out of the car and immediately diagnosed the problem:

"Damn- it's a blowout!"

Ric's face turned bright red.

"We're supposed to meet those dipshits for a fight and you're telling me we have a FLAT TIRE?"

I grabbed my jack and spare tire from the trunk. Right at that moment, the soldiers pulled off the base. When they saw us on the side of the road, they laughed so hard I'm amazed they didn't wreck their jeep.

"Nice Cadillac!" They yelled at Ric as they drove by; slow enough so he could hear them, but fast enough so he couldn't catch them.

His face went from bright red to burgundy.

"YOU MOTHERFUCKERS! GET BACK HERE! LYNNY FIX THAT SHIT!"

I was jacking the car up as fast as I could. Before I could remove the flat, the soldiers returned. Not to fight: they just drove by and hit us with some empty beer cans.

"Maybe one of your imaginary girlfriends should pick you up!"

"THAT'S REAL FUNNY! COME BACK ONE MORE TIME AND SEE WHAT HAPPENS TOUGH GUY!"

They did come back. They were out of beer, so this time they hit us with a McDonald's bag full of trash.

"YOU SON OF A---"

Ric threw his sport coat to the pavement, jumped up and down and unleashed the most profane promo in the history of the English language. By the end, his face matched his maroon tie.

Those assholes never came back, and the next day Ric bought me a new set of expensive tires:

"I don't blame you," he said. "But don't EVER let that shit happen again."

I felt awful- no one wants to embarrass their mentor. But, after all of his teachings, I'd like to think that I finally taught the Nature Boy an important life lesson:

Never get in a Ford LTD with bald tires.

You'd think a 20-year-old kid running with Ric Flair wouldn't even dream about getting married. But remember, we're talking about the same genius that spit on Stan Hansen's boots.

"Country City USA" was a popular Charlotte bar owned by a woman named Lib Hatcher. I guess Lib was a wrestling fan, because she let all the boys drink for free. I was only 20, but thanks to my bulk and beard no one ever carded me- I just filled up on complimentary booze.

Lib had this kid named Randy Traywick who worked for her. Randy was younger than me, but man, that boy could sing! We became buddies and occasionally I'd interrupt his performances with a playful bodyslam or bear hug. Then, he'd go right back to the music and get that place rocking.

It was during one of Randy's shows that I saw a cute girl with feathered brown hair. I was buzzed and feeling like hot shit, so I went over and introduced myself. Her name was Tonda. It didn't take long for us to become an item. We eventually got married- way too young and way too soon.

Look, I'm not going to spend a lot of time talking about this, because the marriage was probably doomed from the start. We were both young and immature. Meanwhile, I was always on the road. Marriage is hard enough for responsible adults who live in the same home; imagine two young kids who never see each other.

We lasted maybe three years- honestly I can't remember. I only bring my first marriage up because it seems important. Tonda will pop up a couple more times in this book, but I'll spare you the rest of our marital woes.

By the way, that Randy Traywick kid? He eventually moved to Nashville, married Lib and changed his name to Randy Travis. Last time I checked, he had sold about 25 million records, so I guess he's doing alright.

By the age of 20 I was a world traveler. I wasn't one of those kids that you hear about, backpacking across Europe to "find myself". I was just trying to find a break in the wrestling business. This damn sure wasn't some sightseeing tour.

I spent six weeks in Germany wrestling for that country's biggest star, an *Arschloch* named Axel Dieter and his promoter Edmund Schober. Dieter embodied the fun-loving humor that is so closely associated with his native country.

"Hey American!" he would snarl. "You need to leesten!"

Of course, Dieter would never chastise my traveling partner. Moose Morowski was a tough hombre from Western Canada, and had become a mentor of mine in the Carolinas. Moose got me booked with Dieter, and on our Trans-Atlantic flight, he wouldn't stop talking about another young wrestler who would be joining the tour.

"His name is Dynamite Kid," he said in almost reverent tones. "He may be the greatest wrestler I've ever seen."

For days on end I heard about this incredible specimen who was Lou Thesz, Harley Race and Evel Knievel all rolled into one. When he finally walked into the locker room one day, Morowski acted like the Pope had arrived.

"He's here!"

I was convinced Moose had lost it. This supposed physical specimen was maybe an inch or two shorter than me and about 70 pounds lighter. Nothing about his sleepy-eyed demeanor reminded me of Ernie Ladd, Dusty Rhodes or any of the other top stars that I admired. When he said hello in his thick British accent, I couldn't help myself.

"Wow Moose," I joked. "Are you sure this is the great big tough guy you've been talking about?"

In an instant, Dynamite closed the space between us and got within an inch of my face.

"You got a fucking problem?" he asked.

I was caught completely off-guard.

"Wait--- I was just…"

"Step outside right now and we'll see who the tough guy is."

I put my hands up in a show of peace.

"Sorry man, I was just joking."

"Well, I'm not joking- outside now."

Thankfully, Moose got between us.

"Sorry Tommy, he's a good kid. Didn't mean anything by it."

Out of respect for Moose, Dynamite nodded, shook his hand and walked off. I didn't say a peep until he left, and made a mental note to never again throw sparks at Dynamite's short fuse.

Of course, when I saw his match later that night, I understood what Moose had been raving about. I had never seen anything like this man- half acrobat, half wrestler and completely ferocious. Forget about a British Bulldog, Tommy Billington was more like a flying pit-bull.

"That was incredible," I told him after his match. "I really apologize for what I said earlier. I didn't mean any disrespect."

"That's alright brother," he said. From that moment on, we were friends. On the tour, we tagged together, and I would just sit in the corner and watch Dynamite do moves that seemed physically impossible. Nip ups into back flips into handstands into missile dropkicks. Then when it came time to sell, the guy would take a beating like nobody's business.

We were the same age, but unlike me, Tommy had been fighting for most of his life. He was a bona fide "shooter", meaning if a fight became real he could hurt someone in an instant. Backstage, he was always playing practical jokes, but if he ever felt disrespected, Dynamite was ready to brawl.

"You can never back down from a confrontation," he told me. "I would rather have someone leave me bloody in the middle of the locker room floor than cower in the back and let someone disrespect me."

Of course, I had been disrespected just about every day of my wrestling career. But, thanks to the Dynamite Kid, I would finally stand up for myself- in the locker room and in the ring.

Wrestling in Germany was a bit strange, as they used a round system, similar to boxing. The referee Peter (aside from Dieter Axel, the only German on the tour) would come to me before each match with my instructions:

"Tree und a half rounds- he goes ovah!" The guy sounded just like one of the guards on *Hogan's Heroes*. One night I misheard Sgt. Schultz and did the job a round earlier than instructed.

"American!" he screamed in the locker room. "You ver told tree rounds- you vent two! You not understand English?"

Is that what that's supposed to be?

The next night, I was scheduled to take on an Italian wrestler named Salvatore Bellomo. Here came Peter again:

"Tree und a half rounds. He goes ovah!"

"Hold on a sec," I said. "You're saying *three* and a half rounds right? I want to make sure I understand what you expect from me."

At this point, my opponent interjected.

"Just-a shut up fat- boy and do-a the job!" Bellomo said.

Great- so now I had to deal with a German asshole *and* an Italian asshole. It was like World War II all over again (And "fat boy"? Art Nelson was calling me a beanpole less than a year ago).

61

I was lacing up my boots a few minutes later when Dynamite sat next to me.

"This is what I've been talking about," he said. "You can't let him talk to you like that."

"Who- Sal or the ref?"

"Either one," he replied, "In this business, you can't let anyone walk all over you. If you do it once, you'll be doing it for the rest of your career."

I sat up and exhaled in frustration.

"So what should I do?" I asked. "Go over there and kick Bellomo's ass?"

"You could do that," Dynamite said with a shrug. "But there's other ways to handle it. Maybe you should show him what a "fat boy" can do in the ring."

With that suggestion my gears started turning. How could I repay their disrespect *in the ring*? Hmmm….

During the match I could hit Sal with some stiff shots, but he would probably just hit me back and nothing would come of it. It would be better if I could embarrass the prick in front of everybody. When it was time for the match, I had a plan: I was going to "blow up" Salvatore Bellomo.

In pro wrestling, great cardio conditioning is essential, or you will quickly run out of gas. A lot of guys will use rest-holds like headlocks and armbars to pace themselves. I knew Sal couldn't hang with me from a conditioning standpoint, so I made that *cazzo* work his ass off for the entire match.

There were no rest holds. I wouldn't allow them. Just run, run, run and run some more. If I knocked Sal down, I picked him up with no time to catch a breath. If he knocked me down, I was back on my feet right away and sending him to the ropes. We're talking non-stop running, jumping and bumping.

"Slow-a this shit down," Sal demanded. He was sucking wind like crazy. "What-a the fuck is wrong with you?"

By the fourth round, Bellomo looked like a dying fish. He was supposed to win, so we went to the finish as instructed. I damn near had to pull the bum on top of me. After scoring the pinfall, Bellomo grabbed the second rope and tried to get to his feet, but he couldn't even stand. I jumped to my heels and looked at him with a smirk. While Salvatore lay there gasping for air, I did ten air squats in the middle of the ring, jumped over the top rope and walked back to the locker room. Meanwhile that idiot won the match and didn't even have the energy to raise his hand.

"Vut are you doing shtupid American?" Peter shouted when he found me backstage. I could barely hear him over Dynamite's roaring laughter.

"You know, maybe you should keep Sal's matches to two rounds," I replied.

With that I packed my bag, shook Dynamite's hand and headed to the hotel. The next week I bid *Auf Wiedersehen* to Deutschland.

After four years in the wrestling business, I had two major problems:

1)   I wasn't pretty enough to attract young girls.

2)   I wasn't ugly enough to scare little children.

I knew I could work, and felt good about my interview skills, but I needed a persona or "gimmick" to transition from a mid-carder to a main event talent. Just being another guy in tights wouldn't cut it.

My first real gimmick came in Stu Hart's Calgary Stampede Wrestling. I had heard that it was a good place for an up and comer to work, because a lot of the veterans didn't want to drive thousands of miles to icy Alberta. Fewer vets meant more openings at the top of the card.

With Dynamite Kid's blessing I debuted as "Dynamite" Len Denton. I bleached my hair blonde, which combined with my black beard gave me a pretty unique look. Remember, this was 1980 and I was surrounded by a bunch of flannel-wearing cowboys and blue-collar Canadians. The plan was for me to feud with Tommy over our shared name, but as soon as I arrived, he left for a tour of Japan.

"Hey- eh kid…. eh… welcome to Calgary."

Stu Hart was in some ways the Paul Bunyan of Calgary- a larger than life legend born out of the frigid plains of Western Canada. He was revered as a great family man and community icon. But in the wrestling business he was best known for making giant men cry with his arsenal of submission holds.

We were in the basement of his home. I had needed a place to work out, so Stu's son Bruce had ushered me into a room with a collection of free weights and one very grimy and soiled wrestling mat. If you know anything about Stu Hart, you know the nickname of this place.

I was in The Dungeon.

"So…. eh… Lenny…" Stu began rubbing his hands together. "How would you… eh… like to learn a few new moves?"

He gestured to the mat. It was smeared with blood (at least I hope it was blood) and god knows what else. The walls were even worse- bodily fluids permanently stained the wood paneling. A few nails stuck out for good measure.

"I appreciate the offer sir," I finally answered. "But… I feel pretty good about my wrestling and how should I put this…"

There's no way in hell I'm getting tortured on that filthy germ hotel?

"…I just need to work out. But, thank you."

Stu looked at me as if I had just cancelled Christmas. Then, the light returned to his eyes and his let loose a deep "heh-heh."

"Welcome to our home," he said. "When Bret gets back, you'll be working with him."

Today wrestling fans know Bret Hart as a Hall of Famer and multi-time world champion. But back in 1980, there was only one legend in the Hart family and that was Stu. Bret was just one of eight sons hoping to follow in his father's sizable footsteps (Stu had 12 kids total which may be one of the reasons he was so damn tough).

My first few weeks in Calgary, Bret was working in Japan, so I would go on TV and call him out:

"I came to Calgary hearing all about the Harts," I would say, "But as soon as I got here that chicken Bret Hart ran off to Japan!"

The promos started building some serious heat with the Calgary fans, and they were eager for Bret to return and shut my big mouth. At one TV taping, I went out and delivered my typical anti-Bret promo:

"They call this place Stampede Wrestling. Well, when I got here that chicken Bret Hart stampeded across the Pacific Ocean!"

I went back to the locker room, and looked at the rundown for the rest of the show. According to the sheet, I was scheduled for another promo in the following segment. So, I went back out in front of the cameras:

"So no one has seen that chicken Bret Hart?" I asked. "No, they haven't seen him, because Dynamite Len Denton rules this roost!"

I went back and checked the sheet again. I was scheduled for *another* interview. What the hell was I supposed to say in a third promo? I called Bruce over.

"I appreciate you guys giving me all this exposure," I said. "But do you really need me to cut a promo every ten minutes?"

Bruce looked at the sheet in my hand. He scrutinized the handwriting and then called back over his shoulder:

"OWEN!"

Stu's youngest son- a skinny, blonde teenager, walked over.

"Did you change this sheet?" Bruce asked.

"Well, kind of," Owen admitted. "I just really like his interviews."

Bruce shook his head and sent his little brother on his way.

"Well, at least your promos are getting over." he said.

Yes, all those lessons with Ric Flair and my old man had finally paid off. Of course, Owen would go on to become a great professional wrestler himself (and a legendary ribber). And, excluding my wife and family, he was probably the only fan of "Dynamite" Len Denton.

When Bret finally returned from Japan it was *on*.

First, we shot some TV angles to build interest in our feud. I had one idea that I thought could really up the intensity.

"I've been calling him a chicken all this time," I explained to Bruce and Stu. "What if I choke him out with a rubber chicken?"

They loved the idea, and the next week I arrived at the T.V. taping ready to strangle the future Hitman. That's when Stu handed me my chicken. Not a *rubber* chicken, mind you. It was just a plain old dead bird- complete with feathers, feet and a head.

"You want me to choke your son with *this*?" I asked.

"Eh…. you boys will be fine," Stu assured me.

So, that night we went on television and I wrapped that dead clucker around Bret Hart's throat. The crowd was thoroughly repulsed and by the end, Bret looked worse than the bird. Our matches ended up being a series of bloody brawls throughout the province of Alberta. We eventually settled our issues with a no-holds barred televised showdown. The match, like our previous confrontations, was extremely physical (while working in Japan and Germany, Bret had learned to work "snug". In other words, I *really* felt his shots. Don't feel bad- I returned the favor).

After kicking the crap out of each other for maybe ten minutes, Bret back-dropped me over the top rope. Usually, for a move like that I would grab the ropes and slow my descent. But my hands were so sweaty they slid right off the ropes. So, instead of a controlled fall, the back of my head bounced off the ring apron and I crashed tailbone-first on to the cement floor.

Bret rolled out of the ring and tried to lift me to my feet. But he couldn't move me- I was knocked out cold. At this point, he could have tried to slap me back into consciousness or maybe thrown a fan's beer into my face. But Bret had a better idea: he slammed a steel chair right into my skull.

That did the trick.

I popped up to my feet and we wrestled another ten minutes. Of course, I don't remember any of this. The only reason I know what happened is because I eventually went back and watched the match on tape. Looking back, I must say that I put on a pretty good performance- especially when you consider that I probably didn't know my own name at that point.

The feud with Bret was my first sustained main-event run. Eventually, Stu teamed me up with a wrestler named Dave Patterson (his real last name was Canal). Dave would become better known as "The Cuban Assassin" Fidel Sierra (in Portland he dropped the "Cuban" as was known simply as The Assassin).

We became close friends and eventually won the Stampede Tag Team titles. But I didn't feel like a champion. After working on top for a few months I was making 500 bucks a week (Canadian dollars of course). Once my pay hit 500, the tax rate jumped and the Canadian government started taking huge chunks out of every check.

"Stu, this is crazy," I said backstage after one house show. "I'm a champion. I'm in the main event. But after taxes, I'm making what I was when I was jerkin' curtains back home."

"I know kid…" he replied with some compassion. "Eh… wish I could help you."

"It's not enough," I insisted. "Can you raise my pay so I'm clearing five hundred *after* taxes?"

"Sorry," Stu said. "You're a good hand… but I can't do that."

We had that conversation a few more times, always with the same result. I eventually discussed the issue with my wife. She was already miserable in Canada and missed her family in North Carolina. Making jobber money for main event work didn't make things any easier- I decided a change was necessary.

So, one early morning Dave and I paid a visit to a couple of our buddies on the Stampede Roster. We were each holding a championship belt when I knocked on their hotel room door.

Bobby Fulton opened the door in his underwear, shielding his eyes from the sunlight. His tag-team partner Tom Stanton was still sleeping off a long night.

"Man, what do you want at this hour?" Bobby asked. "It's not even 9 A.M."

"I got something to show you," I replied as we worked our way into the room. "Now- put me in a small package."

Bobby looked at me, probably trying to decide if I was drunk or high or both.

"Seriously," I said. "Roll me up in a small package, just like you were catching a pinfall in the ring."

Probably wanting to end this bizarre wake-up call, Bobby complied and rolled me up- pressing my shoulders against the floor. In a flash, Dave dropped down, slapped the floor and made the count:

"1- 2- 3!"

Bobby let me go and I leapt to my feet.

"Congratulations," I said. "You guys are the new tag team champions!"

I handed my belt to Bobby and Dave tossed his strap on to the snoring Tom Stanton. Then I got in my car and said goodbye to Dave, Canada and "Dynamite" Len.

Whatever success I had in Calgary meant less than nothing when I returned to the Carolinas. I had been back in Mid-Atlantic for a month when I found myself driving down Interstate 74 and planning my exit from the wrestling business.

"I'm done," I told my traveling partner Don Kernodle. "I told Tonda when we came here this was my last shot. If this didn't work I was getting out. Four years is my limit."

Four years. Damn, that seemed like a long time. My return to Charlotte brought a return to the bottom of the totem pole: once again I was getting paid pennies to make other guys look good. It wasn't a surprise. Outside of my stint in

Stampede and a couple of other blips on the radar, I had been running in place since day one.

"My old man says I can work for him," I continued. "He's going to retire soon and I can take over. It ain't glamorous, but at least it's a real job."

Don nodded his head. He was a native North Carolinian and had been a local college wrestling star. With his blue eyes and curly brown hair Don looked every bit the babyface.

"You're a good worker man," he eventually said. "You just need a hook- the right gimmick."

He was right. The whole "Dynamite" thing worked fine in Calgary, but part of the reason it clicked was because I had borrowed a name from one of the promotion's top stars. Also, my bleach blonde locks weren't unique in Ric Flair country.

"You ever thought of wearing a mask?" Don asked. "I kind of want to try it, but since I wrestled amateur here they won't let me do it. Want to capitalize on the name I guess."

I *had* actually wrestled in a mask before. In Georgia, Ole had me compete as "The Challenger" (a fitting name since I would never be known as "The Champion"). The mask gimmick was just a way for me to work twice on the same card- once as Len Denton and once as The Challenger.

Wrestling in a mask wasn't something that I enjoyed. When you do it the first time, it's almost a claustrophobic experience. If the mask doesn't fit just right, it can be difficult to breath- especially during a long match. Also, your peripheral vision is severely limited. Still, guys like Mr. Wrestling II, The Destroyer and Mil Mascaras had become huge stars while wearing "hoods". If a mask meant a big payday…

"I even have a name picked out," Kernodle said.

Don's words broke my train of thought, and visions of main event purses morphed back into the Interstate's passing traffic.

"What do you mean you picked a name out?" I asked.

"For if I ever got to wear a mask," he answered. "I couldn't be Don Kernodle. I figured I should have a name that represented my wrestling background."

"So what is it?"

Don arched his eyebrows. He spoke in a voice that you might hear in a trailer for a cheap slasher film:

"The--- Grappler!"

That name just hung in the air for a few seconds: *The Grappler*.

"Damn," I finally said. "That *is* a cool name."

Don just swatted the compliment away.

"Doesn't matter," he said. "I'll never get to use it. I'll be Don Kernodle for the rest of my career."

I knew exactly what he meant. My role in the wrestling business had been preordained. I'd be Loser Lynn Denton until the day I finally hung up my boots. And as far as I was concerned, that day couldn't come soon enough.

For two weeks Tonda and I prepared for our move to Texas. She wasn't thrilled about it: she was from Charlotte and liked living near her family. But the move meant money, stability and an end to changing addresses every six months.

I was wrapping up my commitments with Crockett and professional wrestling was essentially in my rear-view mirror. There were just a few dates left on my calendar when Mid-Atlantic held a big card at the Norfolk Scope. I don't remember a lot about that night- who I wrestled, or who handed me the phone backstage. What I will never forget is the conversation that changed my life.

It's weird, if I hadn't been walking down that hall at that exact moment, I could right now be a construction worker in Houston. Instead, one of the boys (I wish I could remember who it was) stopped me and held out the receiver of a payphone.

"Hey Lynny, I got someone here that you should talk to."

I said hello and instantly recognized the voice at the other end. Buck Robley was the booker for Tri-State Wrestling.

"Actually, it's called 'Mid-South Wrestling' now," he informed me. "Watts broke away from McGuirk- changed the name and everything. Anyways, we've seen some of your work. Looks like you're doing good."

I lied and said, yes, things were going good. I didn't mention that in the last three years I had gone from being a job guy in Tri-State to being a job guy in Mid-Atlantic. Robley continued:

"Bill and I have been talking and I think we've got a spot for you here."

Just what I needed: to move hundreds of miles for more humiliation and more shitty paychecks.

"Thanks Buck," I said. "But I think I've been squashed by Big Cat and Kox more than enough times. Besides..."

"You've got it all wrong," he interjected. "This will be big. We're talking some real money."

Now he had my attention. We discussed the idea for a few minutes, and by the end of the conversation my construction career was put on hold. Then, Buck had one final question:

"Have you ever worn a mask?"

I looked down the hall for Don Kernodle. Was this some sort of rib? No. This was really happening. The opportunity of a lifetime was staring me in the face and all I had to do was answer a simple question.

"Yeah, I've worn a mask," I informed Buck. "Hell, I've even got a name picked out."

When he asked me for my alias, I spoke slow and made the moment count:

"Just call me *The Grappler*."

CHAPTER FOUR

A MASK, A BOOT, A BELT

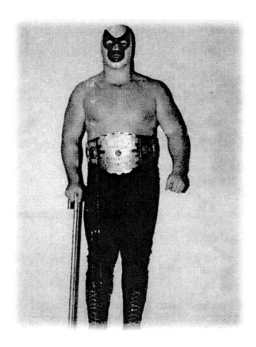

T he Grappler was born a few months after the greatest star in the history of New Orleans wrestling. The Junkyard Dog made his Mid-South Wrestling debut in late 1979. By the time I arrived in the spring of 1980, JYD was breaking attendance records and setting the territory on fire.

The Dog and I traveled similar paths to Mid-South. Like me, Sylvester Ritter had worked for Watts in a previous stint that was not very distinguished. He then went to work for Stu Hart, where he experienced his first run as a main event star. When he returned to Mid-South, The Cowboy repackaged Sylvester as The Junkyard Dog and made him a top attraction.

Overnight he became a folk hero to the large black populations in Louisiana and Mississippi. Even the white good ol' boys cheered for the Dog. With his endless charisma and entertaining interviews it was hard not to love the guy.

There was just one problem: The Junkyard Dog didn't have the ability to work a match longer than five minutes. That's where I came in.

"Dog is gonna draw great crowds," Watts told me. "You're here to have great matches."

Bill, Robley and I were in the KTSB newsroom (the place where Karl Kox had aimed a gun at me four years prior). It was my first night back in the promotion, having moved to Baton Rouge a few days earlier. Watts continued his instructions:

"I need a wrestling heel," he said. "Look, Dog is a great babyface and will bring in the people. But his matches are going to be short. I need someone that can deliver a long, solid match and give the people their money's worth. If things go well, I'll have you working with Teddy."

"Teddy" was Ted Dibiase, a second generation star and the territory's current champion. He was one of Watts' top young workers, along with my old friends Jake Roberts and Paul Orndorff, who were also back in Mid-South. I assured Bill that I was more than ready to put on some great matches with the whole roster. Then Robley made a request:

"Can we see the gimmick?"

The word "gimmick" has infinite meanings in professional wrestling. It can refer to a wrestler's persona, wardrobe, move, catchphrase, a prop, a match stipulation or about a million other things. In this case, Robley wanted to see my mask.

I reached into my duffel bag and pulled out a glittery silver hood with black accents around the eyes and mouth. I had planned to buy a mask before I left Charlotte, but they were pretty expensive. So, my wife (an accomplished seamstress) made one instead. I wish I could say there was some cool story behind the colors or the design. In reality, she just went off of some pictures she had seen in a wrestling magazine and used materials from a fabric store. The finished product looked like something a crazy fan would wear to an Oakland Raiders game.

"That'll do the job," Watts said. "Now it's on you to make it work."

He was right. I had waited four years for this opportunity. Now I had to navigate the road ahead if I wanted to become a top star. Thankfully, one of my predecessors had left me a map.

In the early and mid-70s a masked wrestler named Dr. X was a champion in what was then known as Tri-State Wrestling. He was a solid wrestling heel who feuded with top stars like the legendary Danny Hodge. X was portrayed by a man named Jim Osborne, who was eventually fired (rumor was that he left a show after being told to job to Thunderbolt Patterson). Despite his backstage drama, Dr. X had been a steady draw for Tri-State. The Cowboy's plan was to recreate his success with the younger, more reliable Lynn Denton. So, when The Grappler made his television debut, the comparisons were immediate:

"This Grappler is an incredible talent," the announcer Boyd Pierce would say. "He reminds me of a young Dr. X!"

For the first three weeks, my TV matches were outright squashes. I would use a variety of technical holds to subdue my outmatched opponents, and Pierce would put me over big time. Then I would cut a promo and say that Pierce was holding back: I was the greatest wrestler that this promotion had ever seen! The intent was simple: to establish The Grappler as a jerk who could *really* wrestle.

It worked. The fans bought into this newer, younger version of the great Dr. X. In less than a month, I was in Jackson, Mississippi facing the most important audition of my life.

Believability meant everything to Bill Watts. A heel could never, ever be seen outside of the arena with a babyface. If people saw you fighting each other on TV and then laughing together over a beer, they would know that your wrestling feud was an act- the worst fear of Watts and pretty much every promoter at that time.

That same line of thinking went into the staging of Mid-South Wrestling events. Even in buildings where there was only one locker room, heels and

74

babyfaces would enter the arena from different locations. Heels were absolutely forbidden from being seen anywhere near the babyface entrance and vice versa. That's why I was shocked when fan favorite Paul Orndorff walked back through the heel entrance about thirty minutes before our scheduled match.

"What are you doing man?" I whispered. "I'm supposed to wrestle you tonight! Watts will flip his shit if anyone saw you come back here."

"I made sure no one was watching," Paul assured me. "Brother, I got some big news."

I waved him over to a quiet corner, and glanced around to make sure no lookie-loos were about.

"Watts is here." Paul told me.

That may not sound like a big deal (he was the owner after all), but Bill rarely attended non-televised house shows. His headquarters were in Tulsa and his appearance meant that he flew down, likely for a specific reason.

"He's here to watch you," Paul said with a smile. "Lynny, they're talking about putting the belt on you."

Mid-South had several titles including the Mississippi State title and the Louisiana State title. But "The Belt" was Dibiase's North American Heavyweight Championship- the promotion's top prize.

"I overheard him and Robley," Orndorff continued. "Watts wants to see what you can do in person. We're supposed to go to a 35 minute draw. If he likes it, it sounds like you're in."

This was *insane*- two months ago I was a jobber ready to quit for good; now I was being considered for the #1 spot in the territory. It took everything I had not to dance a jig. But celebrations had to wait- if our match sucked, this conversation wouldn't mean a damn thing.

"Let me call the match out there," I told Paul. "He'll want to see what I can do."

Paul nodded. He was a good guy and an incredible athlete- but if Paul got excited, you could get hurt. Once, he kicked me in the junk so hard that I fell out of the ring and ended up limping for a week. But as I long as I was controlling the pace and the spots, I knew that Paul would make me look like a champion.

"I've got your back brother," he said and slapped me on the shoulder. Then, he cautiously surveyed the scene and made a stealthy return to the babyface locker room.

The match was fantastic. We went the full 35 and Paul did everything I asked of him and more. Afterwards, I should have been exhausted and hurt, but the adrenaline negated all of that. I walked through the back curtain to find Bill Watts waiting for me.

"I don't mean to alarm you boss," I joked. "But you're in the heel locker room."

The Cowboy no-sold the joke and told me we had business to discuss.

Professional wrestling is an industry filled with great minds, and the greatest minds are usually stealing great ideas from other great minds. Watts and Robley had already drawn comparisons between The Grappler and Dr. X. Now, they wanted me to adopt X's infamous weapon: the loaded boot.

It was a gimmick (there's that word again) where a wrestler supposedly had some illegal weight in the heel of their boot. By kicking the mat and "loading" the toe of the boot, the wrestler would then have the power to knock out any opponent. At least, that's what the announcers would tell the television audience.

"But you can't just walk out there and start kicking people with it," Watts told me. "You'll need a reason to start wearing the boot…"

"I could get my foot injured or something," I offered. "Say the boot is for a medical condition."

The Cowboy crossed his arms and exhaled. He didn't have to say "no shit"- his eyes saved his lips the work.

"You're wrestling Teddy next week. I want you to come up with an injury angle for that match," he commanded. "Call me with your idea tomorrow. It *better* be good."

Our meeting ended just like that, and I didn't sleep for the next twenty-four hours. I was excited about the prospect of a championship feud, but terrified of pitching some crappy idea to my hardass boss. Hell, the last time a promoter picked my brain for an angle I ended up choking his son with a dead chicken. The next afternoon I finally had a plan (after a million mental re-writes of course). I called Watts and explained the scenario I had envisioned. His reaction was short and sweet:

"Fucking fantastic. Tell Robley I want the finish exactly like that."

The match took place in Monroe, Louisiana. Fans who only know Ted Dibiase as "The Million Dollar Man" might be taken aback by his 1980 persona. He was an articulate, clean shaven babyface that always played by the rules. But unlike the very limited JYD, Teddy could have a great match with anybody. There were even rumors in the Mid-South locker room that he was being considered for an eventual NWA World Title reign. Backstage, I laid out the plan for our match. It was the same injury angle that Watts had approved.

"That's pretty good- if we can pull it off," Teddy joked. "You ready?"

"No," I answered honestly. "But I've got too much riding on this to quit now."

I wasn't exaggerating. The goal of the match was for me to suffer a serious injury, which would then set up a big title rematch with Teddy down the road. If Watts liked the match, that's exactly what would happen. But if he hated it, that "injury" could end up being a career ender for The Grappler.

The match began as a scientific wrestling contest, with Teddy usually coming out ahead in each exchange. Of course, me being the asshole that I was, every once in a while I would rake an eye or pull some hair to get an unfair advantage. We probably went 20 minutes before setting up the big finish.

At a designated time, the referee got knocked out (big surprise right?) and I decided to capitalize on the situation. I smacked Teddy with a steel chair and the place went apeshit. Unlike today's wrestling, Mid-South didn't show chairshots on TV every week, so when you used one it really meant something. Fans started pelting the ring with garbage as I climbed the top rope. I could hear the fans' pleas from the front row:

"Get up Ted!! GET UP!!!"

All hope appeared lost: Teddy was vulnerable and his title was mine for the taking. I planted one foot on the top turnbuckle and prepared to drop a knee across his throat.

But before I could lower the boom, a funny thing happened- I "slipped". Suddenly, I was dangling upside down, with my right leg trapped between the rope and the turnbuckle. Teddy rose to his feet, his face painted with fury. He grabbed the steel chair and began whacking my defenseless knee and ankle. The ref called for the disqualification but Teddy kept up the attack. It took half the locker room to eventually wrest the chair from the crazed Dibiase. At that point I was carted out on a stretcher, much to the fans delight (in their eyes my evil tactics justified the babyface's illegal attack).

Because Teddy was such a pro, my leg felt just fine afterwards. In fact, backstage I was walking with some extra spring in my step: I knew we had pulled it off. I ran into Buck Robley who confirmed my hunch:

"*That* was a big money angle."

The nice thing about a worked injury is that you get a couple weeks off to sell the beating to the public. For most wrestlers in 1980, it also meant wearing a cast or sling anytime they left the house. Thankfully I wore a mask and didn't have to worry about any of that. I spent my days working out, drinking beers and preparing for my big push. My mini-vacation ended in the KTSB newsroom, where I was introduced to one hideous piece of footwear. It looked like any other wrestling boot, but its sole was several inches thicker than usual- like a massive strip of fat on an otherwise average steak.

"I have to wear that nasty-ass thing?" I asked Buck Robley.

"Looks ain't everything," he replied. "Try it on."

I laced it up. The damn thing was as uncomfortable as it was ugly. Honestly, it might not have been so bad if I wore two boots with those giant soles. But only my right foot was elevated, so I was walking around lop-sided. It was like having a permanent limp.

Fortunately, I would only have to wear that boot every day for the next twenty years.

"We're calling it your "orthopedic boot." Robley said. "This next month, we're gonna get that thing over big time."

Mid-South's television show was somewhat ahead of its time. On every episode, important angles would take place that would lead to another angle the following week. Of course, that's like every wrestling show in 2014. But in 1980, other territories' shows were mostly made up of meaningless matches and promos; you had to watch Mid-South *every week* to keep track of the storylines (we didn't call them 'storylines' back then, but that's what they were).

So, the first episode of my return, I hobbled out to the interview set with a cane and my new "orthopedic boot". I informed the audience that Dibiase's chair attack left me with a serious injury- my right leg was now several inches shorter than my left leg (please don't ask me to explain the science behind this).

"But," I continued, "The Grappler is a competitor. And I will defy the odds and return to wrestle next week."

Of course, the crowd laughed at my ridiculous cane and boot, but I kept my word and returned the following week.

"How can you people make fun of a handicapped man?" I cried. "It's a miracle I can even walk! But, now, I will show all of you how tough I am. It's time for The Grappler's triumphant return to the squared circle!"

The fans were still heckling me as I locked up with my opponent. But later in the match, when I started kicking the mat (behind the referee's back), they knew something bad was about to happen. After all, most of these people had watched Dr. X do the exact same thing.

WHAM!

With one swift kick to the noggin, I earned the victory and the fans' vitriol. The next week brought questions:

"Grappler, what is in that boot?" Boyd Pierce asked. "Is there some sort of illegal object in there?"

"How dare you ask me that question?" I replied with disgust. "I have returned from a career-ending injury! I should be celebrated for this, but instead you come at me with ridiculous accusations. I don't need to cheat- I'm the greatest wrestler in the world!"

Then, the greatest wrestler in the world entered the ring and stole another win with an illegal punt to the skull. This dance continued for a few more weeks, until a number of Mid-South babyfaces decided enough was enough: it was time to stop The Grappler and his lethal lead foot.

Most wrestling fans don't realize this, but I actually competed at a big domed supershow where Andre the Giant wrestled Hulk Hogan. No, I'm not talking about Wrestlemania III. This show took place August 2nd, 1980 at the Louisiana Superdome and Andre vs. Hogan was just a mid-card contest. The main event that night was The Junkyard Dog vs. Michael Hayes in a steel cage match. A few weeks prior, The Dog had taken part in a tremendous angle where he was "blinded" by Hayes and The Fabulous Freebirds. They drew nearly 30,000 fans to the dome that night, solidifying JYD's status as one of pro wrestling's top draws (at least within the city of New Orleans- Dusty and Andre both competed on that card and were bigger global stars).

I continued building my heel momentum that night with a match against a true legend. Wahoo McDaniel was simply one of the toughest men to ever walk this planet. Period. I'm not sure that you could actually hurt the man but he could damn sure hurt you. Don't get me wrong: he would take it as much as he would give it. The only problem was he would give you a whole shitload of it.

I'm not saying Wahoo was a bad guy- on the contrary- he was a beast in the ring and a prince in the locker room. But after a match with Wahoo, you felt it brother. Anyone who doubts wrestling's authenticity should be required to take just one of his chops. That ain't the worst of it. Several years later I would wrestle Wahoo in an Indian Strap Match. Holy Shit. There's a reason you never see me without my mask.

Anyways, I did all the evil stuff that the Mid-South fans had grown to expect and attempted to knock out Wahoo with the loaded boot. He evaded the move, and then went into a rage, eventually getting himself disqualified. The outcome was great for both of us: Wahoo saved face and showed his legendary fighting spirit while I notched a win over a pro wrestling icon. With that signature victory, there was just one mountain left to climb.

The Shreveport Municipal Auditorium is known worldwide as the venue that launched Elvis Presley's musical career. In the early '50s the future king earned $18 for performing on the Auditorium's "Louisiana Hayride" music show. Thankfully, I earned a much bigger paycheck on the night I was crowned king of Mid-South Wrestling.

It was September 19, 1980 and sharp-eyed Shreveporters might have guessed that something big was about to go down. After all, there was a television camera at ringside- a rare sight for a normal house show.

"You don't think that will tip anyone off?" I asked Robley.

"Nah," he assured me. "We'll just say on TV that we were fortunate to have a camera crew on site for this incredible moment. Besides, don't you want everyone to see you win the Heavyweight Title?"

Praise the Lord, it was really happening. Watts had told me about the title change a few weeks earlier, but in pro wrestling plans change and promises are broken every day. I never assumed anything would happen until it actually did.

"You and Teddy go over the finish?" Robley asked.

We had. Once again, Watts had tasked me with booking the match's final sequence. After hearing my pitch, he gave his stamp of approval and ended our talk with a stern admonition:

"Once you wear that belt, you represent this company," he told me. "We are telling everyone you are one of the toughest men on the planet. Don't you *ever* jeopardize that image. If you go into a bar, you better be able to kick everyone's ass. The second some Joe Average knocks your teeth out, you're fucking done. I'll personally stomp the shit out of whatever's left and you'll never work in this territory again."

Later, I told Dick Murdoch about Watts' warning.

"Thank God I wear a mask," I said. "At least if I do get my ass kicked nobody will know."

"Fuck. I'll tell them who you are," Dickie replied. "I'll tell everybody."

Captain Redneck was always joking, but this was no rib. Given the opportunity, I knew he really would have stooged me out. Wrestling friendships are weird that way.

The Auditorium's air was thick and muggy as hell that night. The mask kept sliding across my perspiration-soaked face as Teddy and I went to work. It was a good 25 minutes of back-and-forth, up-tempo wrestling. He'd hit me with a shot that seemed like the end and then I'd kick out at 2 and a half. Then I'd pull some heel move, make the cover and Teddy would barely escape. The crowd was fully invested in the match. When I rolled out of the ring for a breather one psycho old granny yelled at me:

"You're gonna get what's coming to you boy!"

Oh, I was going to get something alright. I just had to take care of one piece of business first.

Somehow, I had been able to come up with a controversial finish that did not involve knocking out the referee. After a hot series of false finishes, Teddy and I came off the ropes and our heads collided. We simultaneously fell to the mat, like Stallone and Carl Weathers at the end of Rocky II. The ref began his count.

"ONE! (long pause) TWO! (longer pause) THREE…"

If he reached ten, the match would be a draw. But at about five, the ref circled towards Teddy and turned his back to me. That was the signal I was waiting for. While lying on my stomach, I kicked the mat several times with my right foot. The fans had never seen this before: I was loading the boot from a prone position. Psycho Granny started screaming at the ref from ringside:

"He's messin' with that damn boot!"

Like any good wrestling referee, he was oblivious to my cheating. He reached nine, and Teddy and I both made it to our feet, the crowd trying to warn the babyface about my evil intentions.

"He loaded the boot Ted! He loaded the boot!"

We traded punches in the middle of the ring. After a couple of exchanges, Teddy blocked a shot and hit me with a right hand. Then another block and another right. Then a right, a right, a right... the fans were euphoric. Psycho Granny looked like she was having a seizure. Finally, Teddy threw me to the ropes. I bounced off and he lowered his head for a backdrop. Everything went according to plan.

WHAM!

My right foot caught him square on the jaw. Teddy fell like a stone. I made the cover and it was over.

Immediately following the three count, all I could hear was the ringing bell and Psycho Granny's curses. Then, everyone started screaming at the ref. When he turned away to retrieve my new title belt, I made a big show of slamming my heel on the mat. I stopped just as the ref turned back around, holding the strap in his left hand. Finally, he could hear what the fans were saying:

"Grappler loaded the boot! He hit Dibiase with the loaded boot!"

The ref looked at the fans, and then back to me.

"Did you use a loaded boot?" he yelled. He added big, obvious gestures to the question, so everyone in the arena would understand what he was asking.

Of course, I made an equally exaggerated plea of innocence. The ref looked back to the fans and then demanded that I lift my right foot. He dropped to a knee, grabbed the boot's toe and felt around for some sort of illegal object. As the TV announcers would explain the following week, by slamming my heel on the mat I had "unloaded" the boot. So, as far as the fans were concerned, there was nothing in my toe for the referee to detect- I had concealed the evidence. When he finished his foot frisking, he raised my arm and handed me the belt.

"The winner and NEW North American Heavyweight Champion... The Grappler!"

I raised my new title overhead, and made a b-line for the aisle. Instantly, a pair of enraged fans started swinging at me. I swung back. Hell, if they wanted to hate me, I'd give them a reason. Eventually, a pair of police officers came to my side and escorted me safely to the dressing room.

I decided to hole up in the back for a while. There was a good chance some lunatic fan (or fans) would be waiting outside the Auditorium, hoping to take a shot at the new champion. Yeah, they probably didn't know what I looked like, but I didn't see the need to take any chances. So I just sat on a bench and admired my sweaty reflection on the belt's chrome surface.

When the building finally emptied, I found Teddy and thanked him for putting me over. He said it was his pleasure and he meant it. For a pro like Ted Dibiase all of this was just another day at the office.

Then I grabbed some quarters from my bag and called my parents with the big news. My dad had always been stern and emotionally distant when I was a kid. But for some reason, as he grew older, Edward Denton became much more expressive and sentimental. Maybe he finally decided that he didn't want to wind up like *his* old man (the curmudgeon who gave me grief about losing to Ernie Ladd). Whatever the reason, I knew my father meant it when he said:

"I'm proud of you son... and Lynny... I love you."

When the janitorial staff started turning off the lights I decided to make one final phone call. I hadn't spoken to the man in years and hoped he had the same phone number. When he picked up, I didn't have to ask if I had reached Joe Mercer; I recognized his gruff "hello".

We began with some small talk- how are you, how's the family- all that B.S. Then we talked wrestling.

"I want to thank you for breaking me into the business and being my teacher," I said. "I think you'd be happy to see where I am today. Also, you were right about one thing."

In this situation, a normal person might respond with a "What?" but not, good ol' Joe Pizza. I had a mental image of him mean mugging his telephone.

"When we first met, you said I would never make a dime in pro wrestling," I reminded him. "Well, you were right about that."

Still more silence. I was about to give up when Joe finally took the bait.

"I was right about that huh?"

That's what I was waiting for; I had booked this whole conversation in my mind, as if it were a wrestling match. Joe gave me the set up, and I went to the finish.

"Yes, you were right," I told him. "I'm not going to make a *dime* in pro wrestling… I'm about to make a *fortune*."

CHAPTER FIVE

CHAMPION

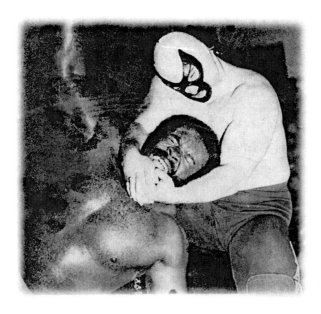

T he Mid-South North American Heavyweight Championship was created in the Autumn of 1979 (when it succeeded the NWA Tri-State Championship) and was laid to rest in the Spring of 1986 (when Mid-South became the Universal Wrestling Federation). These are just *some* of the legends that held the title during its brief but distinguished history: Bill Watts, Ted Dibiase, Jake Roberts, Paul Orndorff, Junkyard Dog, Butch Reed, Magnum TA, Nikolai Volkoff, Mr. Wrestling II, Ernie Ladd, Dick Murdoch and Hacksaw Jim Duggan. After reading those names, can you guess what wrestler had the longest Mid-South North American title reign? Here's a hint: you're reading his autobiography.

For nine months, I wore the promotion's top belt and worked in front of sold out crowds everywhere. I can't take all the credit for the sellouts- Dog was the promotion's top draw. But my lengthy reign showed that Watts had faith in my ability to consistently deliver solid matches. It was my job to legitimize the heavyweight title by wrestling my ass off each and every night.

I didn't have a single "day off" the entire time I was champion. I would perform in eight different cities every week (with two shows on Sundays). Even Christmas and Thanksgiving were workdays. The hard work paid off- in one year's time I went from surviving on bologna sandwiches to making six figures a year. My job, my career- my entire life- revolved around feuds and matches with the heroes of Mid-South Wrestling.

"You know, I thought you would never amount to shit," Killer Karl Kox told me. "Now look at you. Just goes to show, I'm an excellent judge of character."

I shared a laugh with my former tormenter in the Superdome locker room. Kox was my first big challenge as heavyweight champion. For years, he had portrayed a sadistic heel, but Karl was so crazy and unpredictable in the ring, that eventually the fans couldn't help but cheer him (yes, even black fans rooted for KKK). Now, they all wanted him to put an end to The Grappler's evil ways.

We had a series of title matches throughout the territory. Now that I was no longer in constant fear of the man, I learned something almost every night. Karl was a *master* of working the crowd. A small turn of the head or gesture to the fans would elicit a reaction that he could milk for minutes. Together, we had matches that were methodical but exciting. I don't mean to sound like an old codger, but these young guys today flying around and killing their bodies could learn a lot from Killer Karl Kox. There's a reason he wrestled on top for 20 plus years- the guy could make something out of nothing.

We spent a lot of time on the road together, and I finally got to know the man behind the wildman façade. His history was fascinating- Herb Gerwig (Karl's real name) was a Marine who had served in the Korean War and fought in the Battle of Chosin Reservoir. During that fight, more than 30,000 UN troops fought their way through 67,000 Chinese troops. 836 Marines died during the 17-day-fight, but it's estimated that as many as 35,000 Chinese were killed. Karl would never talk about exactly what he did in Korea, but after surviving a scene like that, pro wrestling must have felt like a cakewalk.

Our matches on the Mid-South loop built to a Superdome main event in front of 25,000 people. Kox, a legend who was nearing the end of his career, was going to "do the job" on the big stage.

"Remember when you came after me with that gun all those years back?" I asked.

"Of course I remember," he quipped. "Damn shame the thing jammed. I wouldn't have to put your dumb ass over tonight."

Of course, Karl was joking. He was always joking. That night, he took the loaded boot and cemented my status as a champion to be reckoned with. But thankfully, we weren't done yet.

A series of "I Quit" contests were scheduled to settle our issues. The idea was that you had to beat your opponent so badly that they would say "I Quit" into the ringside microphone. It sounds horrific, but the end result was actually hilarious.

Whenever I would get Karl in a submission hold, the ref would stick the microphone in his face. With the entire arena listening, KKK would cuss like a sailor (or in this case, a Marine):

"FUCK!!!... NO!!! OW-OW-OW MOTHER FUCK!!! HOLY SHIT!! YOU MOTHERFUCKING DOG SHIT…"

Brother, if you could have seen those faces at ringside. The bluehairs all turned bone white. Mothers were covering their kids' ears and waiting for the profanity to stop (it never did). The whole time, I was trying to keep the submission locked in while my body shook with laughter and tears ran down my mask. The whole episode was as funny as a Richard Pryor concert, and twice as profane.

When our program ended, I could tell that Karl was proud of the progress that I had made as a wrestler. Of course, he would never be serious enough to admit it. But, I couldn't help but feel good when the old Marine put his arm around me and said:

"Someday you might actually be worth a shit."

I don't know if I believe in fate, but it seems to me that "Killer" Karl Kox was destined to be a professional wrestler. He was just the right kind of crazy.

One night I was on the road with one of professional wrestling's scariest faces and sharpest tongues. Ox Baker's tweaked eyebrows were in a constant scowl and his Fu Manchu mustache made him look like the white Genghis Khan. He was 350 pounds of muscle, but wrestling fans knew Ox to be as eloquent as a poet. That is, if poets wrote sonnets about decapitating people.

"Kid, this Grappler thing is great," he said in his deep, gravelly timbre. "But you're still missing something."

I wasn't sure what that could be. After Kox, I had moved on to fight a rotation of other top babyfaces: Jimmy Garvin, Don Diamond and the great Dick Murdoch. The houses were good and the money was great.

"Look at Flair and Dusty," Ox continued. "Top guys have a catch phrase. Something that's their signature. For example, when I cut a promo you know I'm going to say…"

"Let me guess," I interjected. "I like to hurt people!"

"Exactly!"

Ox was a promo machine. You could just give the guy the mike and let him do his thing for five minutes… six… ten… it didn't matter. The man could work the stick like nobody's business.

"I think my promos are pretty good," I said. "People react to them."

"Yeah- but they don't *remember* them." Ox said. "I'm going to change that right now."

At that point, he put his hands in the air, like an old movie director envisioning a scene. Ox licked his lips and his eyes flitted about as if he was searching for the right words. Suddenly he found them and his voice shook the windshield:

"They've got a name for you when you're the greatest wrestler in wrestling today!" he bellowed. "They don't call you a great wrestler... They call you THE GRAPPLER!"

He kept his hands in the air and glanced back at me, ever so briefly, when inspiration struck once more. Ox turned back to the horizon and finished his thought:

"BEAT ME... IF YOU CAN!!!"

For a few seconds, the only sound was the car's humming motor.

"Damn Ox," I finally said. "That was good."

"Yeah, I know," he replied. "It's all yours."

That catchphrase would punctuate every Grappler interview for the rest of my career. I've used it in just about every state and even in countries where they don't speak English. Hell, I'm still saying I'm "the greatest wrestler" and I haven't wrestled in years.

I know what some of you are probably thinking. Yes, I got my name from Don Kernodle, my boot from Bill Watts and my catchphrase from Ox Baker. There's a lesson here for young wrestlers: always listen to creative people.

Incidentally, for a guy who worked almost exclusively in the territories, my motto caught on pretty good. In 2013, a friend of mine told me to watch an interview from a recent UFC fight. The interviewee was one of the top stars in Mixed Martial Arts:

"They've got a name for you when you're the greatest fighter in the world today," he said. "They don't call you a great fighter- they call you Chael Sonnen!"

Chael is an Oregon native, who obviously grew up watching me on Portland Wrestling. He is one hell of a fighter and one hell of a promo. But Chael, remember brother: no one delivers that line better than The Grappler (with the possible exception of Ox Baker).

In 1981, Mid-South Wrestling's top draw was a Dog, but I spent most of my nights tangling with a Snake.

While JYD worked 5 to 10 minute contests against guys like Ernie Ladd and The Freebirds, Jake Roberts and I were tasked with delivering long, laborious matches in the sweltering heat.

"We may not be making the money," Jake would say. "But we're damn sure making the time."

We had similar yet divergent paths to the top of the card. Unlike me, Jake was a second-generation wrestler (his dad Grizzly Smith was one of Watts' lieutenants). But we had both started out as job guys in Tri-State Wrestling in the late 70s- losing to guys like Ladd and Kox. Eventually, we both caught breaks in Stampede Wrestling. While in Calgary, Jake worked with a man named "Big Daddy" Sylvester Ritter. The two would return to Watts where Jake became "The Snake" and Sylvester became Junkyard Dog.

Unlike Dog, Jake could work his ass off in the ring. Our matches were a minimum of 30 minutes in length, and usually closer to 45. Jake could do whatever you asked of him, and I would ask a lot. Watts watched our matches, and if we let up for a second, The Cowboy would chew our asses out.

"It's your job to give the people their money's worth," he would tell us.

Of course, most of that money wound up in JYD's pockets. I took pride in delivering long, believable matches, but it might have been nice to just shake my butt, hit a powerslam and then collect a giant paycheck. Oh well.

Jake and I were working in the Lake Charles Civic Center one dreadfully humid night. It was one of those times where you were sweating just from walking to the ring. As we locked up, you could already see the perspiration seeping through my mask.

The match began with a series of amateur wrestling exchanges. Yes, The Grappler was a notorious cheater, but I was also hailed as one of Mid-South's top mat technicians. So, every match would begin with a display of my technical acumen: we flowed effortlessly from arm bars to go-behinds to hammer locks. When we hit the fifteen minute mark, the pace picked up.

"Get me in a front facelock," I whispered.

Jake complied and clamped his right arm around my head. Wrapping his left hand around his right wrist, he took me down to the mat and waited for me to call the next spot:

"Sit out, two tackles, hiptoss, get it back."

With that, I spun out of the hold, landed on my butt and bounced to my feet. I came off the ropes and Jake rose just in time to get dropped by a big shoulder.

BOOM!

He dropped to the mat and popped back up in time to catch another.

BOOM!

The third time I came off the ropes he was ready. Jake stepped to the side and dug his right arm under mine, flipping me in to the air. I landed with a loud thud, and Jake cinched in another front facelock.

By this time, we were sweating like pigs in a slaughterhouse. Jake could barely wrap his arm around my neck because we were both so slippery. As the ref checked my arm, I caught a breath and panted out more commands:

"Big knee… drop down… backdrop… get it back."

We got back to our feet and I sent a hard knee right into his ribs. Jake staggered back as I bounced off the ropes. Before I could hit a tackle, he hit the mat and I jumped over him. When I returned, Jake rose to his feet, dropped his head and flipped me over.

BOOM!

I landed, popped back to my feet, lowered my head and charged right back. Jake was waiting and grabbed me in another front facelock. There was just one problem. Our bodies were so slick with perspiration that Jake couldn't get a firm grip on the hold. As we slid around like a couple of lubed-up oil wrestlers, we both tripped and fell to the mat. In one motion, Jake dropped me right on my head.

"OHHHH!"

The crowd's reaction was like nothing I had ever heard. They weren't cheering or screaming. It was as if they had all simultaneously gasped in horror. My head was throbbing, but the fans' response put all of that pain on hold.

"Buddy, did you hear that?" I whispered to Jake.

"Yeah man," he replied. "Let's do that again."

So, we got back to our feet, and after a couple of exchanges, Jake got me back in the front facelock. This time, he slapped me on the back and fell backwards. I was able to protect my head on this second attempt, and it drew an even bigger reaction than the first.

"We've got to remember that one," Jake said as he covered me for the pinfall attempt. I escaped the count at two, and we went on to finish the match.

The next night, we decided to use that falling front facelock again. We would go on to use it in the rest of our matches that week and the next. It wasn't used as a finisher- just as a high spot that would get a reaction from the crowd. Each time, I would kick out of the pinfall attempt and the match would continue. But after eliciting huge reactions every night, Jake concluded that he had literally stumbled onto something special.

"I'm going to use that as my finisher," he told me. "So let's not use it in our matches anymore. I'm going to get it over on TV."

And that's how the DDT- one of pro wrestling's most famous finishing maneuvers- was born. Jake turned our sweat-fueled fuck-up into wrestling's equivalent of a one-punch knockout. In some ways, it is the most emulated move of all time: a quick-strike finish that can occur at any time. The Stone Cold Stunner, Diamond Cutter, RKO and other famous moves are in many ways descendants of the DDT.

Now, I've heard in recent years that Bill Watts has said this is not how the DDT was created. Of course, he doesn't say *how* the move was actually conceived- he just doesn't think it happened this way. I don't know what the hell he is talking about. Jake says this is how it was invented, and I remember it all very clearly (despite the fact that I got dropped on my damn head). Trust me, the DDT was born on that sweaty and slippery St. Charles night.

I left so many buckets of perspiration in the ring, eventually The Cowboy had to put his boot down.

"What the hell is wrong with you?" he asked as I returned from another 45-minute epic with Jake. "Do you think this is some bodybuilding contest?"

I was no bodybuilder, but after months of working long matches in the humidity, I was definitely looking cut. I was down to almost no body fat and was maybe thirty pounds lighter than I was when I joined the territory. No matter how much I ate and worked out, I couldn't keep any weight on.

"Bill, I'm working for an hour in a damn sauna every night," I pleaded. "How do you expect me to not lose weight?"

Rhetorical questions like that almost never worked with The Cowboy. He knew what he wanted and damn it, he was going to get it- reason and rationality be damned.

"I don't care how you get bigger- but you better do it fast," he said. "I'm planning to have you work a program with Dog. I can't do that if he outweighs you by eighty pounds!"

A program with Dog?

Now Watts had my attention. Working with JYD meant:

1) I would be drawing bigger paychecks.

2) I would be working shorter matches.

After months of sweat-soaked marathons, this all sounded like a nice change of pace.

"Don't worry Bill," I said. "I'll bulk up right away."

"Oh, I know you will," he replied. "You've got three weeks to put on twenty pounds."

Of course, Watts being Watts, he couldn't leave the room without putting this little cherry on top:

"Do it or you're fired."

Needless to say, for the next 21 days I stuffed my face like Abdullah the Butcher in a Tucumcari buffet. My life was an endless procession of double cheeseburgers, cold beers and workouts that would make Porkchop Cash weep. After three weeks of gorging and grunting, I was finally ready for Mid-South's top star.

In 1981, wrestling Junkyard Dog in New Orleans was like cursing the Pope in St. Peter's Square. You were just asking for a holy ass whuppin'. Dog was so beloved in the city that his opponent was instantly the enemy of the people. Don't get me wrong- he was popular throughout the entire territory. But there was something about his bond with the folks in New Orleans. They would have *killed* for JYD. In fact, one of them almost did.

"Who Dat? Who Dat? Who Dat Say They Gonna Beat That Dog?"

I was set to face the Dog on his home turf: the New Orleans Municipal Auditorium. Years before "Who Dat" became a phrase associated with the NFL's Saints, it was the battle cry for JYD's NOLA fans. While Mid-South's biggest cards would take place a few times a year in the Superdome, every week thousands of fans would pack the Auditorium, chanting and cheering for their hero.

He gave them plenty to cheer about. Dog was unlike any black wrestler that had come before. There had been great ones- Bobo Brazil and Rocky Johnson immediately come to mind. But no African-American had been so heavily pushed as a major promotion's top star. From the start, JYD was beating every top heel (white and black) in less than ten minutes a night. Part of that was necessity- he just didn't have the ability to work a long match. But regardless of the reasons, the booking made him appear like a real-life superhero. When you consider what black folks in the south had been through, it's easy to see why they were so proud of the Junkyard Dog.

"You're losing that belt tonight Grappler!"

As I walked to the ring, I got a good look at the crowd. The grannies were cursing me out and so were the little kids. One drunk idiot threw a lit cigarette at me while another fan in a trench coat just gave me the evil eye. From nowhere, a flying battery smacked the side of my head and a half-full beer followed right behind. That's how it was in the Auditorium- Dog's fans didn't mess around. And this night, there was some extra fuel for their fire.

Since his debut, JYD had held every title in Mid-South Wrestling- except for the North American Heavyweight Title. His fans were convinced that he would beat me and finally claim the promotion's top prize. When the first notes of "Another One Bites the Dust" played over the loud speakers, the chant reached deafening levels.

"WHO DAT? WHO DAT? WHO DAT SAY THEY GONNA BEAT THAT DOG?"

He strode down the aisle, slapping hands and clutching the trademark chain that hung from his collar. While the crowd cheered and bobbed to the music, I was visualizing my gameplan. There was a simple flow to a JYD match: the heel would (through some sort of illegal chicanery) get the early advantage. Then, after a few minutes of getting his ass kicked, Dog would make a super-human comeback to end the match. In just a few minutes, the crowd's emotions would swing from anger to fear and finally, to ecstatic joy. As Dog walked through the ropes, I knew what I had to do.

Time to crank up the heat.

I blindsided JYD with a stiff knee, knocking him through the ropes and out of the ring. He hit the arena floor and I followed right behind. Then I grabbed his chain while the crowd screamed bloody murder:

"Stop that motherfucker!"

At first, I could hear their individual curses. But when I wrapped the chain around Dog's neck and pulled back, their voices blended into a chorus of shock and rage.

It was the most beautiful sound I had ever heard.

I yanked back on the chain, "strangling" JYD as hard as humanly possible. He sold my attack like a man gasping his last breath. The crowd's cries became even more panicked and confused. Then I heard screams of honest-to-god terror.

"OH MY GOD—NO!!!!!!!"

I glanced over my shoulder and saw the fans were no longer screaming at me. Two men in the front row were grabbing each other and rolling around, and the crowd's attention had completely shifted to their scuffle. Meanwhile, some other fans were running away and even ducking behind their seats.

Damn it!

When a fight breaks out in the stands, there is really nothing that you can do to get the fans' attention. You just have to wait until the commotion ends. So, I tossed Dog back in the ring and put him in a reverse chinlock. When the hubbub finally died down, we resumed the match as planned.

I was frustrated as hell. All the heat I had built with my chain attack had disappeared in a flash. But despite the distraction, we still had a decent little match. I ended up getting disqualified- retaining my belt in the process. Dog got the moral victory and thumped my ass right out of the ring.

I limped back to the locker room as JYD led the crowd in a post-match celebration. When I passed through the back curtain, I found a pair of uniformed security officers waiting for me. Their smiles suggested that they were sharing an inside joke.

"You need to thank this man," one of the men said, gesturing to his partner.

"*I* need to thank him?" I said, trying to stay in my heel character. "What are you talking about?"

"Did you see that man at ringside- the shifty-looking one in the trench coat?" he asked.

I *did* remember that guy, I told him. He had been sitting in the front row and staring a hole right through me.

"When you attacked Dog with that chain," the officer continued, "That fella pulled a gun from his coat and pointed it right at you. My buddy here wrestled him to the ground and got the gun away. It was a .357. Right now, he's in jail and you're lucky to be alive."

Holy Shit. That wasn't a fight that interrupted our match- it was some homicidal wrestling fan. I knew that my attack would build heat with the crowd, but not THAT much heat!

I shook the officer's hand and thanked him several times. One six-pack later, my nerves were finally calmed and I joked with JYD about my near-death experience.

"Next match," I told him, "I ain't laying a damn finger on you."

Sylvester's deep laughter filled the dressing room. The Junkyard Dog had one hell of a bark… but it wasn't half as scary as his fans' bite.

The Dog and I would clash again in New Orleans, on a night that was probably the highlight of my Mid-South tenure (if not my career). It was during the Superdome tag team title tournament that you read about at the beginning of this book.

Super Destroyer (Scott Irwin) and I had been put together as a tag team several weeks prior. We were a perfect match and not just because we both wore masks. Our skills complimented each other: I was the ring technician and Scott was the tall, muscled monster. While I didn't need a "mouthpiece", Frank Dusek had been Super D's manager, and so he rounded out our trio.

At the time of the tournament, I had already been North American Champion for seven months. I was also the reigning Mississippi State Heavyweight Champion (Mid-South had secondary titles for both Mississippi and Louisiana).

The tournament was set up after JYD and Dick Murdoch were stripped of the tag team titles. The bracket included the former champions, their hated rivals Ernie Ladd and Leroy Brown, along with superstars like Andre and Dusty, the Wild Samoans and The Freebirds. I arrived at the Dome that night with no expectations of leaving with a third championship belt.

When the tournament began, all we were told was what would happen in our first match: we would beat Jake Roberts and Jimmy Garvin. Fair enough. I don't remember exactly how that match ended, but I do remember coming backstage afterwards and looking at the updated booking sheet. It showed us in the semi-finals against Andre and Dusty (they had just beaten Afa and Sika).

"Well, we're obviously not winning that one," I told Scott.

It just seemed obvious. Yes, I was the promotion's champion, but I was still a 22-year-old kid and this was Dusty Motherfucking Rhodes and Andre the Motherfucking Giant. We would do the job, and feel fortunate to do it.

Instead- and forgive me for rehashing the prologue- Watts dropped the bombshell that *we* were going over. Of course, if Andre and Dusty didn't want to comply with his orders, they didn't have to. They were the two biggest stars on the card (if not in the entire world), and no one, not even Bill Watts, could make them lose to a pair of young punks like Scott and me. But they were both pros, and fortunately, I had great relationships with both men. So, in our match they made us look like we actually belonged in the ring with two first ballot Hall-of-Famers. For that, I will always be grateful.

That win pitted us against Dog and Murdoch in the tournament finals. I fully expected to lose that match as well. As I've already stated a million times, JYD was Watts' golden goose. Meanwhile, Dickie was, for my money, the territory's best worker. The guy could have been as good as Harley Race- except for the fact that he was always acting goofy in the ring. For example, during one match he was on the mat and told me to kick him in the head. When I did, he started spinning on his side and making sound effects ala the Three Stooges. When I kicked him again, he spun in the opposite direction, just like Curly in his prime. I'm not kidding. That shit drove Watts up the wall.

Anyways, instead of giving JYD and Dickie the belts, the Cowboy decided to give us the surprise victory. I would pin the Dog in the same city where he damn near got me murdered. I wondered: if there was one trigger-happy JYD fan in the teeny-ass Auditorium, how many would there be in the Superdome? I politely informed Dog that I would *not* be choking him with that damn chain.

99

Thankfully, no firearms appeared during our match. The only surprise was one that we were expecting, but it caught the fans off guard. A giant African-American in a mask (who bore more than a passing resemblance to Ernie Ladd) ran into the ring and hit Dog with an attack from the top rope. I made the cover and three seconds later I was a triple-title holder.

Back in the locker room, after thanking Andre, Dusty, Dog and everybody else, I shared a quiet moment with my three championships. It wasn't that winning belts was a big deal- it was about what they represented. Four years earlier, Joe Mercer had told me I would never be a successful professional wrestler. Now, I owned almost every title in Mid-South Wrestling. Not only that, Bill Watts had me defeat two of the biggest stars in the world and his #1 attraction *all in the same night.* This had to mean something, right?

The way I looked at it, there were two possible reasons for my success:

Reason #1: I had worked hard, listened and honed my craft for several years. As a result, I had earned respect and opportunities. Watts put me over as a champion because he thought I could help contribute to his already successful promotion.

Reason #2: Watts put me over because he *needed* me. I was that damn good. Shit, JYD couldn't work a match so what the hell would Mid-South do without The Grappler? I was irreplaceable and deserved everything I got. Fuck that- I deserved more.

Reason #1 is a conclusion that one might reach when they are rational and have some perspective. Reason #2 is a conclusion that one might reach when they are 22 years old and making shitloads of money.

Guess which conclusion I reached in 1981?

"Fuck this," I told the American Dream. "I'm done with Watts and this whole fucking place."

I was driving Dusty down I-10 to another show in New Orleans. Dream wasn't a territory regular like I was, but he still worked several big Mid-South cards a year. It was early summer and I was no longer North American Heavyweight Champion, having dropped the belt to Jake Roberts in a match that I can't remember (it's funny how I recall every detail of my title *wins* but those title *losses* are fuzzy).

Dropping the title didn't bother me in the slightest- that's how the business worked and Jake deserved it. But I was extremely miffed when, a few weeks later, I heard what some of the other boys were earning for their payouts.

"Dog's pulling two, maybe three grand more a week than I am," I told Dusty. "Hell, even Dickie's making more."

My passenger nodded knowingly. I wasn't the first wrestler that had bitched to Dusty Rhodes about money, and I wouldn't be the last.

"I'm the guy working damn near an hour every night," I continued. "I'm telling Watts he can either up my pay or I'm out of here."

Dream let loose a faint chuckle and then turned to me with a question:

"Baby, how old are you?"

"22," I said with a shrug.

"Uh-huh... and how much money did you make last week?"

"We just had that Dome show- so, three grand."

Dusty flashed his famous smile at me. It was an expression that said *I know something you don't know.*

"Lynny... how many 22 year olds do you know make three grand a week?" he asked. "In fact, how many people- of any age- do you know make three grand a week?"

I didn't offer an answer.

"It's none of my business," The Dream concluded, "But I would reconsider your strategy."

I had all the respect in the world for Dusty Rhodes, but I knew he was wrong. This whole thing was about age. I had been the workhorse of Mid-South and Watts was underpaying me just because I was young. It wasn't right. That's exactly what I told The Cowboy when I saw him later that week.

"You're not happy with your pay?" Watts asked incredulously. "You're fucking serious?"

"Yes sir," I tried to sound determined but respectful, "I got three grand last week, and most weeks I'm lucky to pull down two."

He looked at me as if I told him that I had four eyeballs.

"Two grand a week?" he said in a voice that was as furious as it was sarcastic. "That's not enough for you? You don't appreciate that?"

Bill was an immense, intimidating presence- his voice alone could bring grown men to tears (and often did). But Lynn Denton was no longer a skinny kid getting slapped around by Swede Hanson. I was a wrestling star that was going to stand my ground.

"I appreciate what you've done for me," I told Watts. "But if you can't pay me more then I'm leaving."

"Then I guess you're leaving," he snarled. "Finish up your bookings and you're free to go."

And that was it. I would work in Mid-South for two more weeks and then move on to the next territory. Where I would go remained an open question. But after my successful run with Watts, I had no doubt that promoters would be breaking out their checkbooks to land The Grappler. My hunch was soon confirmed by "Super Destroyer" Scott.

"Watts got us booked," he told me before a show in Lake Charles. "We're heading to Crockett."

It was a good thing Bill was talking to Scott, because Watts hadn't said a peep to me since I quit the previous week. The Cowboy was pissed, but apparently he wasn't so pissed that he couldn't find me work.

"They've got big things planned for us," Scott continued. "Watts said they're giving us the tag team titles."

Now *that* was more like it. Another title reign was exactly what I needed for my post-Mid-South career. I knew that main events- and a lot more money- were right around the corner. My only obstacle was the calendar.

"One more week and we're out of here," I told Scott. "Let's hurry up and get our asses to Carolina."

A few weeks later I arrived at the TV studio in Charlotte and met Mid-Atlantic's new booker: Ole Anderson.

I hadn't seen him in years and braced myself for the usual nastiness. Thankfully, Ole had mellowed out a bit. He told me that he was happy for my recent success and apologized for being so hard on me in the past. We shook hands and went to a nearby bar to share some cold beers and warm memories. From that day on, we were friends and confidantes.

Actually, I'm just messing with you. Ole was still an asshole.

But I had no problem dealing with the usual insults since I knew that big things were on the horizon. At least, that's what I thought when we first arrived. But after a couple of weeks, it became clear that we were *not* being prepared for a title run. Scott and I were working mid-card matches, winning some but losing more. One month into our stay we drove 3000 miles in seven days. My paycheck for that week was just over 300 bucks.

Three. Hundred. Dollars. After reading those numbers, I clenched the check so hard that I damn near ripped it in half. My face was radish-red when I finally tracked down Ole.

"What the hell is this?"

I waved that piddly-ass check right in Ole's face. The bearded bastard just smirked at me.

"Is something wrong with your paycheck?" he finally asked.

"Are you shitting me?" I asked rhetorically. "I've got a wife, man- this ain't nearly enough. My family's going to starve! What the hell am I supposed to do with three hundred bucks?"

Ole replied with a calculated coldness:

"Well... I guess you're going to starve."

That was it. The blood began rushing to my face and my fists. I didn't care who this guy was- I had paid my dues and *nobody* spoke to me like that.

"YOU GOT A FUCKING PROBLEM?"

I shouted with all the menace I could muster, but Ole didn't appear intimidated by my words. Instead, he just grinned at me in amusement.

"You can get mad and want to fight," he finally said. "But remember- all of this is your fault."

MY FAULT? I began preparing a witty comeback but Ole never gave me an opening. He just kept talking and tore me to shreds:

"You had a great thing with Watts. And YOU chose to leave. Why? Because you're some hot shit wrestler? Let me tell you something: no matter how good you *think* you are, you are always replaceable. *We* run this business. *We* make the rules because *we* take the financial risk. You don't know about any of that shit- you've just been wrestling, chasing girls and believing your own hype. You were given a great opportunity but you were too cocky to realize it. Now, you're learning a very expensive lesson."

Ole Anderson was one of the biggest pricks to ever enter the squared circle, but I'll be damned if he wasn't speaking the truth.

I realize that now. Looking back on my whole Mid-South departure, I can't help but shake my head at how dumb and green I was. OF COURSE Junkyard Dog made way more money than I did. He was the territory's biggest draw and the reason all those people packed the arenas. It's the same reason guys like Hulk Hogan and Steve Austin were the top earners during their heydays. Man, talk about pro wrestling 101.

Besides, it wasn't like I was some charity case. Like Dusty said: I was making great money for a kid who had only been in the business for a few years. There were talented veterans that would have killed for two grand a week. But instead of appreciating what I had, I was convinced that my cup was half-empty.

I had no comeback for Ole, so I slinked out of his office and eventually slinked out of Mid-Atlantic altogether. Anderson would eventually take Super Destroyer Scott to Georgia where he did in fact become a tag team champion. I ended up crawling back to Mid-South where The Cowboy paid me about a quarter of my previous salary. There were no more main events and it would be a long time before I saw another two thousand dollar check.

There is no question in my mind that Watts and Ole conspired to teach me some humility. I don't have any evidence, but that's how wrestling was in the territory days. Because promoters didn't consider outside territories their "competition" they would often band together to keep problematic workers in line. Some people might call that collusion, but in my case it was probably justified.

Ole Anderson was right: I had learned a very expensive lesson. When 1981 began, I was a well-paid champion living on cloud nine. When the year ended, I was a broke mid-carder stuck in pro wrestling purgatory. I would spend the next few years trying to fight my way back to the promised land.

CHAPTER SIX

TWO GRAPPLERS ARE BETTER THAN ONE

Moving from the outhouse to the penthouse and then back to the outhouse is a dreadful experience. Traveling that loop in one calendar year can be downright traumatic. At the start of 1982 I wasn't sure what, if any, future I had in pro wrestling. Thanks to youthful arrogance, my career was like a ship that had been blown off course, with no land in sight and no compass onboard. Thankfully my wrestling brothers were on hand to point me in the right direction. My guiding lights would include a young wrestler from the hills of Tennessee and one of the greatest heavyweight champions of all time.

After my Carolina debacle, I returned to Mid-South Wrestling in an act of both contrition and desperation. I had accepted a pay cut without any fuss because:

a) I understood why Watts was pissed at me and

b) I didn't have any better options.

Despite the fact that I was no longer making main-event money, Mid-South was still the place where the Grappler name had some cache. So, Watts would use my name recognition to get other wrestlers over. In other words, up-and-comers like Steve Williams and Tim Horner would get "signature wins" over the former North American Heavyweight Champion. It wasn't the greatest situation for me financially, but I always took pride in making other guys look good. Besides, the demotion was probably what my young ego needed at the time.

Following months of mid-card jobs, I went to Japan for a tour where I got to tag on several occasions with my old buddy Dynamite Kid. We had a series of matches against the Japanese wrestler Tiger Mask (who every night would tag with a different Japanese star). Tiger and Tommy were in the middle of a legendary run, working groundbreaking matches that were fast paced and high-flying. I'd try and describe the moves they used in our matches, but my vocabulary is a bit lacking. The phrase "Holy Shit" comes to mind. Suffice to say, it was an honor to be in the ring with two genuine wrestling prodigies. It was also nice to be in matches that actually mattered.

When I returned to Mid-South, I was ready to add more losses to my wrestling resume. Instead, The Cowboy offered me a new career path.

"We're going to put you in a tag team," he told me. "What do you think of that Anthony kid?"

Tony Anthony had arrived in Mid-South Wrestling a few months prior. He was a couple of years younger than me, and a really good worker. On paper, the two of us tagging up made a lot of sense. Despite his solid work, Tony was still waiting for his first big push. Meanwhile, my career was stuck in neutral. A new partnership could pull us out of our respective ruts.

I told Watts that I liked the idea.

"Good," he replied. "You guys will be The Grapplers. You're Grappler #1 and he's Grappler #2."

The Grapplers? Plural? Hold on a sec.

I was happy to tag up with Tony- but share my gimmick? That thought hadn't occurred to me. After all, I had busted my ass to make The Grappler a name that meant something. Now, Watts just wanted me to hand it off? I decided that I would need to talk with my new tag team partner about this. When I found him, Tony's reaction sealed the deal.

"Sir, it would be an honor to work with you," he said. "I really appreciate the opportunity and I promise I won't let you down."

I decided then and there that if I was ever going to share my Grappler gimmick, it was going to be with this guy. Besides, I had stolen my name from Don Kernodle and my boot from Dr. X. I could afford to be generous.

"Welcome aboard Grappler Number Two," I said with a smile.

With that, Tony and I shook hands. It was the beginning of a partnership that would last for the next three years.

We clicked right away. Tony got some trunks and a mask to match mine, and with our similar builds we were almost indistinguishable. Because I was the more experienced wrestler, I would usually call our matches and do all the talking in interviews. But Tony more than held up his end of the bargain. He was a great hand and we made a solid unit.

Our run in Mid-South was fairly uneventful, but because we worked so well together, we decided to try our luck as a team in some other territories. I called around and eventually got us booked in my home state of Texas.

Joe Blanchard's Southwest Championship Wrestling was based out of San Antonio, and the first wrestling promotion to air on the USA Cable Network. Joe's son Tully was the booker and the territory's top star. When we arrived, Tully wanted to establish The Grapplers as a top-tier attraction. But one well-known wrestler had no interest in making new stars.

That bastard's name was Mil Mascaras.

It was one of our first nights in San Antonio, and I was scheduled to face the masked Mexican "legend" in a one-on-one contest. Tully told me the match would be a "Broadway"- a wrestlers' term for a time-limit draw. But when he told Mascaras the plan, the man-of-a-thousand-masks threw a-thousand-hissy-fits.

"No draw!" Mil said, "I win. I go over."

Tully tried to reason with him.

"We're not asking you to put Lynn over," he explained. "Just let him go the distance with you. We want people to buy him as a top guy."

"I go over," the stubborn prick repeated.

I just stood by silently, watching this BS unfold. Tully finally put his foot down.

"Look, the finish is decided," he said. "You guys are going twenty minutes and that's it."

Mascaras threw his hands in the air and spun away from Tully. Then he pointed to me.

"I go over," he said for the umpteenth time. "You do the job."

The rest of the dressing room went quiet. Mascaras may have been an asshole but he was a big star, especially in South Texas. There were probably some other young wrestlers that would have gone along with his demands. After all, there was no shame in losing to a marquee name like Mil Mascaras. But fuck that. I had been taught this business was about respect, and as far as I could tell this prima donna didn't respect anyone but himself.

"Tully told you the finish," I finally said. "We're going to a twenty minute Broadway."

"No- I go over."

"You can try," I said. "But brother, that ain't happening."

With that, we headed to the ring for a match that quickly devolved into a legit street fight. I would hit Mascaras as hard as I could, and he would fire right back. The match probably looked a little funny to the fans in attendance. We were still doing some normal wrestling spots, but we did it while nailing each other as hard as possible. No punches were pulled. The whole time I kept thinking:

Twenty minutes. I have to last twenty minutes.

Meanwhile, Mil was trying to get me in a compromising position so he could win in a shoot. For the entire match I played defense- making sure that he didn't get me in any kind of pinning or submission hold. If he tried to grab my ankle- WHAM!- I drilled that SOB as hard as I could. It was like the first *Rocky* movie- I just wanted to go the distance.

When the bell finally rang, I was exhausted and sore as hell. Instead of Talia Shire running from the stands, my tag-team partner made his way to ringside. Tony put my arm around his shoulder and helped me to the back. I had gone the full twenty minutes, just like I said I would. You know that saying "Don't Mess with Texas"? Well, that night I had sent my own message to Mil Mascaras and the entire Lone Star State:

Don't fuck with The Grapplers.

When Tony and I finally got established in SCW, life was great. A mouthy ex-wrestler named Don Carson became our manager and we worked with great talent like Tully, Gino Hernandez and the Guerreros. During this time I lived in Houston, so I could be near my family. The drive from Houston to San Antonio was more than two hours, but I was just glad to be home. My dad even bought a ring and began promoting some small shows for the Blanchards. He quickly gave it up when he discovered that it's a lot more fun to watch a wrestling show than to promote one.

Tony was a lot of fun to work with, and we became close right away. He was not only a great worker, but he was also an easy guy to get along with. In three years traveling together, I don't think we ever had an argument. This was despite the fact that I gave Tony plenty of reasons to get mad at me. Consider this:

One night we had finished a show in Austin and were driving back to Houston. It was a rainy evening in the Texas Hill Country. And when I say it was raining- I mean it was RAINING. We're talking a Noah's Ark downpour.

I was driving Tony's new car down the interstate, struggling to see through the sheets of precipitation. I was looking for a shortcut that I knew would save us time, but I could barely see five feet ahead. When an off-ramp sign magically appeared, I hit my turn signal and got ready to take the exit. Immediately, Tony spoke up:

"Lynny, you can't take this exit."

"What are you talking about?"

"Didn't you see the signs earlier? That road is closed for construction."

I waved him off.

"Man, did you grow up in Texas?" I asked. "No. I did. This is my state- I know where I'm going."

"But…"

"I GOT IT MAN--- RELAX!"

Tony quit protesting and I took the exit. My foot pushed hard on the accelerator and the car cut through the deluge and onto the highway. We were making good time.

Then the damn road disappeared.

Tony was right- there *was* construction on that highway and the pavement came to an abrupt end. We blasted off the road and into the air like we were the Dukes of Hazzard. But this wasn't some cool slo-mo stunt with a miracle landing. Tony's brand new ride dropped like a brick into four feet of water.

SPLASH!

Tires popped, windows shattered and brown sludge poured into the cabin. We weren't hurt, but the car was toast.

We had to wade out of the giant puddle and then hike a couple miles (in the wind and rain) to the nearest gas station. It was miserable. When a tow truck finally retrieved the car it was too late. The water landing had destroyed Tony's car (along with the brand new cowboy boots that he had been wearing).

He could have- and probably should have- called me every name in the book. But I apologized, he accepted my apology and that was it. I'm sure he was furious, but he didn't let that affect our friendship. And believe me, that wasn't the only time he forgave one of my fuck-ups. My tag team partner had the patience of Job.

We spent maybe half a year in San Antonio, and held the tag team titles for a couple months (we lost the belts when Don Carson was "bribed" by The Sheepherders and turned on us). It was a nice little run, but it ended prematurely. Our departure was all thanks to one swift kick to a wrestling's fan face.

It happened at a show in Corpus Christi. Tully Blanchard had just wrestled a match and was making his way down the aisle. He was about halfway to the back when this fella in the crowd started screaming at him. Tully stopped and the two started jawing back and forth. This fan was a big son of a gun- bigger than most of the wrestlers on our roster. He started bowing up like he was ready to fight. Meanwhile, Tully wouldn't back down- he had a tough-guy reputation to protect. Tony and I were watching all of this from behind the curtain.

"It's time to stop this," I said.

We ran down the aisle and just before we reached Tully, the fan took a swing at him. Tully ducked and, in a move straight out of professional hockey, he pulled the fan's jacket over his face. The guy dropped to the ground.

I should explain that back then there was a simple code when it came to fan interactions. If someone tried to hurt you it was your job to kick the shit out of him. The same rule applied if he was trying to hurt one of your buddies. It would send a clear message to any other idiot who was feeling tough. So when that fan hit the floor, I reared back and punted him right in the kisser.

CRACK!

Teeth flew and that dude dropped like a box of hammers. Tony grabbed Blanchard and we hurried him back to the dressing room. When his adrenaline finally subsided, Tully shook our hands.

"Thanks for having my back," he said.

I took a shower, changed into my street clothes and got ready to leave. To get to our car we had to leave through the auditorium. So, Tony and I passed through the back curtain and found that giant fan was *still* laid out on the cement floor. A couple of people were trying to revive him and there was blood everywhere.

Oh, fuck.

Tony looked at me with a terrified expression and I'm sure I looked equally panicked. Thankfully, somebody had already called 911. EMTs arrived and loaded the guy into an ambulance. He was unconscious the entire time. I'm not a super religious person, but I said a little prayer and asked God to save the big fella.

Fortunately, the fan did survive. *Un*fortunately, he decided to sue the shit out of the Blanchards.

"He wants 150- thousand dollars," Tully told me. "All cause of that damn kick."

150 Grand? I felt like I got *my* teeth kicked in.

"Tully, I'm sorry. I was just trying…"

He raised his hands in a "shut the hell up" expression.

"I know you didn't mean to do it," he said. "But we gotta let you go. It's just too much heat."

And that was the end of The Grapplers' stay in San Antonio. I don't think the fan ended up getting all that money, and to this day I still regret that I messed him up so badly. So, if you're reading this Mr. Toothless 350-pound Wrestling Fan, please understand that I never thought that one kick could do so much damage.

Hell, I didn't even load the boot.

After the Alamo City, Tony and I moved north to his home state of Tennessee. In 1982, Jerry Jarrett's Memphis territory had received national attention for its groundbreaking feud between comedian Andy Kaufman and local hero Jerry Lawler. When we arrived in mid-83 Kaufman was still making sporadic appearances and Lawler was the reigning King of Memphis (don't get upset Elvis fans- we're just talking wrestling here).

The plan was to continue our run as a heel-tag team, and that meant we would join up with a duo of mouthy managers. Just about every heel that arrived in Memphis was immediately paired with Lawler's on-air rival Jimmy Hart, and the "Mouth of the South" was just the start. Not long after we arrived, a kid named Jim Cornette became the "vice president" of Hart's First Family.

So now we had two mouthpieces and man, could those guys draw some heat. I was a really strong promo by this time, but even I was impressed by their mile-a-minute words. Every interview was a collection of of soliloquies: I'd talk trash for a couple minutes, then Hart would take over and Cornette would bat clean-up. Meanwhile, Tony would stand there nodding for ten minutes, just waiting for the match to start. When we did get to wrestle, we were paired with a new team that was destined for greatness.

"We just put Ricky and Robert together," Lawler told us a few days after our debut. "I think you guys could have a good program with them. It would help put both teams on the map."

"Ricky" was Ricky Morton, a high-flying babyface that we had worked with during our San Antonio run. "Robert" was Robert Gibson, another agile wrestler that had tagged with numerous partners throughout the South. Together they became "The Rock-n-Roll Express". With their long hair and pretty-boy

114

looks, the RnRs were an instant hit with female fans. They were also the perfect opponents for a team that was so nasty they had to wear masks.

Ricky and Robert were two really good guys and a lot of fun to work with. Their locker room nicknames were "Punky" and "Hoot". Ricky was "Punky", probably because of his spiky blonde hair. I'm not sure why Robert was "Hoot"-maybe someone thought he looked like an owl. For several months we wrestled them just about every night and Ricky and Robert were a cohesive unit from the start.

For my money, they were the best tag-team in the business- but there was a glass ceiling in their way. At that time, "The Fabulous Ones" Steve Keirn and Stan Lane were the territory's top babyface team. They had received the on-air endorsement of Memphis legend Jackie Fargo and became instant headliners. Like the RnRs, Steve and Stan were popular with the ladies and good workers, but they couldn't do what Ricky and Robert could do in the ring. Punky and Hoot were on a different level.

But it didn't matter: The Fabs were over with the fans and Keirn's friendship with the territory's decision makers ensured that they would stay on top. So, while The Grapplers and RnRs would work together on some big cards, we were often relegated to the "spot shows" in smaller towns.

No matter the size of the crowds, we always put on one hell of a show. Those guys would sell the shit out of our offense until the ringside teeny-boppers were damn near crying. Then when the Express would make their big comeback, the girls would scream like groupies at a Motley Crue concert. As you can imagine, Ricky and Robert were never lacking female company. But the RnRs weren't just a couple of pretty boys; they could really *work*. Every match we had with them was up tempo and unpredictable. With one notable exception.

It happened at one of those spot shows in Middle-of-Nowhere, Tennessee. We were in the locker room preparing for a match in a high school gymnasium when the local promoter gave us the news:

"We don't have a ring."

Tony and I waited for the punchline.

"What the hell do you mean we don't have a ring?" I finally asked.

"It was in a truck that broke down a couple hours out of town," he said as if he had already explained this a hundred times. "We're just going to have to make do without it."

It's important to note here that professional wrestlers are used to "making do" without a lot of stuff. Sometimes, you'll misplace your tights or boots and have to borrow some from one of the boys. I can remember one Arab wrestler using a hotel towel as a turban when an airline lost his luggage. So, we're pretty resourceful people by necessity. But not having a ring- the one central piece of equipment for a wrestling show? That's like playing basketball without a hoop.

However, that old adage "the show must go on" is a central tenet of professional wrestling. Shows are almost never cancelled- especially when there are already paying customers waiting outside. So, that evening the promoter dragged out some old gym mats and we got ready to wrestle without the use of a "squared circle."

"What the hell are we supposed to do?" Tony asked me. "Ricky and Robert are always running the ropes and jumping off turnbuckles. All that stuff is out. And how the hell are we supposed to take bumps on that skinny ass mat? That thing is maybe a quarter-inch thick- we'll break our necks!"

"We'll be fine," I assured him. "I'll call the match- just follow me."

And with that, about 150 fans were treated to the suckiest tag match in the history of professional wrestling. Dropkicks, arm drags and hip tosses were replaced by headlocks, armbars and more headlocks. The whole thing looked like a high school wrestling meet because that was all we could do- the mat was paper-thin, and every bump was like landing on cement. So I directed the "action" and even dusted off some old mat wrestling sequences from my days with Joe Mercer. We still went a good twenty minutes plus. After working Ricky a bit, I tagged in Tony and called the next spot:

"He's gonna hit you with two bodyslams and two dropkicks."

Tony started running full-speed at Ricky and then stopped dead in his tracks. He turned back to me with a confused expression.

"Two bodyslams and two dropkicks?" he whispered through gritted teeth, "Are you trying to kill me?"

Ricky and I started cracking up. I pointed at Tony with the international sign of *"I'm just messing with you."* He shook his head and our boring-ass match continued. Punky finally scored the win with one of the most devastating inside cradles of all time.

The Rock-n-Roll Express weren't long for Memphis. They went to Mid-South where they became headliners and by the mid-80s they were one of wrestling's most decorated tag-teams. They deserve all their accolades; Ricky and Robert were fantastic babyfaces and I think every aspiring wrestler should study a DVD of their work. Although if you ever run across a match where they're rolling on a gym mat with a couple of masked fellas, you should probably hit fast forward.

After our run with Punky and Hoot, Tony and I finally got our shot at The Fabulous Ones. This was all textbook booking: a heel team enters the promotion, they beat the crap out of some babyfaces and eventually earn a shot at the top dogs. Thanks to some good old-fashioned heel tactics, we did in fact capture the tag team belts. But, we knew our reign wouldn't last long: the Fabs would eventually win the gold back and move on to the next challengers. Meanwhile, we would move to the mid-card or another territory altogether.

That was my role in the pro wrestling food chain. I was what the boys called a "carpenter". Carpenters weren't the glamorous stars of the show- but they were just as necessary. It was our job to "build the house" by making a territory's top guys look like a million bucks.

Of course, I had been a "top guy" a few years earlier in Mid-South (even if I did harbor some delusions of grandeur), but by 1983 I had finally accepted that main event spots and fat paychecks were just pleasant memories. It was now my job to make other guys into stars and I would still make decent money for the work.

117

Of course, I still felt like I had the ability to be "the man" in a promotion *somewhere*. But for that, I would have to find the right opportunity…

That opportunity did not appear in Memphis. After our run with the Fabulous Ones, Tony and I began a program with fellow Jimmy Hart-proteges The Bruise Brothers (a team that included Troy Graham and my old lifting coach Porkchop Cash). The feud was just starting to take off when we received an unusual- and unwelcome- request.

It was Saturday, December 31st, and we were getting ready for the weekly TV taping. The focus of that week's episode would be a special New Years Day show at Mid-South Coliseum where (among other matches) Tony and I would face the Bruise Brothers for the third time in three weeks. When we arrived at the studio, Eddie Marlin took us aside for some instructions. Eddie was the on-camera authority figure for the territory, and in real-life he was Jerry Jarrett's right hand man.

"We want you to cut a promo for tomorrow's show," he began. "Tomorrow is going to be a hair versus masks match. So if the Bruise Brothers lose they get their heads shaved, but if you lose the masks come off."

I looked at Tony and his expression was as dumbfounded as mine. If we lost *our masks were coming off?* That was the first I had heard of this shit.

"Tell me Eddie," I finally replied. "Is Troy shaving his head… or Porkchop… or both?"

Marlin got a good laugh out of that one.

"Yeah right," he snickered. "We all know how that match is ending."

He shook his head as if we had all just shared a very pleasant inside joke. I responded with my best 'this-shit-isn't-funny' tone:

"If you think we're taking these masks off, you're out of your fucking mind."

Eddie's laughter died a sudden death.

"What's the problem?" he asked with a shrug.

That's when I lost my shit.

"Man, I've been busting my ass with this Grappler gimmick for almost FOUR YEARS!" I roared. "I killed myself to make this mask and this name mean something- it's my livelihood! Now you're telling me to flush all of it down the crapper on a whim? Hell- would we even get paid extra for this?"

He avoided eye contact and answered my question at the same time. Marlin then tried to make his unreasonable request sound more reasonable:

"It's just at this one show…"

"There's gonna be a bunch of people at ringside taking pictures," I said, cutting him off mid-sentence. "If a picture of us without the masks appears in some wrestling magazine our gimmick is *dead*. Who's gonna book a couple of mystery men when there's no more mystery?"

My rhetorical question received no reply.

"We'll gladly put those guys over any day of the week," I continued. "But we <u>ain't</u> losing these masks!"

Eddie just nodded silently and went off to relay my message. I kept venting to Tony, and even tracked down Porkchop to fill him in on the situation. I had all the respect in the world for Bobby, and thankfully he understood where I was coming from.

"Man, if I was you I wouldn't drop my mask either," he said. "They should have ran this BS by us first."

After talking with the head honchos (Lawler and booker Bill Dundee), Marlin returned with some updated instructions.

"We're sticking with the hair versus masks stips," he said. "Just cut a promo for that match. Tomorrow, we'll have a finish figured out so everyone is happy."

I wasn't remotely optimistic that this story would have a happy ending, but what the hell else was I supposed to do? So, we went on camera and I cut loose on the mike:

"Man, they better have a barber ready tomorrow! When we're finished with them Cash and Graham are gonna be balder than Kojak!"

When we arrived at Mid-South Coliseum the next day I didn't even bother to get dressed. The fans were filing into their seats when Marlin approached us backstage.

"So... who's head is getting shaved?" I asked without humor.

"Just hear me out," Eddie implored. "You guys do the job and take the masks off. We'll have a couple of guys ready to run in and throw towels over your heads. The crowd will only see your faces for a couple of seconds. "

I shook my head. *This* was the great compromise that we waited for?

"Eddie, you can tell the guys that we said no fucking way."

Marlin just threw his hands up as if to say *"Well, I tried"*.

"I guess you guys are done here," he said. "I'll get a check for what we owe you and you're free to go."

After we got the money I waited for Eddie to leave. Then I put on my mask and told Tony to do the same.

"When the show starts, they'll have the Bruise Brothers go out there and say that they ran us out of town," I explained. "We're going to walk out through the crowd and let everyone know that we're leaving on our own terms."

And that's exactly what we did. Before the opening bell, Tony and I walked out of the dressing room, hopped over the railing and waved goodbye to the fans who almost certainly figured this was part of the show.

"Memphis ain't big enough for us!" I yelled to anyone who would listen. "We're going to a place where we can challenge some real champions!"

Those weren't just words. One week after our walkout I received a call from my old Mid-South boss Buck Robley. He was now the booker in Kansas City and looking for new talent. So, Tony and I packed our bags and began the drive from Memphis to Missouri.

The Grapplers were trading Graceland for Raceland.

When I met Harley Race in 1984, I felt like I was shaking hands with John Wayne.

His gravelly growl and battle scars gave Harley the air of a legendary gunfighter that had sent a thousand men to their graves. Like Wayne's old marshal in *True Grit*, Race knew that his best days were behind him (his record-setting 7th NWA World Title reign had recently ended at the hands of Ric Flair). But Harley Race at 80 percent was better than most men at one hundred and- like The Duke- he could still gun down any young punk that got in his way.

The comparison with movie stars ends there because Harley's tough guy persona was not some Oscar-winning performance. He was the real deal- a legit fighter that feared no man and was universally respected. People sometimes ask me who was the toughest pro wrestler I ever faced. It's a difficult question to answer when you try to compare guys like Wahoo, Dynamite Kid and Bruiser Brody. I'll just say that Harley Race is, at the very least, tied for first place.

Tony and I had been in Kansas City for a few weeks when Harley approached us backstage during a TV taping. It was the first time we had seen him in person, as he had been on a tour of Japan when we made our debut.

"I'm glad to have you boys here," he said in his famous raspy delivery. "Lynn, I wonder if we could have a word in private?"

A lump instantly appeared in my throat.

See, Harley was not only a wrestler, but he was also part owner of the Central States wrestling promotion. He was partners with Kansas City's long time promoter Bob Geigel (who was president of the National Wrestling Alliance). Geigel and Race also owned the historic St. Louis territory, which they had purchased in 1982.

I didn't know why Harley wanted to talk with me, but I played it cool and followed him into the private room that he kept in Memorial Hall. He directed me to a seat. The whole time I was sweating like a kid who had been summoned to the principal's office.

"I've got some news," he said while settling in behind his desk. "Robley just quit."

Aw, crap.

Buck Robley was the whole reason I came to Missouri. Because of our history together in Mid-South, I had expected to do well in Kansas City. But, if he wasn't booker anymore, my outlook was much gloomier. Harley Race didn't know me from Adam.

Shit, am I getting fired?

I was afraid to ask the question, but it turns out I didn't have to. Harley Race was about to change the trajectory of my career.

"I'm looking for a new booker," he said. "And I think you could be the man for the job."

Gobsmacked Silence.

*Who's the man for the job? Me? I'm twenty-four years old and one of the greatest wrestling champions of all-time is talking to **me** about booking his promotion?*

"I've heard that you have lots of good ideas," Harley continued. "Being a booker is more work and more responsibility. But it's also more money. So, what do you think?"

What do I think? Fuck. I better say something.

"Sir… it… would be an… honor," I stammered. "I have so much respect for all you… all of your… um, accomplishments. Just to work… for you in every… I mean, any position. But… your booker… that would be a great… opportunity."

In his open-collared suit, Harley looked just like the champion I had watched in countless interviews- right down to the gold necklace and mini-afro. But he was wearing one accessory that I had never seen on TV:

A smile.

"Wait here," he said.

Harley stepped out of the office and returned a minute later with Bob Geigel. The promoter was a former wrestler who was now identified by his thick glasses and shiny pate.

"Tell Bob what you just said," Race commanded.

I repeated my praises (in a more coherent fashion) and said how humbled I was to be considered for such a prestigious position. It was one of those "it's an honor just to be nominated" speeches. When I finished, "Handsome" Harley grinned in affirmation and turned to his business partner.

"Geigel," he said, "Meet our new booker".

Being a booker was the closest I had ever been to having a "normal job". That is, if any job in the wrestling world can be considered "normal".

For the first time in my life I had regular office hours, just like any working stiff. Every weekday at 9 AM I would arrive at Memorial Hall, where Geigel, Race and I each had private offices. I worked about five hours each day, and spent most of that time trying to get wrestlers on the phone. In the days before cell phones and email, that could be an all day process. After that, I would head out for that night's show, arrive at the arena, go over the matches with the wrestlers, wrestle, and then get back to Kansas City by 9 AM the next day. Harley had told me it would be more work and he wasn't kidding.

My main responsibility was booking matches and angles for all the shows and coordinating the talent. I would come up with a plan for a card and run it by Geigel, who would either sign off on the deal or suggest some changes. Harley was in and out of the territory, often wrestling in Japan or some other promotion. But whenever he was in Kansas City, I made damn sure that my plans had his approval.

The whole thing was one hell of a learning experience. Especially since I was 24 years old and expected to give orders to veterans like Wahoo McDaniel and Ox Baker. Like I'm going to tell those guys that I'm their boss? I'll never forget when Ric Flair stopped in Kansas City for a couple shows.

"So Lynny," he said to me backstage, "What do you want me to do tonight?"

What did *I* want *Ric Flair* to do? Go ahead and have a good laugh at that question. I sure did.

When I finally got my sea legs as a booker, I knew that I had to establish some new talent. That was the key to keeping a territory fresh. It was important to give fans the familiar faces like Harley and The Oates brothers. But without some new blood a promotion could get stagnant fast. That's why, with the exception of a few top stars, most wrestlers were in a territory for a year or less and then moved on. It was out with the old and in with the new.

Tommy Rogers and Marty Jannetty were two young workers on the roster that I wanted to push. They were a pair of handsome high flyers and the girls absolutely loved them. Remembering the success of the Rock-n-Roll Express, I had the "Uptown Boys" feud with The Grapplers over the Central States tag titles. Our program lasted several months and we had some great matches throughout Missouri and Kansas.

Considering it was my first booking job, I felt that I had some good ideas and Harley and Geigel seemed happy with my work. Unfortunately, I learned that a booker is both the most popular *and* the most hated figure in a pro wrestling locker room. When you get the job, every wrestler is suddenly your buddy. Then, one night over beers one of these new friends casually mentions that *"Oh, by the way I have some great ideas for a main-event angle that I could be a part of. Not trying to take advantage of our friendship you understand- just wanted to help you out."* Once in a while the guy might have some decent ideas that make sense and you end up using them. But most of the time their counsel is a bunch of self-serving crap and then- when you don't give your new buddy a push- the bad mojo begins.

"Crazy" Luke Graham was a prime example of this. Luke had been a big star in New York and L.A. during the 60s and 70s. When Tony and I arrived in Kansas City, the blonde wildman's career was winding down and he became our traveling partner. We really liked Luke. He was a nice guy who was always making us laugh. And, with the exception of Harley, he was probably the biggest "name" on the Central States roster.

But Luke was way past his prime. He was in his mid-forties, and just couldn't duplicate the in-ring magic of his younger days. On top of that, the guy drank vodka like it was water, which made him very hard to manage. So, despite our friendship, I kept Luke out of main events and billed him as a mid-card attraction.

Luke had been giddy when I was first named booker. But after a few weeks in the mid-card he stopped traveling with Tony and me. Soon, he stopped talking to me altogether. Luke never complained face-to-face about his spot on the card. But he did send a rather large messenger my way.

It happened backstage at one of the Memorial Hall shows. I was looking over some notes from Harley when a beefy right hand smacked the back of my neck and swung my entire body 180 degrees. I dropped my notes and came face to face with a bearded behemoth named Jerry Blackwell.

"My friend Luke Graham is not happy," he said with disgust.

"What's the problem?" I asked.

"You know what the problem is," Jerry grumbled. "He was never anything but nice to you and now that you have some power you're treating him like shit. Who the fuck do you think you are?"

He finally released his grip.

That big fucker hurt my neck.

Normally, any wrestler that roughed up the booker could expect a pink slip. But this was not a normal situation. Blackwell worked in the AWA for Verne Gagne, and was only in town for one night. That meant I didn't have any authority over him. I should also point out that Jerry was an intimidating son of a bitch. He was a couple inches shorter than me but twice as heavy- imagine Andre the Giant's weight on the Dynamite Kid's frame. "Crusher" Blackwell was probably the scariest man to ever have a Napoleonic complex.

"I have no problem with you Jerry," I said, trying to sound firm yet respectful. As booker, I couldn't kowtow to every wrestler with a beef; lines had to be drawn. But at the same time I *really* didn't want to get my ass whupped.

"I like Luke too," I continued. "I'm sorry that he's unhappy. But at the end of the day I have to answer to a man named Harley Race. I put together shows that I think will draw him the most money. That's my concern- not some wrestler's hurt feelings. But… if you want to tell Harley how to run his business, he's not a hard man to find. I'd just make damn sure you don't grab *his* neck."

Our conversation ended right then and there. Even a quarter-ton goliath knew better than to mess with Harley Race's money. Jerry Blackwell just muttered a few choice curses and made for the exit. As I watched him turn tail like a scolded puppy I realized that this whole episode had concluded with a bit of good news and bad news. The *bad* news was that I obviously still had to earn respect as a booker. The *good* news was that nobody wanted to fuck with my boss.

Well, almost nobody.

"I could kill that motherfucker!"

Harley was in one of those moods. We were taping promos for some house shows, but all he could talk about was another promotion's upcoming card.

"Vince Junior is trying to put us out of business," Harley seethed. "He's trying to put us ALL out of business!"

"Vince Junior" is of course the man we all know as Vince McMahon. In the spring of 1984 he was planning the World Wrestling Federation's first-ever show in the St. Louis Keil Auditorium. This meant that the WWF was "invading" a territory that Race and Geigel had purchased from NWA founding father Sam Muchnick. For an old school guy like Harley Race, this kind of thing just wasn't done. Promoters had always respected each other's boundaries.

McMahon's first shot against the territorial old guard had actually taken place in January of 84, when the WWF began taping shows for St. Louis TV station

KPLR. Those episodes replaced the popular "Wrestling at the Chase" show that had aired on KPLR for almost a quarter century. Now, Vince was using that airtime to promote a major show headlined by his new champion Hulk Hogan.

"Get those cameras rolling," Harley instructed. "I'm going to tape a promo for St. Louis. I'm going to call those assholes what they are."

Once he got the signal, Harley unleashed an epic tirade that barely mentioned our upcoming St. Louis show. Instead, he WENT OFF on Vince McMahon's new golden boy: Hulk Hogan was a "plastic" champion. He couldn't lace Harley Race's boots. Everyone knew how Hogan really got those muscles. If he wanted to prove himself, he'd meet Harley in the middle of the ring. It went on and on. As soon as he was done, Harley mopped the sweat from his brow and fired up a heater.

"Boss," I said as delicately as possible, "We can't air that."

Harley's eyes shot at me like switchblades.

"WHAT THE FUCK ARE YOU TALKING ABOUT?" he thundered. "YOU'RE GONNA TELL ME HOW TO HANDLE MY BUSINESS?"

I raised my hands in submission.

"Look, you're Harley Race and I'm nobody," I pleaded. "But I'm a nobody that wants to help you."

Harley's glare told me to get to the fucking point.

"Boss, all you're doing is putting Hogan over," I explained. "Shit, the way you described him- all big and muscled- *I* want to buy a ticket to see that show. We shouldn't mention those guys at all. Just concentrate on what we do and forget about them."

His expression cooled and Harley slowly nodded.

"I know you're right," he sighed. "But I can't forget about them."

He took a long drag from the cigarette. Harley exhaled slowly, his eyes finding mine through the smoke.

"Everything I have is *here*," he said. "As a man, I can't let these people just walk in to my home and kick their feet up on the couch. I don't give a damn who they are or how much money they have. I *can't* take this lying down."

His voice sounded defiant but defeated. For the first time in his life, Harley Race was preparing for a fight that he did not expect to win.

The WWF ended up filling the Keil Auditorium to capacity. I didn't realize it at the time, but that show was in some ways the beginning of the end for so many legendary wrestling promotions. By mid-1984, Vince McMahon had taken over Georgia Championship Wrestling and a few months later, his company promoted its first show in Kansas City. Harley fought Vince and Hogan for as long as he could, but it was never much of a contest.

By 1986, Harley Race was wrestling for the WWF.

After almost a year in Kansas City, the unwritten rules of territorial wrestling dictated that Tony and I move on to our next stop. I made some calls and found that one former employer wanted to give The Grapplers a new gimmick. The idea sounded intriguing, so I gave Geigel and Race our two weeks notice. What followed next is a story that will tell you everything you need to know about Harley Race:

We were at our second-to-last TV taping when Harley pulled me aside.

"I'd like a favor before you leave," he said. "Would you mind putting me over?"

Think about that for a second. Harley Race was asking me- with all the humility in the world- if I would put him over before I left his territory. This is remarkable for a number of reasons:

Reason #1- I was leaving the territory. When a wrestler left a promotion they almost always "did the honors" on the way out. I just assumed that I would be putting somebody over before I left- that was the right way to do business.

Reason #2- Harley was my boss. He didn't have to *ask* me to lose a match. It was my job to follow his orders.

Reason #3 (and as far as I'm concerned the most amazing thing about this request)- This was HARLEY RACE. Asking <u>me</u> if I would mind letting him win a match. What the hell was I going to say? *Sorry Harley, I can't lose to a 7-Time World Heavyweight Champion. Yeah, I know you beat Jack Brisco, Terry Funk, Ric Flair and every other great wrestler of the past twenty years. But I have a reputation to maintain.*

It was beyond unnecessary that he asked me for this "favor", but that's the kind of guy Harley Race was. If you gave the business your heart, he would always treat you with respect. I told him that I would be honored to grant his request.

To set up my farewell match, we shot an angle for TV where I attacked Harley after a match. He fell to the mat, I loaded the boot and it was KO city. The show went to a commercial break. Harley was carried to the back, and the plan was for him to return later in the show and challenge me on-camera.

But first, he wanted a makeover.

"Bust me open Sonny!"

Harley was shouting instructions at Sonny Myers, a former wrestling champion who now worked as a referee. Sonny balled up a fist and, with all the force he could muster, landed a solid right hand on top of Harley's eyebrow.

"What the hell are you doing?" I asked, although I knew the answer.

"Selling your damn boot!" Harley fired back. "How do I look?"

Harley was trying to juice the "hard way." If you hit a guy just right the blood would gush out like an oil well. It was considered the more believable way to get color, as opposed to using a tiny razor blade. You had to be a tough son of a bitch to stand there and take the shot. But of course, we are talking about Harley Race.

"No juice," Sonny said with a shrug. Harley didn't hesitate for a second: "Do it again!"

Another HARD right hand from Sonny. Harley staggered back from the shot and then shook the cobwebs away. His brow began swelling but there was still no blood.

"Again!"

To me, this was insane. Harley was taking this beating to make my boot attack appear extra deadly. But I didn't see the point. I was leaving the territory and he didn't have to make me look good. As Sonny reared back for another blow, I ran to my boss's side.

"Stop!" I pleaded. "Harley, you don't have to do this for me."

"What the fuck are you talking about?" he snarled. "I'm trying to sell our match for next week you idiot! You think this is the first time I've had someone bust my brow? Sonny- get this shit over with!"

Another right hand connected and instantly Harley's forehead began spewing like Old Faithful. I figured he'd be ready for his promo, but instead that tough bastard gritted his teeth and began scouring his new wound with a piece of sandpaper. Within seconds we were all covered in blood.

"Jesus Harley," I finally said. "I hit you with a boot, not a chainsaw."

He disfigured himself with an attention to detail that would rival any great artist- as if Michelangelo was painting the Sistine Chapel in blood. When he had finally achieved that "headfirst-through-the-windshield" look, Harley the Red walked out in front of the cameras and assured the television audience that next week, he would make The Grappler pay for his evil deeds.

Sure enough, the next week Memorial Hall was packed to the rafters for our two-out-of three falls match. Harley snagged the first pinfall and I got the second. I can't remember exactly how Harley scored the win, but it didn't matter. For almost an hour he made me look like I belonged in the ring with one of the greatest wrestlers of all time. I may have lost the match, but it felt like he was putting *me* over.

And that was the thing about Harley Race. Despite his credentials as a World Champion and legit badass, he always wanted to do what was best for business. If that meant mutilating his own body and elevating a wrestler who wasn't in his league, well so be it. Yeah, he had an ego, but he knew when to set it aside, and you always knew he would give you a fair shake.

In the end, the only thing that exceeded Harley Race's toughness was his sense of honor.

After thanking Harley for our opportunity in KC, Tony and I loaded up our cars and pointed them towards the Volunteer State. For almost three years I had been trying to return to main-event status and mostly failing. Now, I was ready to try something drastic:

It was time to introduce wrestling fans to the man behind the mask.

CHAPTER SEVEN

DIRTY WHITE BOY

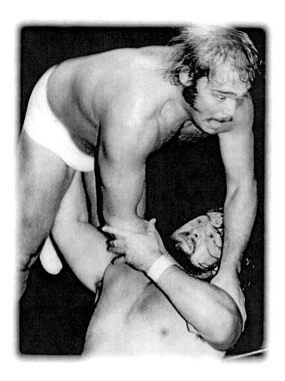

W
hen I returned to Memphis in the autumn of 1984, I traded my name and my mask for some black leather chaps and studded suspenders. I looked less like a wrestler and more like a bouncer on Fire Island. But my old pal Jimmy Hart thought it was the greatest thing he'd ever seen.

"You guys look great!" he howled. "I'm telling you- this gimmick is going to take off!"

When Tony and I walked out of Memphis on New Year's Day, I had assumed that was the last we would ever see of Jerry Lawler's kingdom. But it turned out, we didn't burn that bridge to the ground- just singed it a bit. Hart (who I had stayed in touch with during our Kansas City run) talked Lawler and Jarrett into bringing us back- with a new gimmick that was born from Jimmy's endless imagination.

"Forget about The Grapplers," he told us. "From now on, you're *The Dirty White Boys!*"

The nickname came from a song by the rock band Foreigner. The idea was that Tony and I (wrestling under our real names) would portray a couple of redneck bikers. Jimmy would once again be our manager, and we would be the latest duo to terrorize the god-loving babyfaces of Tennessee. Of course, it was never mentioned that we had actually been wrestling in that same territory nine months earlier. As far as the fans were concerned we were a brand new team that just happened to wrestle, walk and talk EXACTLY like The Grapplers.

I was excited about the opportunity. Kansas City had been a great experience, but in terms of pay and status I was still a long way from my Mid-South heyday. I figured that a new gimmick in a hot territory like Memphis could bring nothing but great things.

But then we shot that damn music video.

See, this was back when MTV was the hottest thing on television. Music videos had made singers like Michael Jackson and Madonna into pop icons, so Jerry Lawler's crew decided to use the new medium to create wrestling stars. Whenever a new wrestler or team would debut in Memphis, they were often promoted on TV with a slickly edited video package.

The pieces were effective in establishing new talent, even though they are (at best) hokey in hindsight. For example, The Fabulous Ones' debut music video was essentially three minutes of Steve and Stan posing in bowties and sequined jackets while a Billy Squier song played in the background. It was Grade-A 1980s cheese, but still a hit with the female fans that eventually bought tickets to see the boys in person.

For the Dirty White Boys' debut, Jimmy Hart oversaw a video shoot outside Memphis' legendary Sun Studio, where Elvis Presley had recorded his first albums. The area was covered in graffiti, and the plan was to show Tony and I in this rough looking place, all dressed up like a pair of thugs from a motorcycle gang. To achieve that "outlaw biker" look we had both pierced our ears and grown

133

beards. Then on the day of the shoot, we wore a couple of different outfits. One ensemble consisted of blue jeans, sunglasses and pastel-colored tanktops. After that, we went shirtless and put on suspenders, fingerless gloves and studded chokers. It was even more hideous than it sounds.

In addition to the outfits, Jimmy had snagged a couple of Harley-Davidson motorcycles for the shoot. I was a little hesitant to hop onboard.

"Jimmy, I've never ridden a motorcycle," I confessed. "I'll do this- but I'm a little worried I'll wreck the thing."

"You won't wreck anything," he assured me. "I just found out these bikes don't even work!"

Yes, the two Harleys were deader than death. Well, that solved one of my problems. But suddenly, I had a new concern: we were going to shoot a video of two badass bikers WHO NEVER RIDE A DAMN BIKE! Still, Jimmy promised that everything would be fine and told the crew to start rolling.

For the next two hours Tony and I posed for the camera. We flexed our biceps in unison, puffed out our hairy chests and sprawled out on our bikes like Burt Reynolds on a bearskin rug. When the shoot was done, Jimmy oversaw the editing process, where the Foreigner song was dubbed underneath this disturbing imagery:

Hey baby if you're feeling down
I know what's good for you all day...
'cause I'm a Dirty White Boy
Yeah a Dirty White Boy
A DIRTY WHITE BOY!

I wish I could describe the finished clip, but I think a quick story will tell you everything you need to know:

Recently, I was visiting a friend and he found that Dirty White Boy music video online. We were watching it and having a few laughs when his wife walked into the room. After a quick glimpse at the screen she turned to me with a puzzled expression.

"So, were you guys supposed to be bears?" she asked.

Bears? Like Polar Bears and Grizzlies? I asked her what she meant.

"You know- 'bears'- big, hairy gay guys," she replied. "I mean with all the leather and studs I just assumed... wait, is one of you wearing handcuffs?"

And that pretty much sums up the TV debut of the Dirty White Boys: we tried to imitate Hell's Angels but ended up looking like the Village People. Incidentally, that clip is on YouTube if you ever need a good chuckle.

On second thought, forget I wrote that. I lied. The Dirty White Boys music video is **not** online.

Please don't look for it.

Once our homoerotic music video made the rounds, it was time for the Dirty White Boys to get in the ring. As usual, we spent our first few weeks in Memphis squashing some of the local job guys. The gimmick was getting over with fans and after about a month on TV, I started getting recognized in public.

This was a new experience for me. As The Grappler, I had always enjoyed anonymity outside of the ring. Fans had no idea what I looked like without the mask. Now that everyone knew my face I was constantly being approached in bars, supermarkets, liquor stores or any other place where I might buy a six-pack.

The worst part of that was half the time the people wanted to talk about motorcycles. Makes sense right? After all, on TV I was the pro wrestling version of Easy Rider. But as we have established, I didn't know the first thing about motorcycles. Just about every day I'd get stuck in a conversation like this:

"Hey, Len Denton! I saw you on TV! What kind of bike do you ride?"

"A Harley."

"What kind? FLT Tour Glide? Fat Bob? Softail?"

"Uh... sure, one of those."

So yeah, I was a pretty lousy biker. Thankfully, I could still wrestle my ass off and my new gimmick was accompanied by one of my biggest pushes in years. After a few months in Memphis, The Dirty White Boys were thrust into a main-event feud with the territory's top stars.

In the fall of 1984, there were no bigger names in Memphis than Jerry Lawler and Randy Savage. The King was the icon of the territory, while the Macho Man was his former nemesis, both on-screen and off. Randy had been the star of his father's "outlaw" promotion ICW. After that company folded, Savage feuded with Jerry as the territory's top heel only to eventually turn babyface. When the Dirty White Boys debuted, both men were waging war against Jimmy Hart's First Family (of which Tony and I were card-carrying members).

I liked both guys. Jerry was an easy-going fella and despite our occasional creative differences (and that one time when I walked out on him) we had a good working relationship. Randy was more high-strung and quick to bark orders, but he was a pro and one electrifying worker.

To continue the duo's feud with Hart's henchmen, Lawler booked a couple of main event tag matches against Tony and me at the Mid-South Coliseum. We set the stage for the first match on TV. In a post-match attack, Tony and I flattened Savage with some stiff chairshots to the face. He bled like crazy, and we went into the Monday night show expecting a nice payoff to the angle. But in pro wrestling, expectations can often fall short of reality.

"The house is down," Lawler informed us backstage. "Again."

Jerry, Randy, Tony and I had been laying out our match when he received the night's attendance numbers. For a few weeks, ticket sales for the weekly coliseum shows had been declining. Jerry estimated that the gate was $10,000 lower than usual.

"We have another match scheduled with you guys," he continued. "So, what can we do *tonight* to put some asses in seats *next week*?"

The room went silent as the four of us racked our brains for a revolutionary idea that would turn things around. The problem was Memphis ran big angles all the time, and there wasn't anything those fans hadn't seen a million times.

"What about if we brawl all over the building?" I finally suggested. "You know, we fight in the crowd, the concession area, maybe the parking lot. Make the whole thing an out of control mess so the people have no idea what we'll do next week."

After chewing on the proposal for a few seconds, the King decided that he didn't have any better ideas. So, he gave his royal blessing and the four of us prepared for a coliseum-wide rumble.

My brilliant plan went into action at the match's conclusion (if memory serves me right, Tony and I were disqualified). Despite the ringing bells, we still went at it- Tony and Randy brawled at ringside, while Jerry and I spilled out into the crowd.

As most wrestling fans know, messing with Jerry Lawler in Memphis was a dangerous proposition. It was like when I tangled with Junkyard Dog in New Orleans and almost got shot. Thankfully, no one pointed a gun at me this time, but the second we were in the audience the fans started punching and kicking me.

"GET THE FUCK OFF ME!"

I began throwing haymakers at those ringside assholes, while Jerry made his way up the steps towards the top of the coliseum. He gave me a subtle nod that told me to follow him. After dropping one drunk dipshit with a back elbow I did just that.

We continued brawling up the steps, and the higher we got the more violent the fans became. Our wrestling angle had devolved into a real mob scene. By the time we reached the top of the coliseum, even Jerry had to deck a guy. I had been in some scary situations before, but this time I actually feared for my life.

"You need to get the fuck out of here," Lawler whispered.

Before I could heed his advice, I felt a shot like a sledgehammer landing on the top of my head. I staggered back against the wall, my vision went blurry and suddenly it sounded like I was underwater. From the corner of my eye, I could just make out the outline of a big S.O.B. in overalls rearing back with a right hand.

Instinctively I ducked and threw my shoulder into his gut. As he gasped for air I grabbed his hair with both hands.

At that point security finally arrived. Two guards grabbed the fan and tried to wrestle him away while I kept yanking on his greasy mop top. After a short struggle, the guards pulled him away and I ripped out two handfuls of hair.

"GO!" Jerry commanded.

I bolted down the stairs while throwing punches in every direction. Most of the fans backed away, but a couple wannabe tough guys tried to block my escape. I jumped a couple of steps and landed on them with a flurry of elbows and fists. When my path was finally clear, I sprinted for the safe confines of the dressing room.

When I finally got to the back, the top of my head was bleeding and I had welts and bruises all over my body. Somehow Tony and Randy had survived the crowd's wrath.

"If that doesn't draw some money I quit!" I told them.

The next week's ticket sales did in fact go up; the increased attendance put an extra two hundred bucks in my pocket. And wouldn't you know it, that big bastard in overalls was sitting at ringside for the rematch and sporting two new bald spots.

I wish I could say that getting clobbered by a pack of drunk assholes was the worst indignity I suffered in Tennessee. Unfortunately, right after that debacle I was introduced to the most godforsaken tradition in all of Memphis wrestling: the tar-and-feathers match.

It all began with a young up-and-comer named Rick Rude. Rick had Tom Selleck good looks, a bodybuilder's physique and was one tough son of a gun (I'll have some examples of that toughness in the next chapter). He had been a heel in Jimmy Hart's First Family, but like all wrestling relationships their partnership went sour and now Rude was an anti-Hart babyface.

I can't remember exactly how it was set up, but for some reason Rick and Jimmy faced each other in a televised one-on-one match. Naturally, the contest consisted of Jimmy running away from Rick and then running away some more. Eventually, he threw some mysterious white powder into Rude's eyes. As any wrestling fan knows, that dreaded substance leaves its victim blind as a bat (its effectiveness is second only to the lethal combination of water and green food coloring).

As Rick staggered around the ring sightless, Tony and I jumped him from behind. With the help of Jimmy's bodyguard (a muscular black fella named "Dr. Detroit") we tied Rude to the ropes. Then the cavalry arrived. Lawler ran to Rude's aid, alongside ring veteran Jimmy Valiant. Once a top heel, "The Boogie Woogie Man" was now a face known for his ZZ-Top beard and jive-talking promos. We went toe-toe for a bit, but with Rude tied up, the heroes were outnumbered. Our fight went to the floor.

Once Lawler and Valiant were subdued, Tony and I produced a couple of jars of molasses and some bags of loose feathers (nobody seemed to wonder why we had these completely random items at ringside). We poured the molasses all over Jimmy and Jerry and then dumped on the feathers. An immobile Rude watched in horror as Boogie and The King were transformed into a pair of ugly ducklings.

So, that was the big TV angle and even a man blinded by mysterious white powder could see where things were headed. A series of "tar and feather" matches were set up on the loop with me and Tony facing various combinations of Valiant, Rude and Lawler. The great news was that it was two weeks of main event money. The not-so-great news was that it was two weeks of us losing tar and feather matches.

Have you ever been eating pancakes or waffles and then accidentally spilled some maple syrup on your pants? It's a bitch right? For the rest of the day you're wearing a sticky, splotchy stain. Well, just imagine all that stuff being dumped on your clothes, in your shoes and down your asscrack. Then imagine that happening again the next day. And the next. And the next. I can assure you there is not enough Head and Shoulders in the world to get all that sticky shit out of your hair.

To make things worse, Tony and I only had two wrestling outfits. So every night we would have to spend a couple hours in a hotel sink, trying desperately to scrub all the molasses off of our pants and boots. As if that wasn't bad enough, you could never get the clothes totally clean and the lingering sugar would attract insects. So, for two weeks straight we had flies buzzing around us like a couple of old turds on the sidewalk.

I guess what's *most* depressing about this story is that the tar and feather series was the highlight of our Memphis run. After our molasses baths, The Dirty White Boys were back in the midcard and then a few months later we were looking for a new home. Tony and I decided to ride our non-existent Harleys to the place where it all began.

I don't think Bill Watts ever cared for the Dirty White Boys gimmick, which just goes to show that the man had some taste. But he brought Tony and I back because he knew a couple of solid workers could help the Mid-South tag division. And in 1985 he needed all the help he could get.

The Junkyard Dog was long gone, having left for the big money of the World Wrestling Federation. Without JYD, the Superdome cards were a fraction of their former glory. Don't get me wrong- Watts still had top talent like Ted Dibiase and Jim Duggan. But Mid-South Wrestling could no longer claim to be the hottest promotion in America.

When we arrived in Shreveport, The Cowboy wanted to tweak our gimmick a bit. Tony and I had always portrayed the Dirty White Boys as a couple of Dixie-bred rednecks- often draping ourselves in the Confederate flag. But Watts wanted to up the ante.

"You guys really need to draw some heat with the black fans," he told us. "I want you to go out there and cut the most racist promos you can. Call them everything but the n-word."

In case you're wondering, Watts didn't say "the n-word"- he used the actual word. But that's a term I don't use in conversation and one I won't put in my book. I wasn't terribly excited to portray what was essentially a motorcycle-riding klansman. There were so many black men that I considered friends and mentors (guys like Porkchop and Abdullah that essentially saved my career) that the "George Wallace on a Harley" thing seemed like a bit of a stretch. But I went along with it, because at the end of the day this was pro wrestling. Watts had made money by giving black folks in Louisiana and Mississippi someone to love (JYD). Theoretically, he could also make money by giving them someone to despise.

So I laced my interviews with all the ignorant shit I could come up with. Tony and I were billed as hailing from Bucksnort, Tennessee, a location that I would reference with racist glee:

"Let me tell you something, where we come from you boys better not show yourself after dark. In Bucksnort, we don't even have black chickens!"

It went on and on. We were definitely booed by the fans- black and white. But it was more of a "get off the damn stage" kind of heat. Meanwhile, my black peers just laughed at the whole thing.

"The Dirty White Boys?" the 400-pound Kamala would say with a chuckle. "Man, I hope you don't think you're scaring anyone."

I knew for sure we weren't intimidating the Ugandan Giant and whatever heat our gimmick drew was for naught anyways. It was obvious from the start that Watts wasn't interested in making the Dirty White Boys a main event attraction. Still, we did manage to sneak into a couple of big matches.

On one Superdome show, Tony and I faced these three teams in a four-corners tag match: The Rock-n-Roll Express, The Fabulous Freebirds and The Road Warriors. Man, you talk about a Hall of Fame field. It was great to work with Punky and Hoot again, but this was the first time we ever worked with the Legion of Doom. After a couple of stiff shots from Hawk I was pretty sure that I never wanted a rematch.

But our most high-profile feud from this period was with Sgt. Slaughter and his tag team partner Terry Daniels. Sarge was one of those workers that you never had to worry about- you knew it was going to be a great match. The feud was settled with a bloody "bootcamp match" at the Superdome. But it's what happened *before* that match that was the highlight of my final run in Mid-South Wrestling.

The show was already underway and Tony and I were backstage shooting the shit. The other boys were milling around the locker room when a familiar voice cut through the crowd:

"Where's that Dirty White Boy at? I want that Dirty White Boy!"

I turned around and could not believe my eyes- that voice belonged to the world's most famous athlete.

Muhammad Ali was walking right towards me.

Watts had brought Ali to the Superdome as a special attraction. The former boxing great was going to be in the corner of a wrestler called The Snowman during his match with Jake Roberts.

Of course, I knew Ali as not just a prizefighter, but also as a political and social activist. For years he had railed against war and racism. Meanwhile, I had just delivered another one of my hyper-bigoted promos, complete with references to watermelon and fried chicken. I noticed the Champ was marching at me with purpose- his fists were balled and his entourage was trying to keep up.

Oh shit.

"There he is!" Ali said, pointing right at me. "That's that Dirty White Boy I've been looking for!"

I'm not a person that is usually speechless but words failed me at that moment. After all, this was a man that I had watched on TV since I was a little kid. Now he was six inches from my face and going off on me like I was Joe Frazier. I didn't know if Ali was pissed about my racist interview, but I really didn't care. Even if he knocked me out, it would still be one hell of a story to tell my grandkids.

"So you're the Dirty White Boy!" Ali said, waving a finger in my face. "You're the one saying all those things about my people!"

I started bracing for a left hook when Muhammad flashed his famous smile.

"Man, that stuff was hilarious! You get on them brothers worse than I do! That line about black chickens- I loved that!"

Ali slapped me on the shoulder, and I finally mustered enough courage to say "thanks" and "it's an honor to meet you." As the champ walked off, two thoughts ran through my mind:

1- *If the greatest promo man in the history of boxing likes my interviews, I must be pretty damn good on the stick.*

2- *If a man like Muhammad Ali enjoys my gimmick, I must be a pretty lousy white supremacist.*

As our short stint with Watts was winding down, it was once again time to take stock of my life and things weren't going great.

My personal life had hit rock bottom- I was pushing thirty, divorced and missing my family. My professional life wasn't much better. Tony and I had been tagging for years and were still stuck with midcard payouts despite some (in my opinion) pretty good work. It was time for a change.

"I'd like to go back to Texas," I told Tony one day. "I'm not sure how much longer this wrestling thing will last, and if it all falls apart, at least I'll be near home."

It turned out my tag team partner was having similar thoughts. Tony was missing his home in Eastern Tennessee.

"I was thinking I could get booked in Knoxville," he said. "It would be nice to live someplace familiar for a change."

We called the necessary parties, and eventually we both got what we wanted- bookings in our home states. Tony and I shook hands and promised that, if things didn't work out, we would tag up again in the future. But, outside of a few occasional team-ups, this was the end of our three-year partnership.

Tony kept the "Dirty White Boy" moniker and eventually became a major star in his home territory. I left my biker gear behind and returned to the Lone Star State with a loaded boot and a silver mask.

The Grappler was back.

CHAPTER EIGHT

BRUISER, BARBARIAN AND THE BRUNETTE

I n the winter of 1985, Fritz Von Erich's World Class Championship Wrestling was a promotion that had reached dizzying heights while experiencing some heartbreaking lows. The territory had been red-hot for several years, with legendary feuds like The Von Erichs versus The Fabulous Freebirds packing fans into the Dallas Sportatorium and, on special occasions, Texas Stadium (home of the Dallas Cowboys). But David Von Erich's death in 1984 was a sad precursor to the dark days that would follow.

After so many hot and (mostly) cold years, I thought World Class might be my last stop in the wrestling business. As I had told Tony, I was now in my home state and if I couldn't make some decent money there I was ready to hang up my boots. It was time to put up or shut up. Booker David Manning had brought me in to be a "working heel"- in other words, I was expected to give the people a quality match every single night. It was essentially the role that I had under Bill Watts, and the *possibility* of some main event money existed. Of course, there are no guarantees in professional wrestling. But at least I was back to my most successful gimmick and paired with a couple of grade-A talents.

Between Memphis and Dallas, I had a brief stint in the Tampa territory. While there, I was paired with a roly-poly heat magnet named Percy Pringle, and his protégé Rick Rude. Percy was a flashy dressing manager who would one day become world famous as The Undertaker's manager Paul Bearer. I knew Rick from our days in Memphis, and we became friends and traveling partners. After a couple months together, Manning brought the three of us into World Class and "The Pringle Dynasty" declared war on the heroes of Texas.

Traveling with Rick was a highlight of those first few months in Dallas. He was one of those "don't-judge-a-book-by-its-cover" kind of guys. On TV, he was portrayed as a handsome lothario who was constantly hopping from one groupie to the next. In real life, he was a reserved one-woman man. Don't get me wrong: the guy could have had any woman he wanted. But Rick didn't go to bars looking for girls- he went there looking for fights.

A lot of people underestimated "The Ravishing One's" toughness because he was such a handsome guy. You know: *"no way that pretty boy could kick my ass."* But Rick Rude was a coiled cobra that was always ready to strike. More importantly, he was a world champion arm wrestler with a grip that could crush bricks. Whenever we went out, Rick would just sit back and wait for someone to try and start some shit. The moment some drunk idiot said the wrong thing, Rude would wrap his hands around his windpipe and within seconds the guy would turn purple.

I don't want to make Rick out to be some kind of bully: the guys he messed up deserved it. He was a good friend and actually a very sensitive guy. But I saw first hand that you didn't want to mess with his touchy-feely side.

One day when we were traveling between shows I was filling up the car at a gas station while Rick was on a call in a nearby phone booth. I went in to pay for the gas and when I came back out he was sitting on the curb with tears streaming down his face. This wasn't some dust in his eye- the man was full on bawling.

"My grandmother died," he said through his sobs. "She helped raise me... I can't believe she's gone."

I sat next to my friend and tried to offer some comfort. Unfortunately, my words were interrupted by an uncaring- and unwelcome- voice.

"RICK RUDE YOU SUCK!"

A wrestling fan was parked at a red light, and yelling at us through his rolled-down passenger side window. Rick's face became so red that his tears almost instantly evaporated.

"Hold on buddy, don't..."

Before I could finish my sentence, Rick was halfway to the car. By the time I got to my feet, he was squeezing the guy's throat and trying to pull him through the open window.

"Rick... stop!!!"

I tried to pry his hands apart but they wouldn't budge; it felt like they were magnetically fixed to the fan's neck. The poor moron was already halfway to indigo. I heard a few stifled gasps escape his mouth and then nothing.

Oh fuck.

"RICK--- YOU'RE KILLING HIM!!!"

The words flipped a switch in my friend's brain and Rick immediately released his grip. With a loud thunk the unconscious fan's head slammed into the side of the car door. He was limp as a wet noodle and hanging halfway out the window. After a few seconds of panicked silence, the guy began choking and panting. While the oxygen returned to his lungs, a pedestrian started yelling from across the street.

"Somebody call the cops! He tried to kill that man!"

Rick was catatonic by this point. He was just staring at the poor sap that he had almost strangled to death. I had to damn near carry him to my car and throw him in the passenger seat. The Good Samaritan kept shouting:

"I'm writing down your license plate number!"

I hit the gas and we got the fuck out of Dodge. Rick didn't say a word. He just stared into space until the memory of his grandmother returned. For the rest of the drive he wept while I wondered about the condition of the wrestling fan with the world's worst timing. The cops never came after us, so I guess things weren't too bad- it was just a case of my buddy getting choked up and some other guy getting choked out.

Rick was the crown jewel of "The Pringle Dynasty" and when we arrived in World Class he was immediately thrown into a feud with the Von Erich brothers. He won the promotion's heavyweight title, while I was the Robin to his Batman (or whatever the bad guy equivalent would be- did The Joker have an intern?).

I embarked on a long feud with Brian Adias over the Texas Heavyweight Title- the territory's #2 championship. I held the belt for about three months- my first singles title reign since I held the North American title four years prior. After so many ups and downs, it was nice to be wearing a strap and making a little extra money. Unfortunately I was in a territory that would soon become synonymous with tragedy.

When I entered World Class one of the top heels was Gino Hernandez, a fella that I had known since my early days in Houston. I never really got along with the guy. From my experience, Gino was one of those main event wrestlers who looked down his nose at the mid-carders. But nobody could deny that he was charismatic and a hell of a talent.

Gino was also at the center of countless backstage rumors. He was a big spender and lived in an upscale part of the Dallas Metroplex- a neighborhood that was pricey even for a main event wrestler. The gossip amongst the boys was that Gino was supplementing his income through some less-than-legal means; drug dealing to be precise. It's important to note that this was the 1980s and cocaine was everywhere, especially in wrestling locker rooms. Plenty of the boys used the white powder. But by most backstage accounts, Gino was more than a recreational coke user.

Whatever his involvement was in the drug scene, anyone could see that Gino was living life on the edge. I can remember at one house show he arrived after the opening match and looked like a zombie. He told a referee to wake him right before his match, then he laid down on a bench and fell asleep in a matter of seconds. It was obvious he hadn't slept in days.

A couple of weeks later, Gino Hernandez was dead. He had no-showed a couple of cards, so a group of World Class officials stopped by his apartment to see what was wrong. Referee Rick Hazzard told me he that he found Gino face down on the floor, holding a glass of orange juice. The coroner found an immense amount of cocaine in his system and the death was ruled an overdose. To this day a number of the boys believe that Gino was the victim of a drug-related homicide. I have no idea what happened; I just know that a great talent died way too young. Sadly, there was more misfortune on the horizon- and it involved the first family of World Class Championship Wrestling.

For Dallas wrestling fans, Kevin and Kerry Von Erich were Sam Houston and Jim Bowie in tights. We're talking living Texas legends. Their younger sibling Mike was also working in the family business, and the three brothers were a study in opposites.

Kevin was the oldest and most level-headed brother. Kerry was an incredible athlete but also a space cadet. Don't get me wrong: nice guy, but a bit out to lunch. I can remember one time when I had driven from a show in El Paso to a show in Dallas. It was one long ass trip, and I was complaining about it when I got to the Sportatorium. Kerry overhead me and piped in:

"You're right man," he said. "Kevin and I just did that drive and it went on forever. What a pain."

"Uh, Kerry-" Kevin interjected. "We *flew* here."

Kerry considered his brother's words. After a few moments of reflection he concluded that yes, he had flown from El Paso to Dallas and it was a rather short trip. He wasn't lying or anything- just a little confused. That was Kerry Von Erich.

In the ring, "The Modern Day Warrior" was great. I've heard stories about Kerry all drugged up during matches, but I can say that never happened with me. In fact, when he lost his right foot following a motorcycle crash, nobody in the locker room had any idea. I worked with Kerry after the amputation and had no clue that he was wrestling with a handicap. He was just as good with one foot as he was with two.

Unfortunately, Mike Von Erich did not possess Kerry's athleticism or Kevin's self-control. Don't ask me to diagnose what was wrong with the kid. I know that he had survived a bout of toxic shock syndrome and obviously the whole family had been deeply affected by the death of his older brother David. Whatever the cause may have been, it was obvious that Mike was in a bad way.

One night, I was scheduled to wrestle him in a one-on-one match. I was backstage talking to referee Bronco Lubich while Mike was sitting on a bench and lacing his boots. Without warning, he fell backwards off of the bench and landed flat on the concrete floor. Bronco and I helped Mike to his feet; he could barely stand and his expression was blank. I don't know if he was drunk, drugged or all of the above but the lights were on and nobody was home.

"What the hell am I supposed to do?" I asked Bronco. "I have to wrestle this guy?"

"I'm not sure what you're going to do," he replied. "But Fritz is watching- so you better make it look good."

I should point out that during my year and a half in Dallas I almost never saw Fritz Von Erich in person. The promotion's owner only attended major shows and TV tapings, with his main focus being his sons' matches. If I didn't make a half-conscious Mike Von Erich look like a World Champion, I'd be looking for a job the next day.

Mike was somehow able to stumble from the dressing room to the ring, but that was about all he could do. As soon as he stepped between the ropes I backed him into a corner. When he collapsed into the turnbuckle I ducked my head and discretely wrapped his arm around my neck. To the audience it appeared that Mike had me in a side headlock, but really I was just trying to keep him on his feet. For a couple of minutes, I "struggled" to escape his debilitating hold. Meanwhile, Mike struggled to stay upright. It felt like I was back wrestling Joe Mercer's broom.

"We need to get this shit over with," I whispered. "Just put me in the claw."

Fortunately, Mike was lucid enough to raise his hand and grab my forehead. I fell to the mat and acted like my skull was going to implode. The referee's three count was a mercy killing for our godawful match. I returned to the dressing room, hoping that Fritz had watched our match. He *had* to see that his son was in bad shape and had no business being in a ring. He had to see that Mike needed help.

A few months later I was driving to a house show when the news came over the radio: Mike Von Erich had committed suicide. He had driven to Lake Dallas and overdosed on sleeping pills and booze. I was saddened but not surprised.

Mike and Gino's deaths introduced me to the dark side of professional wrestling. I had always known that the business could be heartless, but I never considered wrestling a life-or-death proposition. Sadly, many of my peers lost perspective and became slaves to fame, addiction and depression.

I decided that would not be me. Yeah, I'd been through some rough patches- but no job was worth my life. Lynn Denton was not going to wind up some pro wrestling cautionary tale. I was going to find happiness in the business or leave it altogether.

That happiness wasn't necessarily going to come from my place in the World Class food chain. After my run with the Texas title, I was broken away from Percy and Rick and dropped a couple notches down on the card. Thankfully, during this time I worked with a number of men who made the wrestling business fun again. One of those bright lights was the most dangerous lunatic to wear a pair of furry wrestling boots.

Bruiser Brody beat the shit out of me so many times it was almost awkward to have a conversation with him when he wasn't knocking the air out of my lungs. You could say we had an abusive relationship, if not for the fact that Brody abused everyone.

"These fans may wonder what's real and what's not," he told me once. "But they're going to believe *my* matches."

Brody made a believer out of me and pretty much everyone he wrestled. A match with Bruiser was a street fight, pure and simple. The only thing he wouldn't do is knock out your teeth. At least not on purpose. But when it came to punches, kicks and clotheslines the guy delivered more potatoes than the entire state of Idaho.

His wooly hair and wild beard made him look like a caveman, but the man portraying Bruiser Brody was no Neanderthal. Frank Goodish was a sharp fella who knew how to draw money and only unleashed his homicidal alter ego when it made sense for business. In 1986, Frank was brought in to work as the booker for World Class Championship Wrestling (he was also the promotion's top draw that was not named Von Erich).

For a big star that beat the crap out of people without a second thought, Frank was actually a generous guy behind the scenes. He would give me career advice and speak on my behalf to score me extra bookings and bigger payouts. I'm not sure why he was so helpful- perhaps it was because I always treated him with respect. Or maybe he appreciated that I never bitched about his in-ring ass-whuppins.

Because those matches with Brody really did suck- at least from a pain perspective. I can remember one night when I decided to give Frank a taste of his own medicine. We were slated for a one-on-one match and I knew the curb-stomping was imminent. I figured: *what the hell, if I'm going to catch a beating I might as well get a shot in too.* So, before the bell rang I ran across the ring and hit Frank in the face with the hardest punch I could throw. He never saw it coming and I actually knocked him back a couple steps.

In about two seconds the look in his eyes went from surprise to anger to amusement. Then Frank clapped his hands together and his entire face lit up as if I had just handed him a Christmas present.

"Good for you!" he said with pride. "Now, we're going to do this thing right!"

My dear friend and mentor then commenced an unholy bloodbath that made me curse the day I was born.

Brody brought a protégé into World Class that also inflicted severe pain on my person. But it wasn't because of stiff shots- everyday John Nord made me laugh until my sides hurt.

Frank had bequeathed his gimmick to Johnny and was determined to make "Nord the Barbarian" the next generation's Bruiser Brody. To earn that comparison Nord grew a beard, wore some furry boots and worked stiffer than shit. Johnny was about 320 pounds of biceps, traps and quads so when he hit you with his big boot you felt it for days (provided you didn't get knocked out).

But all that monster-caveman shit was in the ring. Backstage, John Nord was a free spirit and one of the funniest guys I ever met. We became very close friends and I loved hanging out with him because he was always leaving me in stitches- and not the kind that you'd get after a match with Abdullah the Butcher.

See, pro wrestling can be a very uptight business. There are so many unwritten rules and codes of conduct that it's very easy for a long time wrestler to take himself too seriously. But Johnny didn't take anything seriously, least of all himself. The guy wanted to have fun in life and wasn't going to let pro wrestling protocol get in the way.

I had first met him when he was a rookie in Mid-South. We all saw this massive ex-football player walk into the dressing room and expected him to be some sort of scary meathead. But then he started joking in his Min-uh-SO-tuh accent and it was obvious that this guy was more Jack Benny than Jack Lambert. He was always playing harmless ribs and lived to take the piss out of the old-timers that treated wrestling like a religion. One time at a Mid-South TV taping Johnny and I were laying down on the floor backstage; we were trying to catch some rest before taping some promos. Bill Watts walked by and dropped one of his customary Wattsims on us:

"You know, if you guys stopped laying around like that you might actually draw money someday."

Normally, that was your cue to get off your ass and let the Cowboy know that you were ready to do anything. But Nord didn't move an inch.

"Aw, come on Bill…" he said, sounding like a third grader pleading with his parents, "We *like* it down here."

The ever-serious Watts just shook his head. Bill didn't bother to lecture Nord because he knew that Johnny wasn't intimidated and would always have a smart aleck retort. Essentially, John Nord was Will Ferrell with a 500 pound bench press. When he arrived in Dallas, he had me busting up every night, which was nice because by early 1987 I had dropped so far down on the card that I needed *something* to laugh about.

My most memorable episode with Johnny happened at the big Parade of Champions card at Texas Stadium. I had a prelim match with a fella named Cousin Junior (the less said about that match the better). Meanwhile, Nord was in the main event and facing Kevin Von Erich for the World Class Heavyweight Title. The match was slated to end in a double-countout. After the bell rang, Kevin and Nord were supposed to keep tussling until a bunch of wrestlers came from the back and pulled them apart. I was the first wrestler that was supposed to run out and try to break up the brawl. Of course, that wouldn't be enough so more boys would keep coming until we could finally restore order.

Well, the match ended as planned and Kevin and Johnny kept fighting after the bell while the referee tried to stop them. When I got my cue, I ran to the ring, which was located at the forty-yard line. From the dressing room entrance it was about a sixty yard sprint to Kevin and Johnny, who were rolling around on the turf. I was five feet away when Nord spotted me out of the corner of his eye. In a flash, he shoved Kevin out of the way and dropped me with a FIERCE overhand right. All the air flew out of my chest and I saw those big and bright stars Texans are always singing about.

The other boys arrived on scene and the pull-apart began while I tried desperately to regain my breath. When oxygen finally returned to my brain, the pain was replaced by anger:

That big fucker wasn't supposed to hit me. Is this some rib? He'll get a receipt for that one!

I looked up and saw that the boys had separated Kevin and Nord. They were each being restrained by multiple wrestlers and struggling to break free. While all this chaos was going on, I snuck up behind Johnny with some bad intentions. Once I was within a few feet I leapt into the air and came down with the stiffest flying elbow I could throw. It landed on the back of Nord's head with a satisfying CRACK. The big galoot flew forward and almost- *almost-* fell on his face. He regained his balance and spun back at me with murder in his eyes.

"YOU MOTHERFUCKER!"

That was my cue to turn tail and run. Johnny was my best friend in the locker room, but a homicidal 320-pound monster is still a homicidal 320-pound monster. So, I did my best Tony Dorsett imitation and sprinted towards the Cowboys' endzone. After a few yards I looked up and saw a peculiar sight on the stadium's Jumbotron: Nord had left his ringside brawl and was now chasing *me*. Bear in mind that Johnny and I were both heels and, as far as the fans were concerned, had no connection to each other whatsoever. I doubt anyone in the stadium knew why Nord the Barbarian had abandoned his hated rival to chase some mid-carder that had lost to Cousin Junior. The whole incident was completely unprofessional and, in hindsight, pretty damn funny.

Nord tackled me at the five-yard line. He then unleashed one of those big brother/little brother beatings where you scream a few words after every three punches:

"DON'T YOU (punch, punch, punch) EVER HIT ME (punch, punch, punch) THAT HARD (punch, punch, punch) AGAIN!"

Once he decided that I had suffered enough pain and humiliation, Johnny ran back to ringside to resume the pull-apart. I would have laughed if I wasn't in so much damn pain. When we got to the back Brody (our booker and boss) was livid.

"What the fuck were you two idiots doing?" he screamed. "I have to go talk to Fritz and if he saw that shit- you guys are going to be done here!"

When Frank left, Johnny and I busted up laughing. We had just beaten the shit out of each other for our own personal amusement and now we could end up losing our jobs. Please don't ask me why we thought that was so damn funny- it was just the kind of shit that could only happen in a pro wrestling friendship. Later that night, Nord and I were getting ready to leave when Brody returned with some important info. It turned out Fritz had not seen our little chase, so we were in the clear. And there was more good news.

"I need you to stay after the show tonight," he told Johnny. "We're going to put the Heavyweight Title on you at the next TV taping. I need you to stay here and tape some promos."

After sharing some more instructions with Nord, Frank left and I congratulated my friend on his imminent title reign. Johnny shrugged it off.

"Fuck it, let's go to the bar." he said.

"Didn't you hear what Frank said?" I said, somewhat dumbfounded. "They want you to tape promos to build for your title change. You're getting the Heavyweight Title!"

"I don't want to be champion of this place," Johnny said, somewhat annoyed. "I don't want to tape promos. Hell, I don't want to work here at all. Now, let's get drunk."

I tried to talk some sense into him, but his mind was made up. So we went out and got sloshed. Johnny had traded a title reign for a night on the town with his friend. A few days later, he was out of the promotion altogether. It was weird: most young wrestlers would have killed for a chance to beat Kevin Von Erich for the World Class Heavyweight Title. But then, Nord the Barbarian wasn't like most young wrestlers and that's what I loved about the guy. You've heard of people marching to the beat of their own drum? Well, John Nord was listening to a different instrument altogether.

Unlike Johnny, I didn't have any main event angles to no-show. After more than a year in the territory I went from being a secondary champion to a complete afterthought. My job was to put guys over and- in certain cases- teach the younger guys how to work. Despite my "carpenter" status, everyone knew that I was a solid in-ring performer. So, from time-to-time, Brody would pair me up with a young talent in need of improvement.

"That Jim kid has a great look," he told me one day. "But he can't work a lick and is beating the hell out of everybody. I want you to teach him a few things."

That "Jim kid" was Jim Hellwig, a super-buffed, face-painting greenhorn who wrestled as "The Dingo Warrior". I didn't know anything about the kid and had no idea why he was named after an Australian wolf. But if *BRUISER BRODY* said he was stiff I had no doubt that the Dingo was one dangerous doggie.

I was paired with Jim for a couple weeks of on-the-job training. Essentially, we would work a match on a card and I'd give him a critique and some pointers afterwards. I came to like the kid. Some of the other boys thought Jim was conceited because he kept to himself in the locker room. I didn't mind that. Yeah, he was quiet but he was also respectful and willing to learn. Which was a good thing because Jim had *a lot* to learn.

After just one match I realized that Brody wasn't exaggerating about Dingo kicking the crap out of people. Jim was strong as a bulldozer and just as subtle. His clotheslines made Stan Hansen's lariats feel like love-taps while his "gorilla press" made you wish you were wrestling an actual gorilla.

See, press-slamming a person is usually a two-person job. The "pressee" straightens his body and essentially becomes a human barbell. Then the "presser" lifts him overhead with one hand on his sternum and the other on his upper quad or lower abdomen. That's how it's supposed to go. But because Jim was so strong, he did the press all by himself. Before I could straighten out, his left hand cinched around my throat and his right hand jammed into my groin. When Jim thrust me overhead his grip tightened on both my windpipe and my "little Grapplers". It felt like I was getting a vasectomy and asphyxiating at the same time.

Thankfully Jim was willing to take directions, and after a couple weeks together we were able to correct some of his flaws. I wasn't able to fix everything- his clotheslines would still loosen your fillings. But at least The Dingo Warrior learned how to perform a gorilla press without crushing his opponent's testicles.

Three years later, Jim- who changed his name to The *Ultimate* Warrior- used that press slam to win the WWF title from Hulk Hogan at Wrestlemania VI. I like to think that, in some small way, our time together prepared Jim for that big day. At the very least, my teachings prevented some serious agony for Terry Bollea's "little Hulksters".

Ultimately, my time in Dallas was most memorable for what happened *outside* the arenas. Bruiser, Barbarian and Warrior were no match for one pretty waitress and two adorable girls. Like most pro wrestling fairytales, this story begins in a bar.

Manhattan's was a Fort Worth nightspot where pro wrestlers drank for free. The Von Erichs were A-list celebrities in the Dallas Metroplex and the bar's owner figured that the World Class roster would bring in the crowds. So, he gave us the run of the place and in return we drank him halfway into bankruptcy.

By this time I was divorced and on the prowl. Nord and I would roll into the joint and within minutes I'd be handing out free drinks to every girl in a fifty-foot radius. The bar's owner eventually instituted a policy where I could only give freebies to one gal a night, but that didn't stop me from occasionally going table to table with a tray full of complimentary Crown and Cokes.

One night, I spotted a new face in the crowd. She was a dark-haired beauty with brown eyes and she was serving beers to a couple of the boys. Brother, I *had* to meet this girl. So I grabbed a sip of liquid courage and walked over to say hi. Her name was Katie, and after a few minutes of small talk she gestured to my buddies.

"You're not one of those wrestler assholes are you?" she asked. "I've heard about those guys."

Damn. That was a problem. But one that (in my slightly buzzed frame of mind) was surmountable. All I needed was the right gimmick.

"I'm just friends with those guys," I said. "I'm actually a pro football player."

Shit, I figured if I was going to lie I might as well make it count.

"You play for the Cowboys?" she asked. "How come I've never heard of you?

This girl knew her stuff. Good thing I knew how to work an angle.

"I'm on the practice squad," I said with all the sincerity of a used-car salesman. "I'm hoping to make the main roster one of these days."

Looking back now, I realize that weaving a tapestry of complete and utter bullshit may not have been the best way to start a relationship. But at least my lies were good enough to score Katie's phone number. Another bonus: she hated her waitressing gig and quit the next day. I wouldn't have to worry about anyone at Manhattan's telling her about my real job.

159

We started dating and things were great from the start (outside of the fact that I was lying to her on an almost hourly basis). Katie was smart, funny and, like me, a recent divorcee. She had two young daughters named Brandi and Heather. The girls were cute as a button and, with their biological dad out the picture, I happily assumed the role of father figure. Yes, we were quite the quartet: Katie, her daughters and her professional football player boyfriend.

You may find this hard to believe, but eventually my dumbass lies caught up with me. It all started innocently enough- I was having a few beers with some of the boys at my apartment. Then they called some friends who called some friends who called some friends. Next thing I knew, there was a full on rager at my place and I was bouncing quarters into a glass of beer while two girls (neither one named Katie) were sitting on my lap. Cue the knock on the door.

When Katie walked in, I expected her to be pissed about the girls, and I guess she was. But for the most part, she was fixated on a picture that was taped on the wall behind me. I don't know who put it up there, but staring back at Katie was an 8 X 10 glossy of The Grappler. She looked at the picture, then back to me, then back to the picture. Before you could say 2 plus 2 equals 4, she had completed the equation.

"You're one of those fucking wrestlers!"

The boys all had a great laugh at my expense while I tried every verbal trick in the book to get myself out of the idiotic hole that I had dug. Thankfully, we had been dating for well over a month and Katie had already fallen under the spell of the legendary Denton charm. I mean, she's only human. She forgave me and I promised that I would never lie to her ever again. And I never did.

You believe me right?

In all sincerity, meeting Katie was the best thing that ever happened to me. Because we had both been divorced, we decided not to marry. But we made a vow to stay together and her daughters became my daughters. Brandi and Heather didn't have my blood, but they had my heart. After a decade of running around the world in tights, my new focus was on being a partner to Katie and a father to the girls. I decided that if pro wrestling couldn't provide for my new family, it was time to find a new profession.

My options were pretty slim in the fall of 1987. I knew my stay in World Class would be ending soon, and with territories closing up left and right, wrestling opportunities were scarce. There was always the option of moving back to Houston and getting into the family construction business. I wasn't sure how I was going to put food on the table, but I knew that the clock was ticking. That's when I got a call from The Crippler.

Rip Oliver and I had briefly worked as a tag team in Tampa, under the management of Percy Pringle. Rip was a great heel who had worked all over the world and was a bona fide legend in the Pacific Northwest. He and Billy Jack Haynes had an epic feud that spanned years in Don Owen's Portland Wrestling promotion. But now Rip was chasing "the big money".

"I just signed with Vince," he told me over the phone. "You won't believe what they're paying me."

I congratulated Rip on his good fortune. He was just the latest territorial star to sign with the WWF. To those of us working for a couple hundred bucks a night it seemed like Vince McMahon had a bottomless bank account.

"There's going to be an opening up here," Rip said. "I told Don he needs to bring you in."

As Rip explained it, the territory needed a top heel and a booker. He said Owen never actually had a full-time booker before; most of the top guys would just book their own angles. But Rip had convinced the promoter that he needed to hire one person to oversee the entire card. With my experience, he figured that I was the best man for the job.

Nine years earlier, I had asked Bill Watts to get me booked in Portland, but it never happened. It was a dream opportunity at the time, but back then I was a 19-year-old kid with no responsibilities. Now, I was a family man and this job would require me to leave the comfort of my home state. Katie said she would be okay with making the move, and I was definitely excited about working as a "top heel" again- it had been years since I had been a "top" anything. But the situation had to make sense for my family- I wasn't moving the kids thousands of miles so we could all remain broke.

So, I called Don Owen and we discussed the job, and more importantly, the pay. He threw out a number and I threw one back. We haggled and haggled until finally he came up with a figure that worked. I put in my notice to World Class and got ready for the big drive.

I tried to keep measured expectations about my new job. It sounded like a perfect opportunity, but that had been true of so many other promotions where I ended up jobbing to the big boys. I told Katie that the likely scenario was that I would get a year of work, and then move back to Texas where I would try to find a real job. Turns out that my prediction was a bit off.

As of this writing, I have lived in Portland, Oregon for almost three decades.

CHAPTER NINE

A GRAPPLER'S GAMBLE

NEW PACIFIC NORTHWEST HEAVYWEIGHT CHAMPION
THE GRAPPLER
Using behind-the-referee's-back tactics and the toe of his infamous boot, The Grappler cheated without getting caught. And Mean Mike Miller lost the Pacific Northwest Heavyweight championship in a Halloween Eve title bout at the

The night I debuted in Don Owen's Portland Wrestling, I felt a little like Davy Crockett arriving at the Alamo. Thanks to Vince "Santa Ana" McMahon, wrestling's old territory system was outgunned and on the verge of annihilation. Long-time promoters like Bill Watts and Paul Boesch were selling their promotions and fleeing the fight. The WWF was an unstoppable juggernaut and many of us old-schoolers thought that Portland was the right place to make a last stand.

Oregon seemed to be one nut that Vince couldn't crack and that was probably because professional wrestling was so ingrained in the local community. Don Owen's family had been promoting wrestling since the 1920s and *Portland*

Wrestling on Channel 12 KPTV was one of the longest running television shows in the country, having debuted in 1953. This was the territory that made stars out of Roddy Piper, Jimmy Snuka, Jesse Ventura and Buddy Rose. Before that, Tony Borne, Dutch Savage and Lonnie Mayne were Northwest icons. Hell, even Gorgeous George got his start in the Beaver State.

With those deep wrestling roots, Portland seemed immune to the *Hulkamania* epidemic that was wiping out wrestling territories. Consider this: in 1986 Hulk Hogan and King Kong Bundy drew fewer than 6,000 fans for a show in the Portland Memorial Coliseum. The previous year, a Don Owen anniversary card- headlined by a returning Piper and Rose- drew 12,000 in the same building. Oregon seemed liked the one place where David had a fighting chance against Goliath.

But there was one problem: by the fall of 1987, David lacked the necessary stones for his slingshot. Owen's early-80s golden boy Billy Jack Haynes was already wrestling for Vince and now another major draw- Rip Oliver- was leaving. Don kept losing big names and as his talent roster shrank, so too did ticket sales. Houses were down throughout the territory, and it was my job to reverse that trend. It would be no easy task, but thankfully I would have the help of a former tag-team partner. Dave Canal and I had once dropped our Stampede tag titles in a Calgary hotel room. Now, Portland Wrestling fans knew Dave as "The Assassin".

"The one thing about Don Owen is that he'll pay you what he owes you," Dave told me. "Don't get me wrong- he's not going to take you out for a steak dinner- or even to McDonalds. The old man is honest but cheap."

Dave was driving me to the Portland Sports Arena for my first show in the Pacific Northwest. He was a broad-chested Cuban-American with dark curly hair and a mustache, although most Portland wrestling fans probably couldn't pick him out of a police lineup. Like me, Dave wrestled under a mask; The Assassin had been one of the territory's long-time heels before turning babyface against Rip Oliver.

"So, what's the old man paying you anyways?" he asked.

I usually didn't discuss money with the other boys- from my experience, such talk only bred jealousy and contempt. But I had known Dave so long that I knew he wouldn't give a damn. Besides, it's not like I was pulling down six figures. After a week of on-the-phone negotiations, Owen had agreed to pay me 800 bucks a week. It wasn't a ton of dough, but more than I had been making in Texas. And thanks to the Portland territory's small size, I would be able to come home after every show. That meant spending less money on gas and no money on hotel rooms- my paycheck would go *a lot* further.

"You got Don to pay you 800 bucks?" Dave asked. "How long do you think it will take before he realizes you're not worth that much?"

Dave was one of those smartasses that was always giving you shit and making you laugh. That's why I figured he was ribbing me when we pulled up outside an old, rundown building that he said was the arena.

"This can't be it," I said. "This looks like a bowling alley."

"It *is* a bowling alley," Dave said without a hint of humor in his voice. "Or at least it was. Don turned it into a wrestling arena 20 years ago."

I thought Dave's use of the word "arena" was more than a bit generous. Look, I had wrestled in smaller and shittier joints- from condemned YMCAs to rat-infested gymnasiums. But those places were usually for spot shows; "The Portland Sports Arena" was the Owen promotion's top venue. It was dank, dirty and smelled of smoke and stale popcorn.

"Don't be fooled by its looks," Dave insisted. "When this place sells out, you can make some nice money. Of course, I can't remember the last time it *did* sell out- but you're going to change all that. Right?"

Dave was messing with me (as usual), but I did have some ideas that I thought could boost the box office. When I finally met Don Owen in person, I told him about my grand plans to bring in new talent and shake things up. My new boss was quick to hit the brakes.

"We're not bringing in a bunch of new wrestlers or changing what we do," Don told me. "These fans have been coming here for years. They'll keep coming as long as you don't fuck it up."

Don was in his mid-70s, gray, skinny and ornery as a polecat. In public he was known as a gentle, grandfather-type but backstage that old son of a gun cussed out more wrestlers than Bill Watts. Of course, in pro wrestling manners always take a backseat to money and that's why so many boys loved working for him; Don was widely known as the best payout guy in the business. But like Dave said, he was also a tightwad and wouldn't spring for new talent any sooner than he would spring for a new outfit (I swear he wore the same suit for five years straight).

Don was right about one thing: those Portland Wrestling fans had been coming to his shows for years- decades even. Every Saturday night you would see the same faces at ringside. I'm telling you, some of those people were probably in the front row when Lewis and Clark debuted in Oregon. Don made it clear that I was expected to fill the empty seats in the back of the building while not alienating the "lifers" at ringside. It goes without saying that I would be doing all of this on the cheap.

The first step in turning things around would be to establish a new main event star and, as you may have guessed, that would be me. This wasn't some sort of self-centered deal- Don had brought me in to be both his booker *and* his top heel. After spending years in the mid-card quagmire, I would finally have the opportunity to be "the man". This was what I had been waiting for and it was time to put up or shut up.

To get things rolling, I booked a TV segment with Rip Oliver and myself in "The Crow's Nest" (the Portland Sports Arena's television interview space). Rip told announcer Don Coss that he was going after his rival Billy Jack Haynes (i.e. heading to the WWF) and introducing a new wrestler that would take his place in Portland. As he put it, The Grappler had won titles all over the world, and was now set to dominate the Pacific Northwest. Then I cut a promo where I probably mentioned something about people having a name for you when you're the greatest wrestler in the world. It was a passing of the alpha-heel torch, and by the end of the interview Portland Wrestling had a new lead villain.

To establish myself as the territory's #1 bad guy I followed the usual playbook: I spent several weeks on TV knocking out fellas with the loaded boot while Don Coss told audiences that I was part Lou Thesz and part Jack the Ripper. From there, the next step was a long run with the Pacific Northwest Heavyweight Championship (the territory's top title). I beat "Mean" Mike Miller for the strap on Halloween and would hold it for almost an entire calendar year. Again, this wasn't some ego trip, it was part of my plan to make money for the promotion. You could call it the Ric Flair philosophy: if you have a champion that people hate, they will always pay money to see him lose.

Going in, I knew that being the promotion's booker and champion would be a delicate balancing act. Usually, if you were the person who decides the winners and losers, some of the boys would see your title reign as some self-serving BS. And let's face it, with some booker/champions that's exactly what it was. Thankfully, I didn't catch any heat for my first championship run; the boys knew that I was a good worker and deserved the opportunity. It's what I wanted to do *outside* of the title picture that riled up the nay-sayers.

See, while Don Owen wouldn't spring for new talent to come in, I knew that the territory still needed new blood at the top of the card. When I arrived in Portland guys like Mike Miller and Coco Samoa were working on top and the shows felt stagnant. Mike and Coco were both good guys and fine workers, but they had been in the territory for years and the fans were bored. And while these veterans were main-eventing in front of half-capacity crowds, the promotion's young talent was dying on the vine.

Steve Doll and Scott Peterson were two babyfaces waiting for a break, and I was eager to give it to them. The guys reminded me of Ricky Morton and Robert Gibson, and not just because their "Southern Rockers" gimmick was a carbon copy of the "Rock-n-Roll Express". Steve and Scott could really work and put on the kind of high-flying tag matches that would bring a crowd to its feet.

Also, I knew their good looks would attract a new demographic (young women) to the Sports Arena.

So, I began putting The Southern Rockers in high-profile tag matches and soon they were one of the promotion's most popular attractions. At the same time, I bumped some of the veterans like Coco and Mike down a couple notches and began using them to put guys over. I knew they wouldn't like it. After all, the same thing had happened to me in just about every other territory and I *hated* it.

"Those rock and roll kids don't know what they're doing," Coco told me. "Why the hell am I doing jobs while they're getting all the glory?"

Mike Miller was also unhappy. He was polite about it, but let me know that he could (and should) be doing more.

"I know you need to get some new guys over," he said, "But I can still draw money for you."

As a peace offering, I came up with a new gimmick for "Mean" Mike: a 2x4 named "Lucille" that he would carry to the ring (and yes, it was an idea that I stole from my old Mid-South co-worker Jim Duggan). Mike would chase heels (like myself) with Lucille and that piece of lumber got over quick.

After a couple months of tinkering, it seemed like the territory was making progress. With an increased focus on youth and new faces, I knew that we had the right people in the right positions. Still, the puzzle was missing quite a few pieces. Then, out of the blue, my boss introduced me to a Polynesian powerhouse.

"You wanted someone new?" Don asked me. "Well, here you go."

We were in his office at the Portland Sports Arena. Don handed me an 8x10 picture of a sleepy-eyed wrestler with long hair and colossal muscles. Brother, you want to talk about being jacked- this guy's traps had traps. The name at the bottom of the picture read *Brian Adams*.

"He's coming here from Japan," Don told me. "I guess he's pretty new because we're getting him cheap."

This was great news. A big guy like Adams could be a monster heel- or perhaps a strong babyface that could chase me for the belt. The possibilities seemed endless. I only had one question:

"Can he work?"

Don snatched the picture from my hand and replied with more than a little disgust.

"Can he work?" he asked, while pointing to Adams' biceps, "Just look at him! He's a giant fucking wrestler! What the hell am I paying you for?" (Incidentally, that 'what the hell am I paying you for' question would become a constant refrain for Don Owen, often replacing "hello" and "goodbye" in our daily conversations.)

A couple weeks later, Brian showed up in Portland and I realized that Don's 8x10 hadn't done the cat justice. Adams was a Hawaiian Hercules that could lift anyone out of the gym (I'll never forget when he military pressed 315 pounds ten times on a bet). He had trained in the dojos of Japan with legends like Antonio Inoki, but you would have never guessed it from his laid back demeanor. Despite Brian's ungodly strength and ass-kicking credentials he was an easy-going islander at heart.

But just because the kid could fling around a barbell didn't mean he could work a lick. So, I put him in a match at a spot show to evaluate his skill level. I don't remember the name of his opponent, and there's a good chance the opponent doesn't remember his name either. A few minutes into the match Brian knocked the fella out cold with a STIFF back kick. This was no work, but a legit Tyson-esque KO. You've heard of a mule kick? Brian Adams delivered a Clydesdale kick.

When the match ended I told Brian that I would like to train him for a few weeks and refine his skills.

"I think you can be a star," I told him. "But first, let's make sure you're not tried for manslaughter."

From then on, I trained Brian in the ring before every show. At first it was painful...for me. The guy didn't know his own strength and wasn't used to pulling punches. But we kept at it. The process reminded me of William Shatner on the old *Star Trek* show: we were switching Brian's phaser from "kill" to "stun".

Eventually, Brian learned how to work a match without maiming everybody and we put him on TV. Because of his time in Japan we called him "The American Ninja" (a late-80s gimmick if there ever was one). The fans took to Brian and he became a powerhouse babyface that chased The Grappler all over the territory. Thanks to our training sessions, I was able to get through our matches with only a few minor concussions. I figured it was a small price to pay for establishing a new main-eventer.

Besides, what was a little brain trauma between friends?

It was sometime in early '88 when I realized that this Oregon thing just might work out. I had originally told Katie to wait with the girls in Texas just in case I bombed in the Northwest. But when it became clear that I wasn't getting fired anytime soon, I told her to pack a suitcase. A couple of weeks later my three ladies joined me in Portland and we moved into a nice little home on the city's east side.

I felt pretty good about the direction of my career and the Owen promotion in general. We had established young talent like The Southern Rockers and Brian Adams, while reinvigorating veterans like Mike Miller. Then some familiar faces appeared: Rip Oliver returned to Portland after his WWF run fizzled, and local hero Matt Borne followed close behind. Don Owen's roster was the deepest it had been in years. Meanwhile, Oregonians had fully embraced their hatred of The Grappler.

I was in the middle of what would be the longest title reign in the 60+year history of the Portland territory. After years of jobbing, I was finally a top guy and it felt great. Of course, my lengthy run may have had *something* to do with the fact that I was also the guy picking winners and losers. But hell, it was working: after two years of flat houses Don Owen's ticket sales were increasing (even if we still weren't selling out).

My main on-camera adversary at that time also happened to be my best friend in the territory. "Assassin" Dave and I had great chemistry together: the guy could cut a great promo and work his ass off in the ring. He was also one of the most creative dudes on the roster and helped me book our Saturday TV tapings. Friday nights we'd meet at my place for marathon writing sessions where the "writing" was often replaced by "drinking", "ribbing" and more "drinking".

I can remember one Friday night where we got completely hammered and passed out without booking a single match. When Katie woke us up on Saturday afternoon we only had one hour to get to the TV taping. Dave and I booked that show while driving to the arena in a blurry hangover. I can't remember any of the matches or angles that we came up with, but they must have been good: the following week the gate went up by a thousand bucks. Dave and I resolved to get blackout-drunk more often.

Of course, creating new stars and binging on Budweisers were just a few of my duties as booker. Job #1 was pleasing my boss and that seemed a damn-near impossible task. Every week, I would present new ideas to Don Owen and every week he would shoot them down. I'd propose a cage match and he'd say no. I'd propose a no-disqualification match and he'd say no.

"Are you trying to kill this territory?" he would ask. "Stop trying to change everything."

"Change" was a dirty word in Owen-land. Don had been promoting since FDR was president and his booking philosophy felt as dated as a fireside chat. He mandated that every TV main event be a simple two-out-of-three falls contest. I was not permitted to ever break from this formula, so our fans would see the same type of match week after week.

What really drove me nuts was that Don would handcuff my booking and then complain about the results. While paid attendance was up, we still had not sold out the Portland Sports Arena- a fact that he would remind me about on a daily basis. In fact, Don would usually point this out in front of all the boys as we

171

received our Saturday night payouts. His verbal jabs would always include a shot at my home state.

"I'm so glad that I hired this brilliant booker," Don would say to the assembled roster. "Apparently, in Texas they don't teach people how to draw money."

After the laughs died down, I would usually suggest a new angle for the following week. *Maybe if you listened to me, we could put some more butts in those seats* I would say. Don would then kill my idea and ask what the hell he was paying me for. This was our Saturday night tradition.

Don couldn't resist change forever and eventually it was thrust upon him. In May of 1988, Billy Jack Haynes launched his own Portland- based promotion called the Oregon Wrestling Federation. Billy was fresh off a run with the WWF and had money to spend. He secured airtime on a local UHF station and hired away some of Owen's top stars like Rip Oliver, Mike Miller and Brian Adams.

"I helped all of those people feed their families," Don fumed. "Now they want to put me out of business."

The old man was on the verge of a nervous breakdown and I couldn't blame him. It was hard enough trying to keep Vince McMahon at bay, the last thing Don needed was another local promotion with star power. I knew the situation was serious when he actually spent some money to bring back the territory's legendary heel Buddy Rose. Don Owen reaching for his checkbook was akin to a cop reaching for his gun- he didn't *want* to use it, but he would if absolutely necessary.

Fortunately for Don, Billy Jack Haynes did not prove to be a successful wrestling promoter. The Oregon Wrestling Federation lasted less than a year and eventually guys like Rip and Brian came crawling back for their old jobs. That was the good news. The bad news was that we still had not sold out the Sports Arena and, after the OWF threat subsided, Don was as ornery as ever. Every Saturday night I heard the same old shit:

"They say everything is bigger in Texas. Except for the money."

"I don't know why they call Texas 'The Lone Star State'. They should call it 'The Can't Draw Any Money State'."

"You know what they say in Texas: Remember the Alamo and forget about drawing money."

On and on and on. It was like I was the guest of honor at a never-ending Dean Martin roast. One night in October, I finally lost my shit.

"Alright you old smartass," I shouted over the boys' laughter, "If you want to sell this place out, then let me do my job. If I can't do it- I'LL QUIT!"

Those last two words brought the laughter to an abrupt end.

"Give me two months," I told Don. "Let me book the shows the way I want. If you stay out of my way, I guarantee that I will sell this fucker out. If we don't fill *every single seat*, I'll turn in my notice and you'll never see me again."

It sounded like the buildup for a loser-leaves-town match, but this was no angle. Don and I came to a gentlemen's agreement: I would have all of November and December to book the TV shows without any interference. I could book any match that I wanted- the only stipulation was that I could not bring in any new talent. If we did not sell out the Sports Arena show on Christmas night, I would leave the territory for good.

"Good luck," Don said as we shook on it. "I hear it's a long drive back to Texas."

It took me about five minutes to realize that I had painted myself into one hell of a corner. Wrestling territories were shutting down left and right and I had very few options- if any- outside of Portland. In short, I was gambling with my career. If that Christmas show did not sell out, I would likely have to move my family back to Texas and try to find a "normal job". The thought sent shivers down my spine.

I have to pack this place to the rafters.

I racked my brain for angles that would draw a big house. I knew that my best opponent for the Christmas show would be Dave, who had recently ditched his "Assassin" moniker and renamed himself "Top Gun" (a handle that was not-

173

so-coincidentally the title of a blockbuster movie). Dave was a strong interview that could hype the shit out of the show; we just needed the right type of match.

I decided that we would do a variation of a coal miner's glove match. Portland legend Dutch Savage had invented the match, and it was one of the territory's most dependable draws. Essentially, the match featured two wrestlers fighting over a steel-lined glove that hung from a pole. The first person that retrieved the glove could use it as a weapon and the fans knew that glove *always* drew blood. At one time, I had pitched the idea of doing a similar match that would substitute my loaded boot for the glove. Don nixed the idea before I could finish my pitch.

"You're going to kill the coal miner's glove gimmick," he said. "What the hell am I paying you for?"

Thanks to our wager, I was now free to pursue my idea and I decided to up the ante: Dave and I would meet in the first ever loaded-boot-on-a-pole steel cage match. Rolls right off the tongue doesn't it?

The match and the opponent were obviously crucial, but they didn't mean a thing without the proper buildup. I mapped out a series of angles that would take place week after week, all leading to that big show on the 25th.

We started the hype with a six-man match: Top Gun teamed with the Southern Rockers against myself and fellow heels Matt Borne and Abudda Dein (in reality a second generation wrestler named Rocky Iaukea). After that match went to a no-contest, Top Gun demanded a singles match against yours truly that, to the shock of everyone, ended with outside interference and a loaded boot.

From that point on, Dave vowed to rid Portland of The Grappler, his henchmen and that loaded boot. He wrestled a series of matches against Borne and Abudda Dein, eventually beating the pseudo-Arab in a Coal Miner's Glove Match. The following week Dave and I scored two big wins that kept us hot: he beat Buddy Rose in a haircut match and I beat Japanese superstar Tatsumi Fujinami to regain the PNW title (he had won the title a month prior). Having conquered every obstacle in his way, Top Gun demanded a Christmas night title match. The contest would take place inside a steel cage (to keep my fellow heels away) with the loaded boot hanging from a pole (so Dave could give me a taste of my own medicine). The stage was set.

All Christmas day the butterflies were flapping in my gut. Even as the girls opened their presents, all I could think about was that night's box office. I had to fill every seat or hit the bricks.

What if we're just 10 short of a sell out? I'll be looking in the Houston classifieds under "Help Wanted". Shit, I don't know how to write a resume!

That afternoon, I rode with Dave to the Sports Arena and the inner pessimism continued.

What if I can't find a job? All I know is wrestling. I'm going to wind up on a street corner holding a "Will Bump For Food" sign...

"Lynny- look at that line!"

Dave snapped me out of my funk as we rolled into the Portland Sports Arena parking lot. It was still several hours until the opening bell and there were hundreds of fans snaking around the building. It was by far the biggest advance crowd I had ever seen in Portland.

Thank you God and Santa Claus!

Dave ended up parking four blocks away so the fans wouldn't see us together. I put on my hood and made the long walk to the arena's front entrance. When the fans saw me, they let it rip:

"Go to hell Grappler!"

"Top Gun is going to kick your butt!"

"I hope that boot gets shoved up your ass!"

Their curses sounded sweeter than any Christmas carol.

The Christmas show was filled to capacity with more than 800 fans turned away at the door. In the subsequent week we sold out shows in Eugene and every other town on the loop. By every standard the Top Gun/Grappler program was a success. The following Saturday we all gathered outside Don's office to receive our payouts. On the heels of our multiple sellouts, I expected a big bonus. I was damn near speechless when Don handed me my usual fee of 800 bucks.

"You better put another grand in my hand," I finally said.

"What the hell are you talking about?" Don snapped back.

I didn't yell, but made sure that I responded loud enough so the boys could hear.

"We made a bet and I sold this place out! Hell, we sold out every town. Where's my cut?"

"Our bet had nothing to do with money," Don replied. "The only thing that was on the line was your job, and you still have it. So take your money or don't take it. I don't give a damn."

The conversation ended there, but the hard feelings did not. True, we had never wagered any actual money but I still felt that I deserved some compensation for giving the old man his first sell out in years. Because I'm a vengeful guy who never forgets a slight, I decided to get some payback.

I knew the only way to really upset Don Owen was to take some of his money, so I planned to do just that. As booker, I had to call wrestlers all the time, and had an expense account for my long-distance charges. In an effort to stick it to my boss, I made a number of calls to Japan (we had recently swapped some talent with New Japan Pro Wrestling) and let those charges add up. Sometimes I'd just leave the phone off the hook. Remember, this was before the days of cell phones and Skype- Don ended up having to pay a thousand-dollar phone bill. Suffice to say, he did not find my rib all that funny.

From then on it was bicker-bicker-bicker between promoter and booker. Until, out of nowhere, Don invited me to have lunch with him at a nice restaurant in Downtown Portland. My wrestler's intuition started tingling right away. In the past year Owen hadn't bought me a cup of coffee and now he wanted to treat me to a French Dip? Something was up.

As I walked through the front door, I saw that my boss was already seated. Don was sitting next to his son Barry and another man that I instantly recognized.

This unexpected guest was a man that I knew well. Hell, every wrestling fan on the planet knew this guy.

When Roddy Piper smiled at me, I knew that I was fired.

CHAPTER TEN

THE FALSE FINISH

For a man who was once the most reviled wrestler in the world, Roddy Piper had an infectious sense of humor. The "Hot Rod" was the kind of fella that could crack up a widow at a funeral. So, it seemed appropriate that we were sharing a laugh at the end of my wrestling career.

"I figured something was wrong when Don offered to pay for my meal," I joked. "I just didn't realize this lunch was going to be my severance package."

As soon I had sat down at the table, Don told me that Roddy was replacing me as booker. I wasn't shocked by my dismissal, but I was a bit surprised by my replacement. Piper was a pop culture icon that had been one of the WWF's top stars. Hell, this was the guy who headlined the very first *Wrestlemania*! I didn't know what Don was paying him, but I was pretty sure it wasn't 800 bucks a week.

I had gotten to know Rod when I worked in Atlanta and the Carolinas. Even back then he was a top draw while I was still a greenhorn hoping for my big break. He never knew me as "The Grappler"; to Roddy I was just a hard-working kid named Lenny.

"It's good to see you bud," he said with a wink and a smile.

Roddy was the biggest star to come out of the Portland territory and lived with his wife and kids on a rural estate just outside the city. He had a soft spot in his heart for the Northwest, and also for Don Owen. When he was in the WWF, Roddy refused to wrestle in Oregon, out of loyalty to his old boss. In March of 1987 he had "retired" from the WWF to focus on his acting career. But a man like Roddy Piper could never *stay* retired- the wrestling business was in his blood. So, when Don asked for his help, the Rowdy One accepted the challenge.

I had always liked Roddy and, despite the circumstances, I was glad to see him again. When our pleasantries (and unpleasantries) were taken care of, I looked over the menu. By now I wasn't feeling very hungry- all I could think about was the drive down I-5 and I-10. It was a pretty straight shot from Portland to Houston.

Well, at least I milked a year-and-a half out of this place. I guess that's something.

"Order anything you want," Don said with a little snicker. "After you finish up your advertised dates, you're done."

That's when the Piper piped in.

"Hold on a sec Don," Roddy began. "I've been thinking. Remember how I told you about those projects I'm working on?"

Owen nodded.

"I'm filming that movie next month, and after that I'm doing a TV shoot," Rod continued. "I won't be here for a lot of shows. I can handle all the big picture

179

stuff but I need an assistant that can be my eyes and ears when I'm gone- someone the boys will respect and listen to."

I didn't make a peep. I *thought* I could see where this was going, but didn't want to jinx it.

"I think Lenny would be the perfect guy for the job," Roddy concluded. "I know him. I trust him. If I'm going to do this, I want him by my side."

Well, I'll be damned.

In pro wrestling a "false finish" is when a wrestler attempts a pinfall that his opponent kicks out of at the last second. Everyone thinks the guy is done for, but in a split second he's back in the fight. Well, at that lunch Roddy Piper delivered a real-life false-finish. I had thought that my career was over, but by the end of the meal Don Owen agreed to keep me on and pay me my old salary.

I was back in the fight, and now I had one hell of a tag-team partner.

That weekend I settled into my new role, which was very similar to my old role. I was still the territory's top heel and handled most of the backstage stuff, the only difference was that I now worked directly under Roddy. Every week we would put the shows together- sometimes in person and sometimes over the phone. He was often out of town during TV tapings, so it was my job to make sure that all the matches and angles met his specifications. We even had a direct phone line installed backstage (nicknamed *The Bat Phone*) so that he could reach me at all hours.

Not only did Roddy save my job, almost overnight he also changed the dynamic of our Portland Wrestling TV tapings. While Don had always shot down my ideas, I found that he would never say no to the Hot Rod. The outdated television formulas that I dreaded were history; Roddy wanted hot angles and big stipulations on the shows and that's what he got. He even persuaded Don to loosen up his purse strings (a bit) to bring in new talent and improve the look of our television production. The man in the kilt was a miracle worker.

In a short period of time, I learned why Roddy Piper was a megastar. I had always assumed that his success was because of his legendary promos and in-ring work, but that was just scratching the surface. Roddy was a wrestling A-lister because of his tireless work ethic, attention to detail and infinite imagination. The guy lived the business 24-7 and could pull a hot angle out of thin air. During our booking sessions, he would throw out a million ideas that ranged in quality from brilliant to insane. And by the end of the meeting, he would convince you that the insane ideas were actually pretty brilliant.

Take the case of Art Barr, a young high-flyer who was the son of referee Sandy Barr (himself a former wrestler). We all liked Art but weren't really sure what to do with him. The kid was one hell of a hand, but he weighed *maybe* 190 pounds with his boots on. Remember, this was before guys like Shawn Michaels and Rey Mysterio became marquee stars. Big men ruled wrestling, and main-event spots seemed elusive for a smaller guy like Art. But then, just a few weeks after becoming booker, Roddy Piper was struck by odd inspiration.

"Have you seen the movie *Beetlejuice*?" he asked me. "That could be one hell of a gimmick."

In the film, Michael Keaton played a sarcastic ghost with snow-white skin and raccoon eyes. I still can't figure out how Roddy watched that movie and thought of Art Barr. Nothing about the kid screamed "undead, albino smart-ass", but Roddy Piper could pull ideas from the most unlikely places. He wanted to turn Art Barr into Beetlejuice, so damn it, that's what we were going to do.

We set up an angle where I assaulted Art in the Crow's Nest, with some help from my muscular henchman Carl Styles. Carl slapped a full-nelson on the poor kid while I slapped him silly. It was typical schoolyard bully stuff until Roddy rode in on his white horse. After a brief verbal encounter (Rod was "retired" and wouldn't fight on camera), the bad guys were sent packing and Art lived to fight another day.

Fast forward one week and Roddy joined Art in the Crows Nest for an interview segment. He wanted to unleash some aggression in the kid and informed

181

the audience that he was going to "create a wrestler" on the spot. With that, Piper ordered Art to strip down to his birthday suit live on camera (to keep the segment PG, Art undressed behind a curtain). When the disrobing was complete, Rod dressed him in an acid-washed denim jacket, rubbed black paint on his face, and dumped a bottle of baby powder on his head. He told everyone that he was creating *"A mean, nasty, crazy little sucker that I saw in the movies one time. You know what his name was? BEETLEJUICE!"* With that, mild-mannered Art Barr instantly transformed into a raving lunatic. He ran around the interview set-convulsing, spitting on his hand and kissing complete strangers. The newly minted Beetlejuice ended the segment by telling the crowd that it was "Show Time!"

If you've never actually watched that segment, I'm sure the whole thing sounds like a bizarre clusterfuck. You might ask: *How drunk were you guys when you dreamed up that bit?* To which I would answer: *Only slightly but that's beside the point.* The bottom line is that Beetlejuice was an instant hit. The kids in the arena began painting their faces and calling themselves "little Juicers". When Art made his ring entrance, Harry Belafonte's "Banana Boat Song" would play over the loud speakers (Day-O! Me Say Day O!). As soon as their hero appeared, the youngsters would leave their seats and run behind him like he was the Pied Piper. Before his gimmick transplant, most fans probably considered Art Barr a nice kid who was bound to get his ass kicked by the big fellas. But that crazy-ass Juicer? Well, that guy was loco enough to beat *anybody*. Thanks to Roddy's imagination and Art's previously untapped charisma, Beetlejuice became one of the most popular acts in all of Portland Wrestling.

Establishing a top young babyface was a great way to kick off the Roddy Piper regime, and we were just getting warmed up. Right around the same time that Beetlejuice debuted, a young worker with curly brown hair approached us backstage at the Sports Arena.

"My name's Scott Levy," he told us in a faint East Coast accent. "I go by 'Scotty the Body'. I talked to Don about working for you guys."

No one had told us that this guy was coming. But, new talent was new talent. We chatted Scotty up for a few minutes and it was obvious that he was pretty bright. Levy was a college graduate with the vocabulary to prove it. Later I would learn that he was also a member of Mensa. Apparently, you have to be a certified genius to join that group. I wouldn't know.

"It appears that you can talk," Roddy said. "How about tonight you go out and do commentary with Don Coss?"

With that, Scotty the Body made his Portland Wrestling debut in the Crow's Nest. From the moment Scotty started talking, it was clear that he could work the stick. His gimmick was somewhat fashioned after Jesse Ventura- he wore all sorts of gaudy outfits and talked about how great he was. Of course, Scotty didn't have the massive physique of a Ventura or a "Superstar" Billy Graham. But what he lacked in size, he made up for with white-hot heel heat.

See, Scotty's on air-persona was simultaneously verbose, conceited and completely annoying. I mean, it was bad enough that he constantly bragged about himself, but he did it in a nasally whine that drove fans up the wall. People really wanted to strangle the guy. To build on that heat, we staged a segment where Scotty was caught picking his nose on camera. From that moment on, the fans would torment him with chants of "Snotty." It didn't take long for Scotty the Body to become one of our most despised heels. And that was just from running his yap. When we finally let him wrestle, in turned out the guy could really work!

It was pretty amazing. When I had arrived in Portland a year and a half earlier, the roster was primarily a collection of has-beens and never-weres. Now, we had veterans like myself, Buddy Rose and Top Gun alongside young stars like the Southern Rockers, Beetlejuice and Scotty the Body. I thought our collective talent matched up pretty good with the few remaining territorial promotions. But Roddy was convinced that we were still missing a crucial ingredient.

"We need a boy that can really shake this place up," he told me. "Someone who will kick everyone's ass and scare the shit out of people."

"I know just the guy," I told him. "But just remember... you asked for this."

At that time, John Nord was wrestling for Verne Gagne's AWA. He and a former arm-wrestler named Scott Norton had formed a tag-team called "The Lumberjacks". I guess "Yukon" John Nord was supposed to be a wrestling version of Paul Bunyan. It wasn't the worst gimmick ever, but the Pacific Northwest already had enough lumberjacks.

"Ditch the flannel and dust off those furry boots," I told him. "Portland needs The Barbarian."

When John arrived in Portland, we wanted him to have an immediate impact. For one of his first appearances, we had him storm the ring unannounced during a battle royal. Right before it was time for his entrance, I handed him a leather strap.

"I want those people to have nightmares about you," I told him. "Go in there and absolutely beat the dogshit out of those boys. Don't hold anything back."

Looking back, I realize that those were the most unnecessary instructions I've ever given a man. John Nord didn't know how to *not* kick the dogshit out of people. By the time he ended up whipping the Southern Rockers, both Steve and Scott were red as lobsters.

Just as we expected, Nord the Barbarian became the most feared man on the Portland Wrestling roster. The fans had no doubt that he was kicking the shit out of his opponents because *he really was* kicking the shit out of his opponents. When a wrestler saw his name opposite Nord's on the booking sheet he would wilt. "*Lynny, are you mad at me?*" one of John's would-be-opponents asked me. I assured him that his imminent maiming was nothing personal.

Nord and I became a team on TV and he kept me in stitches when the camera was off. Despite his terrifying reputation, no one could lighten the mood of a locker room like John. And of course, that big knucklehead was always getting me in trouble.

One day, we were having a few beers at my place. I think it was a Friday. Out of the blue, John decided that he wanted to gamble.

"I want to go buy some scratch tickets," he said. "Spot me some money."

We were scheduled to get paid the next night and funds were low. I told John that I didn't have any money to lend. He corrected me:

"Man, I was just in the kitchen and Katie left her purse sitting on the counter wide open. I saw a hundred dollar bill in there."

You may wonder why my thick-headed friend was checking out my old lady's purse. Well, don't worry. Johnny wasn't a thief, he just did whatever kind of random shit he felt like. I tried to explain to him that Ben Franklin was for groceries and emergencies. We didn't have a savings account; it was literally all the money we had until payday. But once Johnny set his mind to something, he wouldn't give up. He kept pestering me and promising that I'd get my hundred back. It went on and on until I finally agreed to do it just to shut him up. I swiped the bill (while Katie was taking a nap) and we headed to the local convenience store.

Nord the Barbarian didn't do anything halfway, so instead of buying 20 or 30 bucks worth of scratch tickets, he spent the whole hundred (my hundred) in one purchase.

"I guarantee you'll get this money back right away," he said.

He started scratching the cards. Nothing. Nothing. A buck here and there. Then nothing. Nothing. More nothing. There were about twenty tickets left when I really started to panic.

"Katie is going to fucking kill me," I groaned.

"Relax, I'm going to win your money," Nord insisted. While I was sweating buckets, John was still cool as a cucumber. That's probably because *he* wasn't about to spend the next five years sleeping on his couch.

Finally, there was one ticket left. One damn ticket. I mentally prepared myself for the verbal- and probably physical- ass-whupping that awaited me at home. John scratched the ticket.

One cherry. Two cherries. Three cherries. The ticket was a $100 winner.

"I told you I'd get that money back," John said nonchalantly as the clerk handed me back my c-note. "Lynny, you worry too much."

On the whole, John Nord was right: I really didn't have a lot to worry about. Sure, I wasn't making a ton of money and there were problems in Portland Wrestling at the time (which I will discuss in the next chapter), but I was still enjoying the best run of my career. While my title reign in Mid-South had been nice, my time in that semi-main event picture was shortened because of my own pigheadedness.

Portland was pretty much the first territory where things worked out the way that I had hoped. I had spent several years working on the top of the card, while forming a great working relationship with a pro wrestling legend. On top of that, I was still helping to create new stars- many of whom would go on to bigger and better things.

For example, Nord convinced me to bring in his old tag-team partner Scott Norton. The guy was strong as an ox, but when he arrived in Portland I could see that his in-ring work needed a lot of help. So, I gave Scott some private "tutoring" and after a few months he was able to put together a quality match. Later, the tag-team of Ron and Don Harris would also graduate from The Grappler's finishing school. Just like in Dallas with The Dingo Warrior it seemed like I was always helping big, strong guys become better workers. Bill Danenhauer was a tall, broad-chested rookie that I trained from the start. When he finished his training, we dubbed Bill "The Equalizer". On screen he was my tag-team partner, and off-screen we became good friends. After his time in Portland, Bill had a nice stint in WCW as "Dave Sullivan", where he worked alongside his "brother" Kevin Sullivan and Hulk Hogan.

The constant focus on young talent was necessary to keep things fresh in an industry with short-attention spans. But of course, you still needed a veteran who could work quality matches on top and that was my job. My feuds with guys like Carl Styles and Brian Adams did pretty good business. But it was my program with one of Oregon's biggest stars that drew perhaps the most money (and notoriety).

Billy Jack Haynes was still recovering from the collapse of his Oregon Wrestling Federation in the spring of 1989. Up until that point, Don Owen had refused to rehire Billy, or any of his defectors. The old man felt betrayed by the OWF episode.

"They all turned their backs on me," he would say. "To hell with them."

After a while, Brian Adams started calling me and asking for his old job back. I knew that we could really use him, so I sweet-talked Don into bringing him back: *The kid was young and didn't know any better. He feels bad about leaving, and he wants to make it right.* You know, that kind of bullshit. It worked, and once Brian returned to the promotion, he told me about another fella that was eager to come back.

"Billy Jack's just sitting at home," he told me. "He lives here and wants to work. And you know the guy can sell tickets."

Brian wasn't kidding. In some ways, Billy Jack Haynes was to Oregon what the Von Erichs had been to Texas. He was a muscular local boy whose feud with Rip Oliver set box-office records in the early 80s. When he joined the WWF, Haynes represented Oregon on a national level and even wore the state's name on his trunks (which were yellow and green- the school colors of the University of Oregon). Oregonians, many of whom often felt ignored by the national media, loved Billy for his dedication to his home state.

That love did not always carry over into the locker room. See, I had worked with Billy in Tampa and I knew plenty of boys that just did not like the guy. He had one of the most unpredictable personalities of any person I'd ever been around. On Monday, Billy could be happy-go-lucky and chatting up everyone. Then on Tuesday, he'd be completely withdrawn and silent. And when the guy lost his temper- which happened quite a bit- look the hell out.

187

Once, my manager Percy Pringle complained about a stiff shot that Billy had delivered during a match. Billy flew into a rage and slapped Percy as hard as he could and broke his glasses. On another occasion I saw him slap a skinny little camera man because he was angry about some shot that made it on air. That was the kind of crap you had to deal with when Billy Jack was on your roster.

But of course, in pro wrestling bad behavior doesn't mean a damn thing if you're putting asses in seats. And Billy could do just that. Roddy and I agreed that he should come back, and we made the pitch to Don. He did not share our enthusiasm.

"You want me to rehire the man who tried to put me out of business?" he asked. "No way. Let him sleep in the bed he made."

We kept our sales pitch going, and eventually won Don over the only way we knew how: by appealing to his bank account.

"Don, just answer this question," I said. "Would you rather save face or make money?"

For Don Owen, there was only one possible answer.

Roddy and I knew we wanted to re-introduce Billy in some sort of grand fashion. We tried to think of something big that would really ignite the box office. It turned out, Billy had an idea of his own.

"I was thinking we could do something with my dad," he told us.

At first, I had no idea why Billy wanted to involve his dad in a wrestling program. I just didn't see how that would draw any money. But then, Billy explained that his father was a) in a wheelchair and b) completely blind. All of a sudden, I could hear cash registers ringing. Here's the angle we laid out (and please remember, this was all Billy's idea):

We announced on TV that Billy Jack Haynes was returning to Portland Wrestling to make a major announcement. The rumor, Don Coss informed the audience, was that Portland's favorite son would be retiring from professional wrestling. Sure enough, Billy's return show turned into a retirement ceremony. He told the Sports Arena fans that he was finally calling it quits, and even gave away a pair of his wrestling boots. Billy Jack thanked the fans for their years of support. He was joined on-camera by his "inspiration", his dear old, wheelchair-bound, legally blind dad. As father and son embraced, some people in the crowd began to cry. It was a touching moment that obviously had to be ruined.

Later in the show, I came out to brag about a recent victory over my former protege Carl Styles. I had "blinded" Carl with a mysterious mist and was very proud about that fact. After a couple minutes of gloating, I spotted Billy's dad, who was still sitting in the Crow's Nest all by himself. I laughed about how Styles and Mr. Haynes were now in the same helpless condition. A number of tasteless blind jokes followed and I'm pretty sure that I said something about Stevie Wonder and Helen Keller. Then I walked over to Billy's dad, grabbed the handles of his wheelchair, and pushed him to the interview area. By this time, I was joined on-camera by fellow heels CW Bergstrom and Al Madril. We continued tormenting Mr. Haynes with an extremely off-key rendition of *Three Blind Mice*. The crowd wanted to kill us.

But Billy Jack beat them to it.

He flew onto the set and unleashed a hurricane of haymakers. Madril went down. Bergstrom went down. And you know that line in *Three Blind Mice*: "See how they run, See how they run"? Well, that was me. I scampered away while Billy Jack chased me like the farmer's wife with a carving knife. We ran all over the Sports Arena as the crowd screamed for my head. Of course, I ended up escaping (we weren't going to give away that beatdown for free) and Billy returned to his father's side. Roddy came out and told Billy that he couldn't retire now. He had to man up. He had to fight. He had to destroy The Grappler!

The angle worked to perfection. For the next month-and-a-half, Billy and I wrestled in front of sold out houses throughout the state of Oregon. We finally settled our issues with a "stretcher match" in front of a capacity crowd at the Sports Arena. Some people complained that the "Three Blind Mice" episode went well beyond the boundaries of good taste. I can't disagree with that. So, let me state this on the record: making fun of a person's disability is a crass and disgusting thing to do.

And if you're a pro wrestler, it's also a great way to make money.

One night in early 1990, I was enjoying a beer and a rare quiet moment. I had just headlined another sold-out show and it seemed like the right time to reflect on my good fortune.

I'm still here, I thought. *Mid-South is gone, Kansas City, Amarillo, San Antonio and Houston. All gone. The wrestling business I grew up with is gone. But I'm still here. A poor kid from Humble, Texas- working on top in Portland, Oregon.*

I'm one lucky son of a bitch.

It was all true, but the shitty thing about luck is that it always runs out. As the old wrestling territories continued falling one-by-one, I knew that my future was inextricably linked to that of Portland Wrestling. And unfortunately, by the early '90s, Don Owen's promotion was living on borrowed time.

See, while these last two chapters have focused on my successes in Portland, there was another side to my tenure in the Great Northwest. At the same time that I was achieving career highlights, Portland Wrestling was trying to fend off a pair of adversaries with deep pockets and power. One of these entities was the World Wrestling Federation; the other was the Oregon state government.

This was a two-front war that we were destined to lose.

CHAPTER ELEVEN

END OF AN ERA

When I joined Portland Wrestling in 1987, I knew the promotion faced an uphill battle. Vince McMahon was taking over the wrestling world and territories were dropping like flies. While the Northwest had fared better than other local promotions, I didn't kid myself about our chances. I knew that we would probably need a miracle to survive Vince's national expansion. What I did *not* realize at the time was that the WWF was not our only serious threat- another entity was setting its sights on Don Owen's promotion. And while Vince sat in some office in Connecticut, these other guys were in our own backyard.

It was early 1988 when I had my first encounter with the Oregon State Boxing and Wrestling Commission. I had been in the territory for maybe six months when I broke my right thumb during a match. That damn digit had always caused me problems- this was the third time that I had broken it. But pro wrestling doesn't stop for a busted thumb, so I taped it up and wrestled all my advertised dates, including a Saturday night television taping. The following Monday, I went to the Sports Arena to take care of some business with Don. My boss hit me with a bit of unexpected news:

"The guy from the wrestling commission called and said you're being fined $250," he told me. "Something about a taped thumb."

What the hell????

I asked Don to elaborate, but he couldn't offer me any details. He just handed me a phone number and a name: Bruce Anderson. I called the man right away and tried to assure him that there had been some sort of mistake.

"There's no mistake," he informed me. "You had an excessive amount of tape on your thumb. That's a $250 fine."

"My thumb was taped up because I broke it!" I replied.

"You broke your thumb?" Anderson asked. "Well, did you have it examined by a commission-approved doctor?"

The guy spoke all rough and gruff like he was some cop interrogating a suspect on *Hill Street Blues*. I told him that I didn't know a thing about any "commission-approved doctors".

"You're supposed to be examined by a commission doctor," he insisted. "The thing is, I can fine you for the taped thumb and fine you again for not seeing an approved doctor. All this stuff is in the state rulebook."

"WHAT FUCKING STATE RULEBOOK?"

There was a brief pause at the other end of the line. Then Anderson continued on about new rules passed by the legislature and our promoter was supposed to give us these rulebooks and blah blah blah blah blah. I could tell we weren't going to get anywhere on the phone, so I asked if we could meet in person to hash this out.

Later that week, we met for lunch (I paid for it of course) and I discovered that the surly voice on the phone belonged to a gray old man that was scrawny as a stringbean. After a few minutes of chitchat, I learned why Bruce Anderson talked like some character on a TV cop show- it turned out he really was a former New York police officer. He told me that he was also a former boxer.

"A few years back, one young fighter that I knew was scammed out of money by a promoter," he explained. "At the time, the state of Oregon didn't regulate boxing- it was all done on the local level. So, the kid had no recourse and never got his money."

Apparently, that's when Bruce Anderson decided to "clean up" the fight game. He became a lobbyist and pressured the Oregon State Legislature to form a Boxing and Wrestling Commission. They eventually complied and Governor Neil Goldschmidt appointed Bruce as the commission's first Executive Director. Along with that title came a state-funded salary and a new office near his home in Wilsonville (about a half-hour south of Portland).

I had dealt with wrestling commissions before in states like Texas and Louisiana. From my experience they were usually quite powerful and susceptible to corruption. I didn't know if this Anderson fella was corrupt, but I could tell that he had no problem throwing his weight around.

"So, I guess you're the new Judge, Jury and Executioner?" I said.

He insisted that the commission was formed primarily to prevent greedy promoters from exploiting their athletes.

"We're here to protect you guys," he said.

This wasn't the first time I had heard that kind of spiel. I asked Bruce how confiscating one-third of my weekly salary for breaking my thumb was *protecting me*. He didn't have an answer for that. Anderson let me go with a warning, and asked me to look over the rulebook and share it with the rest of the boys. He then told me he would be stopping by the Sports Arena to make sure that everyone was on the same page.

Not surprisingly, Don Owen was not on the same page as Bruce Anderson- they weren't even reading the same book. I was in Don's office at the Sports Arena as Bruce explained the state's new rules. Most of it was white noise for the old man until Anderson brought up the subject of money.

"You have to pay the commission 6 percent of the receipts from every show that you promote," he said. "That's not just here, but any show you run in the state. I know your son Barry and Sandy Barr are promoting shows- we get 6 percent of those gates as well. That's off the top."

As I've stated before, most Portland Wrestling fans considered Don Owen to be a gentle old soul. He was known not only as a promoter, but also as the most endearingly awkward ring announcer of all time. Watching Don stammer through his intros was like watching your grandpa give a toast at your wedding- you just hoped the lovable old fella would find the right words. But that on-air persona was Don Owen's "Dr. Jekyll". When Bruce Anderson told him that he would be forking over thousands of dollars, my boss unleashed "Mr. Hyde".

"Who the fuck are you to come in here and talk me to like this?" he demanded to know. "My father started this company and I've been doing this for fifty years! I'm not paying you a red fucking cent!"

At one point I thought I was going to have to physically restrain the old man. It wasn't necessary because when Don was done cursing, Anderson simply gave a polite nod and walked out of the office. I tried to talk some sense into Don as the blood drained from his face.

"I know that you're not used to this kind of thing," I told him. "But you have to play ball with these guys. I've seen these commissions in other territories- they can make things *very* difficult."

Don wasn't hearing it.

"I don't care who that guy thinks he is," he fumed. "I'm not going to be bullied by some fucking pencil pusher!"

When Don finally calmed down (it took awhile) I left his office to find Bruce and hopefully resolve the situation. I ran into Don's son Marc, who ran concessions in the Sports Arena. I asked if he had seen Anderson anywhere.

"He asked me for a cup of coffee," Marc replied. "I told him we don't serve assholes here."

Well, so much for the peaceful resolution that I had hoped for.

Here was an ironic thing about the Oregon Boxing and Wrestling Commission: Bruce Anderson was a former boxer who had formed the commission to clean up the sport of boxing. Yet there were very few professional boxing matches that took place in the state of Oregon. What we had in abundance was pro wrestling. Don Owen and his associates promoted numerous shows every week, and the commission stood to make money from each one. Accordingly, Anderson spent the bulk of his time focusing his crosshairs on a business that he knew nothing about.

Despite his objections, Don Owen started paying the state their 6 percent cut. He never really had a choice in the matter. But the commission wasn't just collecting money- Bruce Anderson wanted to change the wrestling business altogether.

The first big change for the wrestlers was that we all had to undergo mandatory testing for drugs and HIV. Presumably the HIV tests were because of the bloody matches that could take place in pro wrestling. After all, in the late-80s AIDS paranoia was high and there were still questions about how someone could acquire the virus.

I took the tests like all the other boys and never worried about failing. I knew that the only drug I could test positive for was vodka. But a couple of weeks later, I received a call from Bruce Anderson who said that he needed to meet with me right away. Katie and I drove almost an hour from our home in Northeast Portland to his office in Wilsonville. He greeted us with a somber look on his face and ushered us over to his desk.

"Lynn, we've received the results of your HIV test," he said grimly. "I'm afraid that you have tested positive."

Brother, you could have heard a rat piss on cotton. I couldn't talk. Hell, I couldn't breath. Look, I was a wrestler who had done some stupid shit, but how was this even possible? I expected Katie to start crying, but I could see that she had been stunned into silence.

Then Anderson cut loose with a giant belly laugh.

"I'm just messing with you!" he chuckled. "Your test is fine!"

Katie dropped her head into her hands- she was practically hyperventilating. I jumped up and slammed my fists on the desk.

"You think that's funny you gray-haired motherfucker?" I asked. "If you weren't so damn old I'd yank you behind that desk and beat the fuck out of you! Katie, let's go!"

We headed towards the door and Anderson finally stopped laughing.

"I really do have business we need to discuss!" he called to me. "I have this paperwork that needs to be…"

"Send it to Don!"

We got in our car and I had the steering wheel in a death grip for the entire drive home. All I could think about was beating the laughter out of that old coot. This was the man who was supposedly trying to protect guys like me? I never wanted to see or hear Bruce Anderson again. Unfortunately, I knew that I didn't have a choice. A few weeks after our meeting, Don Owen came to me with more news from Oregon's grand poobah of wrestling:

"Anderson just called," he told me. "He says we can't have any more blood in our matches. If there's any blood we have to stop the match right away."

Unbelievable. I didn't know if Anderson was worried about AIDS or if he just liked messing with us (I figured it was a little bit of both). Either way, "getting color" was one of the oldest tricks in the pro wrestling handbook and a surefire way to add drama to a big match. When you needed to show the audience that *shit just got serious*, red was the gold standard. And now we couldn't use it.

"Why does that asshole care about what we do to our own foreheads?" one of the boys asked me. "Of all the shit that happens in our business *this* is what he worries about?"

That sentiment was unanimous in the locker room, but I knew there was nothing we could do about it. We were already on shaky ground with the commission and defying Anderson could prove to be suicidal. So, I told the whole roster point blank: no more blood was allowed. That edict was promptly ignored.

Matt Borne was a second-generation wrestler and one tough hombre. Matt learned about the business from his legendary father "Tough" Tony Borne and he couldn't have given two shits about some bureaucrat and his regulations. So, during one TV taping in November, Matt told the TV audience that there would be blood in his match next week. But that wasn't enough- he also called out Bruce Anderson on air. Matt said the wrestling commission should be at the Sports Arena for his match so they could see the blood in person. Sure enough, the next week Steve Doll threw Matt into a post and he got busted wide open.

I should point out that I didn't tell Matt to say or do any of this stuff. He came up with all of it on his own. It was kind of ballsy, because the commission could yank Matt's wrestling license for such blatant defiance. Unfortunately, there was also the potential for collateral damage. Sure enough, the next week Bruce Anderson dropped the hammer.

"That son of a bitch is shutting me down," Don said.

The commission had suspended Don's promoting license over the Borne incident, and the entire story was splashed across the front page of the *Oregonian* newspaper. For a business that was still trying to "protect itself", this was the worst kind of publicity. The newspaper article quoted Anderson as saying that Matt had intentionally cut himself with a razor blade. Remember, this was in a territory where many older fans still believed everything they saw on TV. Now, a government official was telling all of them that pro wrestling was a work.

And the bad press was the least of our concerns. Don didn't know if he would be able to promote again. Our planned show on Thanksgiving weekend was cancelled and Owen's lawyers got involved. Incidentally, that cancelled show was when I was in the middle of my "sell-out" bet with Don (detailed in Chapter 9). Because of the suspension, I lost a week of build up for my boot-on-a-pole match with Top Gun. Talk about your shitty timing.

After a couple of days, Don and the state came to an agreement and he was allowed to promote again. I guess Anderson realized that, without our shows, the commission would no longer be able to claim its 6 percent cut. So, we were back in business. But after getting shut down for a week, we knew that we couldn't fuck up again.

That's why a couple months later, I knew we were up shit creek when Anderson laid out another directive: we were no longer allowed to use steel chairs as weapons before, during or after a match. Why? Don't fucking ask me. It was obvious Bruce knew that wrestling was a work, and he knew *how* it worked (the backstage rumor was that Billy Jack Haynes had filled him in on all those details while he was running his OWF). But for some reason, he still wanted to regulate pro wrestling like it was a competitive sport. Chair shots were something that we all knew how to deliver and endure. But this idiot was determined to make us perform under Marquis of Queensbury rules.

By the end of this year, I thought, *We're all going to be wearing headgear and singlets.*

Banning chair shots felt like banning body slams and headlocks. They were an integral part of pro wrestling and one of the easiest ways to build heat. Once that no-chairs decree came down, I *really* had to stretch my creative muscles. At that time Roddy and I were trying to book an angle with Nord and myself against Brian Adams (who we were feuding with). We wanted to stage an epic beatdown that would build sympathy for Brian and make us out to be the rotten assholes that we were. But how could we brutalize the guy without any chairs? I was at a loss, until Nord came up with one the most bizarre ideas I'd ever heard.

"Let's go to the grocery store," he said. "We'll need to stock up on supplies."

That night, the big TV match was Adams versus Nord in a strap match. The two men were connected at the wrists with a leather--- wait, why the hell am I explaining this? If you're reading this book, you're obviously an old school wrestling fan and have seen a damn strap match before. So, as you would expect, Brian and John whipped the shit out of each other. Finally, I interfered in the match and the beating was on.

After blinding Adams with the infamous "white powder", we tied one end of the strap to a ring rope (the other end was attached to Brian's right wrist). Then we wrapped a second strap around Brian's left wrist and tied that to the opposite rope. That left Adams lying on the mat, with his arms pulled in different directions like he was attached to some medieval torture device (and unfortunately for Brian that analogy would prove to be painfully appropriate).

See, by this point Nord was pushing a shopping cart out to the ring. In the cart were some boxes of cereal and several plastic milk jugs. Nord took the milk jugs (each one was a full gallon) and slammed them onto Brian as hard as possible. The jugs exploded on impact and milk sprayed everywhere. Because Brian's hands were tied, he couldn't do anything to cushion the blows. Nord would slam a jug onto his chest, it would bust open and then he would grab another jug and do it again.

Now, I'm guessing that you have never been assaulted with a gallon of milk before (although if you have, I'd love to hear the story). Suffice to say it hurts like a son of a bitch, especially when a monster like John Nord is swinging the jug. Within seconds, Brian's chest was beet-red and he was begging for the forgiving embrace of a steel chair.

Sorry bud- the commission knows best!

Johnny kept swinging the milk jugs until he exhausted his supply. Then, as a final insult, we opened the cereal boxes and dumped the contents all over Brian's dairy-drenched carcass. Cheerios and Lucky Charms spilled everywhere. The reaction from the crowd was pretty priceless: it was a mix of screams, laughter and *what the fuck?* Through the years those fans had witnessed some crazy stuff in the Portland Sports Arena, but they had never seen a grown man get his ass whipped with Corn Flakes and moo juice.

From that day on, Nord and I were nicknamed "The Breakfast Club", and we would use milk and cereal to humiliate our opponents (on one show, Nord even dumped a quart of 2% on Roddy's head). Johnny's idea was a hit and, in my opinion, a unique way to tiptoe around our "no-chairs" restriction. Really, it was a fun episode for everyone not named Brian Adams. I'm pretty sure all those milk jug shots left him lactose intolerant.

The ban on blood and chairs definitely made our jobs difficult. But of all the commission's regulations, it was the mandatory drug testing that was most damaging to our bottom line. On the surface, I'm sure it sounds like a grand idea. But you have to consider what they were testing for... and what they *weren't* testing for.

Steroids and other performance-enhancing drugs were not part of the testing process. Apparently that test was too expensive for the state's bean counters. What they were checking for was street drugs: heroin, cocaine and- the real doozy- marijuana. Now, I'm no fan of Mary Jane, and the test didn't bother me personally. But I would estimate that at least 75% of the boys that I knew smoked weed. Some of those guys just wanted to get high, but for others it was a way to relieve the physical pains associated with professional wrestling.

I know, I know: at the time, marijuana was illegal in all fifty states, with no exception made for medicinal use. I'm not here to debate legalization, but I have yet to meet a person that died from smoking too much weed. Do you know what has killed professional wrestlers? Prescription drugs. It's absolutely criminal how many young wrestlers died because they abused painkillers, muscle relaxers and the like. But under the commission's rules, the boys could down as many pills as they liked, as long as they had a prescription. Getting those "scrips" was easy (you could always find some mark doctor to write one up) and plenty of guys on the Portland Wrestling roster took advantage of that broken system. Their gym bags were portable pharmacies that contained, in some cases, dozens of different medications. As far as the commission was concerned, this was all on the up and up- a wrestler could chase a bottle of Percocet with a fifth of Jack Daniels and not worry about any repercussions. But if that same wrestler lit up *one joint*, he was out on his ass. It was insane.

The marijuana testing became a real nightmare when it came to booking outside talent. In early 1988, Curt Hennig made a stop in Portland to defend his AWA Championship. Curt was a blue-chip talent that had spent his early years wrestling for Don Owen. Now that he had established his name in a larger (albeit dwindling) promotion, he was returning to the Northwest to defend his strap against yours truly. But when "Assassin" Dave and I picked Curt up from the airport, one giant problem reared its head.

"I have to pass a drug test?" he asked incredulously.

See, before anyone set foot in an Oregon ring, they had to go to an approved commission doctor and pee in a cup. But Curt, like so many of the boys, liked to smoke pot. He knew that he would fail the test.

"No problem," I said. "The match is tonight. Just go take the test and wrestle. By the time they get the results you'll be back in Minnesota. They don't test there so no one will care."

"Are you kidding?" he asked. "All it takes is one person to leak that failed drug test to the newspapers or magazines. Then I'll be the dope-smoking World Champion. Verne will lose his mind and I'll be finished!"

Curt had a point. But there was no way around the testing- if he didn't submit a sample (in person) he would not be allowed in the ring. So Dave, Curt and myself tried to think of an approach that would protect both Hennig's career and our main event. And when you hear the plan that we came up with, you're going to think that we were all high.

Dave and Curt ended up going together to the commission doctor's office. But when they arrived, Dave told the lady at check-in that *he* was Curt Hennig and had come to take his drug test. See, Dave knew that he was clean (he already had to undergo the state testing) and there was no photo ID required when you took the test. The only *possible* problem was that Dave was a Cuban with black, curly hair pretending to be a blonde, blue-eyed Minnesotan. For you kids who don't know what Dave and Curt looked like, just imagine Edward James Olmos trying to pass himself off as Brad Pitt.

"YOU'RE Curt Hennig?" the receptionist asked Dave.

"That's me," he replied cooly. "AWA World Champion!"

The one thing we had going for us in this cockamamie plan was that Dave wrestled under a mask, so the general population had no idea what he looked like. Unfortunately, the AWA was nationally broadcast on ESPN, so people all over the country knew Curt Hennig's face. If one person in that office was a wrestling fan, we were fucked.

After checking in, the guys waited in the lobby and Curt covertly helped Dave fill out his medical paperwork. After a few moments, one of the nurses came out, looked at them, and then returned to the back. That wasn't good. The guys started discussing the legal ramifications of what they were doing: *Was it a crime to take someone else's state-mandated drug test? Shit, could we go to jail for this?* Neither Dave nor Curt was a lawyer, but they both knew that getting caught would be bad news. A few minutes later, the nurse returned with a man, probably a doctor, and they shared a few quiet words before returning to the back. As soon as they disappeared, Curt pulled the plug on the operation:

"We're out of here!" he said.

Dave and Curt ran out of the office, hopped in the car and sped off like a pair of fugitives. When they explained the situation later, I knew that they made the right decision. But no drug test meant no Hennig- our advertised main event was history. We ended up putting Curt's arm in a sling and telling the fans that he couldn't wrestle because of an injury. Dave took his place in the main event and Curt was his honorary manager. It was a definitely a letdown for the fans: they had come to see the AWA Champion and instead they watched Top Gun fight The Grappler for the millionth time.

After that testing debacle, the future Mr. Perfect had no interest in ever returning to Portland Wrestling. And Curt wasn't alone. Word spread and soon dope-smoking wrestlers throughout the U.S. (and there were plenty of them) avoided the Northwest like the plague. Whenever I tried to hire some top star from another territory, testing was almost always an obstacle. I couldn't blame them.

Why would they risk their careers for an eight hundred dollar payout? As a result, Don Owen's roster from this era (while loaded with young talent) lacked many of the experienced stars that could have elevated business to another level.

Here's what *really* pissed me off about the whole drug testing thing: while we were jumping through all these regulatory hoops, the WWF was running shows in Oregon with no problems. Again, this was 1989. I knew all the guys in Vince's locker room and I was supposed to believe that *they* were drug free? Shit, half the guys from that roster have written books about all the coke they inhaled. But when I asked the Commission about it I was told that, because they were a traveling company, the WWF was allowed to do its drug testing back in Connecticut and mail in the results.

Gee, nothing fishy about that!

I don't want to get all "Conspiracy Theory" on you, but I always had a sneaking suspicion that Vince was somehow behind the formation of the Oregon Wrestling Commission. After all, Bruce Anderson was just some ex-cop. Who bankrolled his lobbying efforts to create the commission? Perhaps Vince saw it as a cheap way to weaken Don Owen's promotion so he could swoop in and take over.

No, I don't have a shred of evidence to back this up. And yes, I know that the WWF ran plenty of other promotions out of business without the help of a regulatory agency. But I also know that, during a very crucial time, the commission placed Portland Wrestling under intense scrutiny while it simultaneously allowed the WWF to dance around its regulations. This double-standard helped weaken Don Owen's promotion and strengthen Vince's presence in the Beaver State.

(Incidentally, if Vince *did* help Anderson out, the whole thing eventually backfired. After the demise of Portland Wrestling, the commission started clamping down on the WWF and getting more serious about their drug testing. In 1993, Vince decided to pull out of the state and the WWF didn't run any shows in Oregon for a decade.)

The commission's regulations definitely made it hard to bring new talent into Portland. Unfortunately, some of the boys on our roster also made it hard to keep our *existing* talent.

For example, take Billy Jack Haynes. We did good business with Billy when he returned after his OWF debacle, and he garnered even more attention with a heel turn that fans still talk about. The turn was Billy's idea. He wanted to shake things up, and so he cut a rather bitter promo that criticized Portland Wrestling fans for abandoning him during his hour of need (in other words for not supporting his failed promotion and gym). "I've got three words for the state of Oregon," he yelled to the TV audience. "Kiss my ass!" For those of you not from Oregon, this would be like Kerry Von Erich spitting on the Alamo. The fans really reacted to this new "evil" Billy Jack, and for a while the angle helped our box office receipts. But it wouldn't last. Despite some financial success, Billy Jack was soon on Don Owen's shit list. One day I was relaying Don's latest complaints to Roddy via the "Bat Phone".

"That does it," he told me. "Billy Jack has to go."

Billy had no-showed several advertised dates. That was Don Owen's #1 no-no. Unless you were crippled in a car crash, there was no excuse for missing a show. And even in that situation, Don would probably expect you to call 911 and catch an ambulance ride to the arena. Missing the dates was reason enough for a dismissal, but Billy was a guy that was already on thin ice. Don never truly forgave him for the OWF and Billy's "hot and cold" backstage demeanor had alienated others. I'm not saying he didn't have friends, but there were plenty of guys that would be happy to see him go.

I should point out that at this time, Roddy was calling me from the set of a "Love Boat" TV movie shoot. As the booker, it was his responsibility to deal with personnel issues. But, since Rod was sipping mai tais with Captain Stubing and Gopher, that duty fell to me.

"Just walk in there and tell Billy he's done," he told me.

I had a few concerns about being the "hatchet man" for this job:

Concern #1: I had a relatively good relationship with Billy. Sure, we had some disagreements, but we got along alright. I knew that firing him would hurt our working relationship in the future.

Concern #2: We were going to lose one of our top draws, which could negatively impact our ticket sales.

Concern #3 (and if I'm being honest, this was my biggest reservation): I was pretty sure that once I fired Billy, he would kick the ever loving shit out of me.

Look, I'd won my share of fights, but Billy was a strong S.O.B. who- on occasion- had the demeanor of a serial killer. If he snapped, I did not like my odds. But Roddy had given me my marching orders, so I just had to do my job and deal with the (potentially painful) consequences. Billy was getting dressed when I approached him backstage.

"I'm sorry to tell you this," I began. "Don is letting you go."

Billy's eyes met mine. He wore a look of surprise. I decided to lay on the sweet talk while I still could.

"It's entirely Don's decision," I assured him. "I feel bad about this- you're one hell of a hand."

I continued to lay it on thick, as Billy Jack processed the meaning of my words. I waited for Bruce Banner to transform into the Hulk, but it never happened. Instead of throwing fists, the big man just shrank into his chair.

"You're fucking kidding me," he finally said. "What the hell am I supposed to do now?"

And that was it. No screaming. No threats. No shooting the messenger. I continued to offer Billy my condolences, just thankful that this episode had remained peaceful. Unfortunately, other guys on the roster were screwing up, and the next firing I was involved with would be considerably more violent.

That situation involved Scotty "The Body". The kid was a great talent, but also one giant pain-in-the-ass. Granted, he wasn't always like that. When Scotty started with us, he was very respectful and followed directions. We became friends and rode together. It was obvious that he was bright and creative, so he began helping me write the TV shows.

But as Scotty's name grew bigger, so too did his head. He became an insufferable know-it-all. During our writing sessions, he would criticize everything I came up with. I don't mean that in a *here's some constructive criticism* way. This was more of a *shut up old-timer, you don't know what the hell you're talking about* kind of deal. Scotty always had better ideas than me. At least that's what he told me (constantly). And the thing is, maybe he *did* have better ideas- but he expressed them in the wrong way. In professional wrestling a young guy is expected to give a certain amount of deference to a veteran; especially a veteran who is his boss. With Scotty, there was none of that. He had become brash, arrogant and insolent.

I wasn't the only superior that he pissed off. Don Owen really came to loathe Scotty. It was no secret that I had my own disagreements with Don, but I had always shown him the respect that he deserved both as a long-time promoter and as my boss. But Scotty skipped that respect stuff and was constantly mouthing off to Don. Eventually the old man had enough. One night at the Sports Arena, he approached me as I was planning the night's TV taping.

"I want that kid gone," he told me. "Right away."

I didn't like firing anyone, and I wasn't crazy about losing one of our top young stars. But I'd be lying if I said that I shed a tear about canning Scotty. Yeah, we were losing a big draw, but I was losing an even bigger headache. I found him in the locker room and broke the news point blank.

"Don's letting you go," I told him. "You can finish up your advertised dates, but that's it."

His expression was hard to decipher: I couldn't tell if he was shocked, hurt or just pissed off. Scotty tried to bargain with me, but I told him that this wasn't my decision.

"My hands are tied," I told him. "I'm sorry to see you go." (That last line may have been complete bullshit).

As I was leaving the locker room, I ran into my buddy "Equalizer" Bill Danenhauer. We started chatting about some nonsense and I told a dumb joke that made him laugh. Then I headed back to the office. Once I disappeared, Scotty exploded.

"You and your buddy are laughing at me?" he yelled at Bill. "You think it's funny that I'm getting fired?"

Bill had *not* been laughing at Scotty. Our conversation had nothing to do with the guy. In fact, Bill had no idea that "The Body" had gotten "The Boot". He tried to explain that, but Scotty was in no mood to listen. The kid was pissed at the world, and he needed to unleash his anger on somebody. That somebody ended up being "The Equalizer." After a few choice words, Scotty tried to shoot on Bill and tackle him to the ground.

Talk about your poor decisions.

Bill outweighed Scotty by probably 60 pounds of muscle *and* he was half-a-foot taller. The big fella evaded the attack with ease and threw Scotty to the floor. Now *Bill* was pissed, and that was bad news for Mr. Levy. By the time I returned to the locker room (I had heard the commotion from the adjacent hallway), Bill had pinned Scotty to the ground and was raining fists on his face. A couple of the boys pulled him off, but by then the damage was done. Scotty "The Body" was now Scotty "The Bloody".

At that moment, I had no idea what the fight was about. I asked Scotty if he was alright, but he just glared at me. There was no mistaking *that* look: I knew hatred when I saw it. For the rest of his time in Portland Wrestling (he stuck around for maybe two more weeks), Scotty didn't utter a single word to me. Before every show, I would give him the instructions for his match, and he'd just nod and walk off. He still worked every match and did everything we asked of him. But outside of the ring it was the complete silent treatment. In fact, Scott Levy and I would not share words again for seven years. You'll read about *that* encounter in the next chapter.

I had been in Oregon for almost four years when I began to plot my escape from professional wrestling.

"I had a nice run but now it's over," I told Roddy one day. "There's just nothing left for me to give."

As a wrestling territory, Portland had been everything that I had hoped for. I had spent several years working on top and making pretty good money. Sure, there had been headaches, but that was the case in every place I worked. I was proud of what I had accomplished with Don Owen, but I also knew that it was time to move on.

That's just how things worked in the territorial days. You'd work in a promotion for a year and then you would move on to another territory where you were the hot new attraction. It was how you avoided "overexposure"- which can be a killer for any pro wrestler. You know how sometimes you hear a song on the radio that you like, but then they play that damn song over and over until you never want to hear it again? *That's* overexposure. And by mid-1990, I felt like I was one of those annoyingly inescapable tunes on the Portland Wrestling radio. After all, there's only so many times you can watch the same masked guy kick someone with a loaded boot.

I had tried every trick in the book to keep my act from feeling stale: I turned babyface, I teamed with different wrestlers and I even ditched my mask. That was no easy decision- you may remember that I had quit the Memphis territory because they told me to lose the hood. But after 3 years on top, I was desperate for any angle that could keep The Grappler "fresh". It didn't work of course. After the initial shock of the de-masking wore off, the fans went back to being bored of me. And as one fan told me:

"The Grappler without a mask just isn't The Grappler."

I was pretty much going in circles in the Northwest, and ready to move on to another territory. But there was one big problem: only a handful of wrestling territories were still in operation. Obviously, the WWF was the spot where you could make some big money. But they weren't calling me. Ted Turner's WCW (the old Jim Crockett Promotions) was the second best option. They weren't calling either. Once you got past those two, the pickings were slim. Promotions like the AWA and World Class were on life support, and most of the mom and pop territories had already gone under. I felt that I could still make a contribution to the wrestling business, but the job opportunities just weren't there.

"I'm thinking of moving back to Texas," I told Roddy. "Katie and I both have our families there and it will be easier to transition into a new line of work. I can't worry about wrestling anymore- my first concern is what's best for the girls."

I knew that Roddy was one person that would understand my dilemma. He may have had a "wildman" reputation, but the Hot Rod was really a down-to-earth family man that worked hard to provide for his wife and kids. Obviously, he had a bigger bank account than I did. But ultimately, we were two guys chasing the same simple goal: financial security for our families.

"Don't pack up just yet Lenny," he told me. "I think I can help you out."

It turned out that Roddy had been thinking of opening a new business in the Portland area. He didn't know what kind of business he wanted to pursue and he certainly didn't have time to be hands-on with this new venture (in addition to booking for Don, Rod was also wrestling for Vince and making movies). Essentially, he was looking to invest some money in a person that he trusted. That person would then use the funds to build a new business from the ground up.

"I think you're the right guy for the job," he said.

Roddy's proposition was this: I could pick out any business of my choosing. It could be a new restaurant, a new gym- anything that I wanted. He would then spend the money necessary to get the business off the ground. From then on, I would be in charge of the entire operation: hiring, firing, balancing the books. All of that stuff would be my responsibility. We would lease a space, and if the business was stable after a year, Roddy would buy the property.

"Several years down the road we'll sell the place," he concluded. "And split all the proceeds 50-50."

I couldn't believe it. This was exactly what I had been hoping for- a chance to earn a regular, non-wrestling income and provide a future for my family. I told Roddy that I loved the idea, and we shook on the deal right then and there. We didn't need a contract: I knew that Roddy's word was gold, and he knew the same about me. Now, we were business partners. I just had to figure out what kind of business we were in.

After a couple weeks of research, I decided to open a transmission repair shop. I had gotten the idea from a man named Larry Van Zandt, who advertised his own transmission shop on the Portland Wrestling broadcasts. I had gotten to know Larry a bit and saw how he charged $1500 for a job that required $200 worth of parts. Hell, I was no business school graduate, but I knew that was a nice profit margin. I called my dad to tell him about my bright idea.

"You're opening a transmission shop?" he asked. "I've got a better idea. Why don't you just open a place that builds space shuttles? You know just as much about that business as you do auto repair!"

My old man had a point- I knew how to drive cars, but I didn't know the first thing about fixing them. Still, I was convinced that a transmission shop was a can't-miss proposition, I just had to bring in people that knew what they were doing. So, I hired one of Jerry Van Zandt's former employees, and leased a building in Southeast Portland. We fixed the place up and called it the "Piper's Pit Stop Transmission Center" (I figured it couldn't hurt to cash in on Roddy's notoriety).

Once the Pit Stop was up and running, I settled into a new 24/7 schedule. During the day I worked at the transmission shop. During the night, I would attend to my Portland Wrestling duties, either at a TV taping or a house show. Whatever few hours remained were devoted to sleeping and seeing the girls. I knew that I couldn't stop wrestling until the Pit Stop was stable, so I temporarily resigned myself to this round-the-clock workday.

Unfortunately, our first year of business was more than a little rocky. After we had been open a few months, I discovered that some employees were taking advantage of my ignorance and hurting our bottom line in the process. They were ordering more parts than they needed and then selling those surplus parts to their buddies. When I called them out, they would tell me that I didn't know what I was talking about (sadly, they were right). Not only that, but I couldn't fire any of the guys because I needed them to do the repair work. What could I do? Like my dad said, I didn't know shit about fixing cars and now these guys had me over a barrel.

Something had to change. I decided that I would learn how to fix transmissions myself (and yes, that's a skill I should have probably learned *before* I opened a transmission shop). I ended up paying a retired mechanic 500 bucks a week to teach me how to disassemble and reassemble transmissions. Just like my days in Joe Mercer's wrestling school, I was a clumsy greenhorn during my first few lessons but eventually became semi-competent. After a couple months of training, I was a full-fledged pro.

Those lessons changed everything. The employees could no longer get rich off of their boss' lack of knowledge- I kept tabs on all the orders and repairs. If someone tried to pull a fast one, he was out on his ass. When all the embezzlement ended, the Pit Stop began to make money. Within a year it was a viable business and Roddy purchased the property. Everything was going according to plan.

"I just need a couple more months to really get this place established," I assured Katie. "After that, I can finally walk away from wrestling."

I didn't realize that wrestling was about to walk away from me.

I wish I could tell you that there was some big, sexy story behind the death of Don Owen's Portland Wrestling. After all, this is a promotion that survived a World War, a Cold War and a Gulf War- it was a Northwest institution that deserved to go out with a bang, not a whimper. But while I have spent much of this chapter detailing behind-the-scenes squabbles and our tumultuous relationship with the state wrestling commission, ultimately Portland Wrestling's fatal flaw was the same one shared by every other now-defunct wrestling territory: we just couldn't compete with Vince McMahon's checkbook.

Don delivered the news to me late one evening after a TV taping. It was time to get paid and, as usual, I was the last person to receive his money. All the other boys had cleared out, and the only people left in the room were Don, his son Barry and myself.

"I figured you should have fair warning," the old man told me. "We're going out of business."

Now, Don had been telling me he was going out of business every week since the day that I met him. I'm not kidding. During my first meeting with the guy we had talked for maybe twenty minutes when he pulled a newspaper clipping out of his jacket pocket. The article was about the closing of some lumber mill in Southern Oregon. *"See this? This is what's happening to the economy,"* he said. *"Soon, we'll be out of business! You're lucky to have a job."* I swear he made me read that same yellowed, dog-eared clipping every day for five years straight. So yeah, I was used to Don claiming that the sky was falling. Unfortunately *this* night in the Sports Arena, Don Owen was no Chicken Little.

"Vince got our TV," he told me. "It's all over."

As Don explained it, the WWF was taking over our Saturday evening spot on KPTV Channel 12. And unfortunately, we weren't just being shipped off to a different timeslot. After 38 years on local TV, Portland Wrestling was getting kicked off the air.

Here's the crux of what happened. KPTV (at the time owned by a company called Chris-Craft that also made boats) had hired a new General Manager. Don had been close friends with the old GM, who had been an ardent supporter of Portland Wrestling. But like pretty much all TV executives, KPTV's *new* GM was looking to increase revenues while cutting costs at the same time. And Vince McMahon helped him do both.

According to Don, the WWF bought our Saturday night timeslot for approximately $1,500 a week (I can't remember what the exact number was).

Under their new contract agreement, the WWF would air syndicated programming every week, and KPTV was not allowed to carry any other wrestling programming. Why would this be a better deal for the TV station? Well, first you have to consider the business arrangement that Don Owen had with KPTV.

Unlike Vince's new agreement, Don never paid a dime for his TV time. It was all free. KPTV paid the production costs on all the Saturday night shoots (providing cameras, crew, etc.) and made money by selling advertising on the Portland Wrestling telecast. All the ad revenue went to the station- even when sponsors appeared live at the Sports Arena to sell their merchandise. Don made his money strictly by using the TV to promote ticket sales at his shows throughout Oregon and parts of Washington. For decades it had been a win-win situation.

But KPTV had to write a rather hefty check to produce all of those episodes. For every show they had to pay the cameramen, director, audio guy and other behind-the-scenes staff (many of whom were news employees being paid overtime). The station also had to roll out their expensive production van and studio cameras for each taping. Then, when the final TV match ended, a courier was paid to shuttle the tape back to the station, where some other KPTV staffers were waiting to make sure that the show was ready for broadcast at 11 PM. This happened every Saturday night.

I don't know exactly what that process cost per episode, but let's just say it was a nice round number like 500 bucks. It was probably more than that, but just roll with me here. That would mean that KPTV had to sell $2000 worth of ads on Portland Wrestling every week just to equal the $1500 profit that Vince was offering for his syndicated programming. On top of that, the WWF deal meant the station wouldn't have to worry about staffing problems, equipment malfunctions or any of the other headaches that come with producing a weekly TV show. All they had to do was play Vince's tape and cash a check.

Since the fall of Portland Wrestling, I've read a lot of theories about why Don Owen lost his TV slot. Some people say it was because of declining interest in local wrestling. But honestly, our ratings were fine and our houses were still doing good business. Other people claim the cancellation was because local electronics dealer Tom Peterson- a long-time sponsor of Portland Wrestling- was experiencing financial problems. That's not the reason either. Tom could have been making millions and we still would have been kicked off the air. The cold, hard truth is KPTV management cancelled Portland Wrestling because Vince McMahon offered them an easier way to make money. It was that simple.

The cancellation was sad for me on a personal level. After all, I had dedicated the last five years of my life to Portland Wrestling. At the time Don told me the bad news, I was once again working as his booker (Roddy had left a few months prior to concentrate on his WWF and Hollywood obligations). I didn't want to be seen as the captain of a sinking ship, so before the other boys learned about the TV cancellation I passed the booking job on to my pal Steve Doll. *"You've earned this buddy,"* I told him. Poor guy was really touched by the gesture. When he found out the next week that he was the booker of a show that was about to be cancelled, he was less appreciative. But we both shared a laugh about it.

The final episode of Portland Wrestling aired on KPTV December 28th, 1991. Like a lot of things that happened in my career, I don't remember a thing about that particular show. There was no big sendoff or anything like that. For me, the promotion's real farewell happened one week earlier, when Roddy Piper returned to make his final Portland Wrestling appearance.

It was Christmastime and "Piper Claus" brought a bunch of young kids into the Crow's Nest to thank KPTV and the fans for all their years of support. When he was done, I ushered Don Owen onstage with a bottle of champagne (I also made one final, shameless plug for "Piper's Pit Stop"). After a few good-natured jokes, Roddy presented a plaque to his old boss that read: *In Appreciation to the Owen Family for supporting Pro Wrestling for 65 years.*

"We all love you," Roddy told him. "If there's ever been a more fair promoter or a more wonderful man, I have never met him."

Don shut down his wrestling operations a few months after our final episode aired. He had tried to keep running house shows, but without the TV exposure, the ticket sales just weren't there. Don eventually sold the promotion to Sandy Barr. I worked a little while for Sandy, but it was obvious that we weren't going to duplicate the magic (or the money) of the Owen years. Wrestling's territorial era was over and I decided that it was time to hang up my loaded boot.

By the end of 1992, my pro wrestling career felt like a distant memory. The Pit Stop was my full-time job, and I had no time to dwell on an industry that had passed me by. Sure, I could chase bookings all over the world, but I had a family to feed. I wanted to watch the girls grow up and provide stability for their future. That meant concentrating on the transmission shop and turning my back on wrestling.

Of course, I could never *completely* forget about the business. Occasionally, I would look back fondly on my career and accomplishments. As a teenager, I was told that I would never be a professional wrestler. I could have given up, but instead I spent 15 years proving the naysayers wrong. Heavyweight titles. Main events. The respect of my peers. I had earned all of these things. Not a bad showing for a kid from Humble.

In the end, I had only one regret about my wrestling career. Despite all of my success in the territories, I had never worked for a big, international promotion like the WWF. Sure, in the early 80s I had been a job guy for a few promotions with cable deals. But that was before Vince McMahon had transformed the industry with big TV ratings, massive merchandising and giant Pay-Per-Views. At times, I would daydream about what I could have achieved on that global stage.

After a few moments, those fantasies would always fade. My in-ring career was over and I knew that there was no "big money" job waiting for me in wrestling. It was time to accept that fact and concentrate on my new career. But, a funny thing happened on the way to pro wrestling retirement:

The "big money" finally came calling.

CHAPTER TWELVE

THE BIG MONEY

A lot of fans ask me why I never worked for Vince McMahon and the WWF. The answer is simple: sometimes life changing opportunities can appear at the most inopportune times. That was certainly the case in 1995 when I received a phone call from a Freebird.

"I'm calling for The Grappler!" announced the voice at the other end of the line. It didn't take long for me to identify the caller- there was no mistaking the gravelly growl of Michael "P.S." Hayes.

I had known Michael since our Mid-South days. Back then, he and his fellow Fabulous Freebirds headlined shows with the Junkyard Dog while I worked hour-long Broadways with Jake Roberts. Those Dog/Freebird matches would last just a few minutes but they were always extremely profitable. Unfortunately for me, pro wrestling never paid by the hour.

Michael had called me at the Pit Stop. At the time I was expecting a call from some old lady bitching about her Ford Taurus, so my old friend's voice was a pleasant surprise. After we spent a few minutes reliving old memories, Michael told me about his latest career move.

"I'm working for Vince," he said. "I've even got a new gimmick."

Mr. Badstreet was now an announcer called "Dok Hendrix". Michael's long locks and Stars-and-Bars capes had been replaced by a pompadour and tacky suits. His makeover was typical for the WWF at that time- it seemed they were always repackaging stars from other promotions. Sometimes these new personas would work (ala Ted "Million Dollar Man" Dibiase) and sometimes they were disasters (ala Dok Hendrix). But even if you were saddled with a loser gimmick, you could usually find solace in the fact that you were earning the biggest paycheck of your life.

"The guys up here are making *great* money," Michael told me. "In fact, that's why I called you. Vince is looking for new talent and I told the guys that he should bring *you* in."

Me? In the WWF?

You have to realize, at this time in my life I hadn't worked a regular wrestling schedule in a few years. I asked Michael if he had dialed the correct number.

"You could do great up here," he assured me. "You're a helluva worker and have a great mind for the business. So, are you interested in coming up?"

As soon as Michael asked that question, my brain started crunching all the "pros" and "cons" of his proposition. The "pros" were obvious. After all, I had been waiting my whole life for this phone call. The WWF was *the* global giant and premiere brand in pro wrestling. Sure, Ted Turner's WCW was on the rise, but it had not eclipsed the WWF in ratings or recognition. McMahon-land was still the place to earn fame, fortune and wrestling immortality. If I had received Michael's phone call a few years earlier, I would have been on a plane to Connecticut faster than you can say "Dok Hendrix".

Unfortunately, in 1995, there were some pretty big "cons" to accepting a job with the WWF. My biggest problem was that I couldn't leave the Pit Stop. When Roddy bought our transmission shop, I promised him that I would work non-stop to make the thing successful. After a few years in business we were getting by alright, but managing the shop was still a full-time job. I had to order parts, deal with payroll, pay bills and do all that other boring administrative crap- without any assistant to help me with the workload. Sure, I could take a day off here and there. But working for the WWF would put me on the road for weeks on end. There was no way I could do that *and* run the shop at the same time. Michael's proposal was tempting as hell, but Roddy had invested his faith (and money) in me. I wasn't going to let him down.

"That sounds like a great opportunity," I finally told Michael. "But, there's just no way I can do it right now."

My reply was followed by a few seconds of silence at the other end of the line. I don't think WWF guys were used to strapped-for-cash wrestlers turning down job offers.

"Just think about it," Michael finally said. "Again, you can make some really good money up here. We'll call you back in a few weeks after you give it some thought."

I thanked Michael for the call, and assumed that was the end of that. But a few weeks later, he did call me back to see if I had reconsidered. Unfortunately, my situation with the Pit Stop was unchanged so I had to say "no" once more.

"I gave Roddy my word on this thing," I explained. "I have to see it through."

Michael said he understood and wished me well. We promised to keep in touch, but like a lot of wrestling conversations, that was all just idle chatter.

The WWF never called me again.

Today, I'm almost 20 years removed from Michael's call, and I can't help but consider the "what ifs". Did I walk away from the opportunity of a lifetime? What would have happened if I did work for the World Wrestling Federation?

It's hard to say.

There's no question that I would have made some nice money- at least compared to my payouts in the old wrestling territories. I had friends that earned more money in WWF preliminary matches than I did in Don Owen's main events.

That's not an indictment of Don- just an illustration of how much cash the WWF raked in with its massive TV and touring operation.

But the thing is, you never knew how long that money would keep rolling in. At that time, there were not a lot of guaranteed contracts for pro wrestlers. Those were reserved for Hulk Hogan and maybe a few other top stars. A guy like me could be fired anytime. If I blew out my knee or Vince decided he didn't like my "look", I would have been out of a job. That's another reason I couldn't leave the Pit Stop- it was a much more reliable source of income for my family.

Besides, who knows what kind of wrestler I would have been for the WWF? Excuse me, I mean what kind of "WWF Superstar" I would have been? Obviously, my old buddies Jake Roberts, Ted Dibiase and Rick Rude did very well for themselves. But other talented workers like Rip Oliver were completely lost in the WWF shuffle. Hell, Vince turned my old tag team partner Tony Anthony into "T.L. Hopper" the wrestling plumber. I'm sure Tony made a nice paycheck with that gimmick, but I doubt he would list his WWF stint as a career highlight.

So, do I regret never working for the World Wrestling Federation? Sure. I would have loved the opportunity to prove myself on such an enormous stage. But, I'm also realistic about what my chances would have been in Vince's cartoon kingdom. In all likelihood, I would have been a WWF Superstar that most Grappler fans would have never recognized. And if rejecting the WWF's overtures meant that the world never got to see "L.D. Doberman, the Wrestling Dogcatcher", well, that's probably a good thing.

By 1998, I had accepted the fact that I was probably never going to achieve national wrestling fame and earn one of those fat contracts that I kept hearing about. It was a shame, because pro wrestling was red hot. The WWF and WCW were in the middle of the "Monday Night Wars" and with all that Pay-Per-View and merchandise money coming in, it seemed every talented worker was signing a six-figure deal.

But at least one talented worker was still stuck in a transmission shop in Southeast Portland. That wasn't necessarily a bad thing- by this time, the Pit Stop was profitable with capable staff that could run the place when I was out of town. That allowed me to work some independent shows and keep my wrestling options open. In the back of my mind, I held out hope that Michael Hayes would call me back with another offer.

I can do it now! I would tell him. *When can I start?*

Of course, the Freebird never came calling. But here's a cool thing that I have discovered about pro wrestling: if you help someone out in the business, in most cases he will eventually return the favor. It may take a week. It may take a month. In the case of Scott Norton, it took almost eight years. But you know that old saying about good things coming to those who wait? This is what they were talking about.

"I'll never forget all the things you taught me when I was coming up," Scott told me on the phone. "Now I want to pay you back."

After his time in Portland Wrestling (where I helped Scott improve his in-ring work), "Flash" had gone on to become a big star in Japan. He then parlayed that overseas success into a lucrative contract with World Championship Wrestling. I won't divulge the exact number on Scott's deal, but he was making in one year what I might make in fifteen.

"I told Bischoff all about you," he told me. "He wants to bring you in. Brother, this is a chance for you to make some real money if you're up for it."

Unlike when Michael Hayes had called me, I was able to give my friend an emphatic "hell yes!" response. The Pit Stop was on solid ground and I was ready to roll. Scott told me the WCW booking office would contact me to work out the details. I thanked him about a million times and a few days later, I received a phone call from one of the muckety-mucks in Atlanta.

"I'm not sure how these deals work," I told him. "Will you guys be sending me a contract?"

"A contract?" The suit asked in astonishment. "I'm afraid there's been some miscommunication. Before we offer a deal, you have to work in a try-out match."

A try-out match? I thought. *What the fuck is that? You want to see if I can work? I've got two decades of "try-out matches" on tape.*

Of course, I wasn't going to blow a big-money deal on account of pride, so I told the guy that I'd be happy to participate in his little audition. The next week, I was booked on a TV taping for WCW Saturday Night in Thibodaux, Louisiana.

I was feeling pretty anxious on the flight out of Portland. There was so much riding on this one match and I had no idea who my opponent would be. I had no doubt about my own in-ring skills, but if I was paired up with some stiff our match would likely suck and my big fat contract would disappear. That's why I was all nerves until I finally arrived at the arena and saw this match listed on the booking sheet:

Len Denton vs. Eddie Guerrero

Thank you God.

I had wrestled Eddie and his brothers numerous times throughout the years and knew that I had nothing to worry about. Working with Eddie was like taking a night off. You could just kick back while he busted his ass and made you look like Ric Flair. That contract was mine.

Sure enough, we tore the house down. The match went 15, maybe 20 minutes and we were clicking on everything. That is, until the very end of the match. To set up the finish, Eddie planned to hit me with a Tornado DDT. Now, despite the fact that I took Jake Roberts' very first DDT, Eddie's move was one that I was unfamiliar with. But I trusted him. So he leapt off the turnbuckle and latched on a front facelock in mid-air.

Then, just like in that damn Jake Roberts match, I slipped.

Eddie tried to salvage the move, but instead of spinning my body around as planned, he could only ride my skull straight into the mat. Then everything went dark. When I woke up a few seconds later, it felt like an out-of-body experience. I couldn't breathe and I couldn't feel *anything*. I knew that I was in a wrestling match but I felt like an observer not a participant; just a ghostly Grappler watching from above.

Wow. I'm dying.

I seriously thought that. My ticket was punched and I was all done. And here's the really weird thing: I felt very calm about the whole thing. I was going to die any second- in a wrestling ring- and that was OK. There was no pain or sorrow, just a peaceful acceptance of my fate.

Then came the frog splash.

Eddie's finishing move was perhaps the most painful defibrillator in the history of medicine. In a millisecond I was back in the real world and hurting *everywhere*. My neck felt broken, my ears were ringing and I was choking on blood. It was the most excruciating pain of my entire career.

The ref's three count ended the match but not my misery. I got to the back and discovered that my left ear had been partially torn off and my tongue was almost bitten in half. I tried to conceal my agony. After all, my body could be stitched back together; my WCW employment status was much more fragile. So, I mumbled my way through a few painful conversations with some of the agents. They told me the company executives liked my match and as a result I would receive a booking sheet with future dates. That news didn't dull my pain, but it definitely improved my mood. After 20 years in the wrestling business, I was finally going to make some big money.

Becoming part of the WCW/Time Warner machine was something of a culture shock. Back in the territory days, I drove from town to town with my brothers and raised all sorts of hell. Some of those stories I have shared in this book and some others I will take to my grave. But in WCW, there was none of that. It was one big corporate behemoth where "travelling with the boys" meant waving to your co-workers from across a crowded airport terminal. I was happy to be wrestling again, but the camaraderie just wasn't the same.

But hell, I really had nothing to complain about: I was making good money and working for the #1 attraction on cable television! Every other weekend, I was flown out to a TV taping where I appeared on one of the company's lower-tier shows (i.e. not Nitro or Thunder). My Grappler mask and loaded boot were left behind, and I competed as plain old Len Denton. I received a nice fee for each taping and was told that I would eventually be signing a contract to become a full-time member of the WCW roster.

On top of that, I was catching up with a number of my old friends. John Nord, Rick Rude and Brian Adams were just some of the guys working for WCW at that time. After so many years locked up in the Pit Stop, it was great to see my buddies again- although I was dreading some other potential "reunions".

For example, there was Scott Levy. I hadn't seen Scotty since he left Portland Wrestling in 1991. I knew that he blamed me for his dismissal and for Bill Danenhauer leaving him bloody on the locker room floor. Back then, I was Scotty's boss, but in WCW our roles were quite different.

"Scotty the Body" was now "Raven"- a hardcore character that was part grunge-rocker and part cult leader. The gimmick had propelled Scotty to stardom in ECW and then WCW. Basically, he was a hot shot drawing a big paycheck, while I was just another veteran trying to score a contract. I was well aware of both these facts when Scotty approached me backstage at one TV taping.

"Lynny, can we talk in private?" he asked.

You talk about your extreme makeovers- the pretty boy that I knew was *long gone*. The man talking to me now was pierced, scarred and tatted beyond recognition. Scotty was no longer a young kid hoping for a big break- he was a grizzled star staring a hole right through me.

"Sure, we can talk," I said. "Lead the way."

I followed Scotty to a side room and prepared myself for *whatever* was about to go down. Maybe he wanted to talk... but maybe he wanted to fight. I didn't have any beef with Scotty, but I was ready to do either.

If it's going to happen, it's going to happen. I told myself. But then, another thought popped in my head: *Shit, if I get in a fight, that contract may get torn up before I ever sign it.* I wasn't worried about Scotty kicking my ass, but the thought of losing that big payday terrified me.

When we were finally alone, Scotty closed the door behind us. Then, instead of throwing a fist, he extended a hand.

"I'm sorry Lynny," he said. "I'm hoping we can shake hands and be friends again."

Scotty was apologizing to *me*? This was not the conversation- or confrontation- that I expected.

"I was a dumb kid," Scotty continued. "You and Roddy taught me so much. I just want you to know that I appreciate all that you did for me. Thank you."

Wow. With no hesitation I shook Scotty's hand and told him that no apology was necessary. Hell, I had been a pig-headed kid at one point in my career. In the long run, that kind of stuff really didn't matter. What *did* matter is that Scott Levy had become a true professional and a stand-up guy.

"I'm proud of what you've accomplished," I told him. "And proud to call you a friend."

We shared a bro-hug and then I asked my old buddy if he could please talk to Eric Bischoff and get me my fucking contract.

Seriously- after a couple months of work, I was getting the runaround from the WCW brass. I was getting paid, but whenever I asked about my supposed contract I was told to ask this guy who would then tell me to ask some other guy. It always went nowhere. I shared my frustration with Scott Norton, who promised to get answers. A couple of days later, he called me at home with some good news.

"It's a done deal," he told me. "I spoke with Bischoff myself. They're drawing it all up, and you should get it in a couple weeks. Listen to this brother: it's a two year deal- $150,000 a year and you only have to work ten days a month!"

HOT DAMN!

Look, this wasn't Hulk Hogan money- or even Scott Norton money. But compared to my old $800 payouts, 150 grand was like hitting the jackpot! Plus, with just ten shows a month I could spend plenty of time at the Pit Stop to make sure that it remained profitable.

"All I have to do is get through this contract," I told Katie. "Then we can pay off the house. Once Roddy and I sell the shop, we'll actually be able to put something away for the future."

It was kind of strange: I had busted my ass in wrestling, living paycheck to paycheck for two decades. Now, in just two *years*, I would have some financial security for my family.

All those bumps and bruises were finally paying dividends.

As I waited for the Time Warner suits to draw up the paperwork on my new deal, I wondered about what kind of on-camera role I would have in WCW. I figured that I would probably be putting over some of the younger guys on the roster. In a way, it would be similar to what I did in World Class: work with some up-and-comers and help them fine tune their skills. I wasn't concerned about personal glory- that guaranteed money was all the reward I needed.

In early May, I was flown out to Kansas City for Monday Nitro. This was of course the company's flagship show, although I was scheduled to work a non-televised match. That night I was paired up with a huge African-American kid named Teddy Reade. Actually, "huge" doesn't do the guy justice- Teddy weighed 400 pounds and about half of that was in his biceps. He was also greener than goose shit, so I sat him down to make sure that I knew exactly what he could do in the ring. We were mapping out our match when my old manager Jimmy Hart popped his head into the room.

"Lenny, it looks like there's been a change of plans," he told me. "I was asked to come get you."

I followed Jimmy into another nearby room. Waiting for me there were a couple of agents... and Bill Goldberg.

Aw, Crap.

Bill was in the middle of a historic run on WCW television- he had amassed a record of 82 consecutive wins. The vast majority of those wins were squashes, and it was obvious that I was going to be the next sacrificial lamb. This would be my big debut on Monday Nitro: a 30 second drubbing in front of millions of viewers. I introduced myself to Bill and we laid out the plan for our match. It didn't take long.

"I should probably warn you," Bill offered, "I'm going to hit you pretty hard with that spear."

I told Bill not to worry about it, and prepared for my emasculation.

If there was any bright side to my match with Goldberg, it was the fact that I got *some* offense against the big fella. Here's how it went: first he kicked me, then I nailed him with a jawbreaker. Bill staggered for exactly a half-second, then he hit me with a clothesline, six punches, a spear (stiff, just as Bill promised) and a jackhammer. That was it- win #83. The whole thing lasted 52 seconds and 10 seconds of that was Bill hoisting me in the air for his finishing move. Essentially, it took you longer to read about the match than it would for you to watch it on YouTube.

As I walked back to the locker room, I couldn't help but remember my years as a greenhorn putting over big stars. The Goldberg match was a lot like my first televised match when I was manhandled by Dory Funk, Jr. The only difference was that about *5 million people* saw that Goldberg squash- making it the most watched match of my entire career. As you've read in this book, I have wrestled and defeated some of the biggest stars in pro wrestling history. Yet for so many fans, I'm just another forgettable guy who was bulldozed by Big Bill.

"I saw your match," my dad called to tell me. "At least you didn't have to work too hard for that check."

My old man spoke the truth. The Goldberg match was the quickest grand I ever earned in my life. But it was also one of the last paydays I would see in World Championship Wrestling.

From the moment I saw Goldberg waiting for me in that room I knew that there would be no WCW contract. After all- why would anyone job out a guy so decisively (in his Nitro debut no less) and then give him guaranteed money? I had been around the business long enough to see where things were headed.

That doesn't mean that I gave up. At the next TV taping in Orlando, I approached my old Mid-South co-worker Terry Taylor, who now served in a management capacity.

"Terry, help me out," I pleaded. "I've been asking everyone about this contract. I just need to know what the hell is going on."

"Man, that is not my responsibility!" he snapped back. "You've got a booking sheet- just make those dates. I don't have time for this!"

In fairness to Terry, my contract situation really *wasn't* his responsibility. I had approached him in the middle of a TV taping when he had a million other things to worry about, so his response was understandable. But at that moment, none of those facts mattered to me. Terry was still WCW management, and those Atlanta suits had jerked me around for too long. I had gone back on the road to provide for my family. Now, it was clear that I was chasing nothing but empty promises.

"Get your shit together!" I barked at Terry. "Not just you, but this whole fucking company! I'm not asking for the star treatment, but I am asking to be treated like a professional. If you guys don't want me- fine, let me know. Just quit jerking me around- this is my *fucking life* you're messing with!"

I didn't wait for Terry's response, but I did make all of my scheduled dates just as he instructed. After that, I returned to Portland and never received another booking sheet. Of course, nobody from the company contacted me to tell me that I was finished. They didn't even bother to return my phone calls, probably because that would have been the professional thing to do. Instead, my time in World Championship Wrestling- and my pursuit of that elusive contract- ended with a bunch of grown men giving me the silent treatment.

I'll probably never know why WCW management changed their minds about my role with the company. Perhaps Bischoff and his cronies decided that I wasn't "marketable" enough. Maybe it was a dollars and cents issue. Or it could have been that WCW was just a poorly run company where the right hand didn't know what the left hand was doing.

Whatever the reason, I was disappointed but not distraught. Obviously, that Time Warner money would have helped my family's financial situation, but I still had the Pit Stop to provide a steady income. As far as my wrestling career was concerned, I was proud of my accomplishments. Sure, it would have been nice to show my talents to millions of people instead of just taking a spear and a jackhammer. But I wasn't going to cry about it- not after what I had been through.

When I was a teenager, men like Joe Mercer and Art Nelson told me that I would never make it in the wrestling business. Karl Kox threatened me, Ole Anderson cursed me and Bill Watts humbled me. But I busted my ass, never quit and proved those naysayers wrong. I may not have become an international superstar, but I had earned the respect of my peers and fans throughout the country. That was a legacy I could live with.

So, I left the road for good and rededicated myself to building a business and (most important) raising a family. Some guys have trouble making that transition, but I enjoyed it. Being home meant that I was able to watch my girls grow up, an experience that I wouldn't have traded for all the main events in the world. On top of that, Katie and I finally tied the knot. When we first met, we had both sworn off marriage. But after twenty years together, I figured it was time to make her an honest woman.

Now I can look back on my life and say that I enjoyed a great pro wrestling career while staying true to myself and my principles. That may not sound like much, but unfortunately many of my brothers lost their families- and even their lives- in the pursuit of stardom. I'm not judging any of them. I just feel fortunate that I have been able to enjoy my life both inside and outside of wrestling. Fame and money are great- but nothing can replace the laughter of your kids or the love of your wife.

So who is Lynn Denton today? Well, I'm a husband, a father, a brother and sometimes a teacher. Basically, I'm a man that wears a lot of hats.

And on special occasions, I also wear a mask.

EPILOGUE

October 27, 2012
Beaverton, Oregon

The television studio was small, sweaty and standing room only. About 80 wrestling fans were packed under the hot TV lights, their eyes trained on an old Grappler ready for his last ride. We were a long way from the Superdome, but that was OK with me.

The people had come to watch a taping of a local television show called *Portland Wrestling Uncut*. It was main event time and I was scheduled to face a young greenhorn making his in-ring debut. Colt Toombs was a clean-cut babyface with an MMA background and a famous father- his old man Roderick Toombs is better known as Roddy Piper.

Our contest had a "circle of life" feeling to it. This would be the first match of Colt's wrestling career, and the last match of mine. I was retiring from in-ring action, a fact that we did not advertise in advance. After all, I was the heel and good heels don't want any sympathy. So, before the bell rang, I skipped the farewell speech and unleashed a verbal ass-whupping:

"You know something Colt?" I screamed into the camera. "I've wrestled 35 years. I've had many, many injuries and lived with a lot of pain. It ain't all glitz and glamour. I know when you take your shirt off and all the little girls scream and holler that makes you say *I wanna be a wrestler like my daddy, I want to wrestle in Madison Square Garden!* But you know what? To get there, <u>you have to go through guys like me</u>! I promise you after this match tonight, you're going to know why they've got a name for you when you're the greatest wrestler in wrestling today. They don't call you a great wrestler… they call you The Grappler! Beat me if you can!"

Damn, it felt good to say that.

When my WCW contract disappeared back in 1998, I had retreated to a "normal" domestic life. My everyday routine involved working at the Pit Stop and spending time with my family. Some people think it can be a challenge to juggle work, bills and the drama of raising teenage girls. But after you have been slapped by Swede Hanson and berated by Harley Race, those everyday struggles don't seem so bad.

In 2004, Roddy sold the Pit Stop. I had put 14 years of work into the transmission shop and made it a viable business. I'll admit- getting that thing off the ground was tougher than I expected. But thankfully, wrestling prepared me for life after wrestling. Not to get all Dr. Phil on you, but I have found that you can overcome most everyday obstacles by simply working hard, treating people right and staying positive. That approach made me a heavyweight champion *and* a successful businessman.

You may remember that back in 1990, Roddy and I had agreed to split the proceeds of the shop's sale 50/50. That was all a handshake deal, with no contracts. When he finally sold the property, the Hot Rod wasn't legally obligated to give me a nickel. But here's the thing about Roddy Piper- he is, at his core, a man of his word. As soon as the deal closed, he cut me a check for 50 percent of the sale (despite the objections of his financial advisor) and I used that money to pay off the mortgage on my house. After a quarter century of busting my hump and taking bumps, I finally had some security for my family.

After we sold the shop, I joined Roddy on the road as his assistant/bodyguard. The word "bodyguard" is something of a misnomer really; I was there to make sure his personal appearances went smoothly and to keep away the occasional psycho fan. That whole experience could be another book. In 2006 we were working an L.A. sci-fi convention when I received a phone call from my daughter Brandi, who was expecting her first child.

"Daddy- my water just broke!"

That is an incredible phone call for any expectant grandfather- the only problem was that I was a thousand miles from home! I told her not to panic and then (completely engulfed in panic) I tracked down Katie and told her to call an ambulance. She instructed me to relax and get home when I could. A few minutes later I was knocking on Roddy's hotel room door with a suitcase in hand. A father of four, Rod had no problem reading the scene.

"You're leaving aren't you?" he asked.

"I'm sorry," I told him. "I don't think I can do this anymore."

"Don't worry about it," Rod replied. "You go take care of your girl."

That's exactly what I did. Brandi gave birth to a beautiful daughter named Leslie, and Katie and I were instantly in love. There was no way I was going back on the road with Roddy- I wanted to be home to watch Leslie grow up. So, I used my Pit Stop experience to land a job working on motors at a home improvement store. It wasn't the most glamorous job, but it paid the bills and gave me plenty of time with Grandpa's little girl.

You know what's odd? Despite all the crazy things I have done- from wrestling Andre in a dome, to driving down a freeway with the Nature Boy- nothing has given me more pure joy than spending an afternoon with my granddaughter. It's such a basic thing, but it means so much. When I think about my wife, my daughters and my grandbaby, I know that I have done something good in this life.

But don't worry… I still find time to be bad.

Over the past fifteen years, I have worked for just about every independent wrestling promotion in the Portland area. Obviously no one can recreate the glory days of Don Owen and the Sports Arena, but I love the business and wouldn't stay away if you paid me. I was still actively wrestling up until a few years ago, when my doctor told me that I had to stop. Three decades of bumps had left me with serious neck problems and I had to have my 5th and 6th vertebrae replaced. The surgeon, who was also a wrestling fan, did not sugarcoat my prognosis.

"You can't take any big falls like the ones I have seen you take on TV," he told me. "It's not a question of if you'll end up paralyzed. It's a question of if you'll even survive."

That was the end of that. I loved wrestling, but there was no way I was dying for the business. So, from that point on I have worked primarily as a booker and trainer for several local promotions. And since my injuries don't prevent me from cutting promos, I also appear on camera as a manager. The fans still boo the hell out of me, which I love, but my greatest pleasure comes from teaching young workers the art and psychology of our great sport. The Pacific Northwest is home to some great professional wrestlers (I encourage you to look them up on YouTube) and I am proud to have played a part in their collective success.

Which brings me back to my farewell match.

Despite what my doctor said, I knew that I had at least one match left in these old legs and I wanted to give it to Colt Toombs. I had known the kid since he was in diapers and to this day he still calls me "Uncle Lenny." Colt is a respectful, humble young man and, when you consider what his father has done for my family, this job was a no-brainer.

Colt was nervous for his first match, but that's true for any rookie. I wanted to throw up before my debut, and that was in a room full of drunks at the Silver Wings Ballroom. Colt would be working his first match in front of thousands of television viewers while simultaneously trying to live up to the legacy of his Hall of Fame dad. There was a lot of pressure on the kid's shoulders. But he was in good hands.

After all, I had made a career out of making other wrestlers look good, and I didn't even like half of them. Colt was like family to me, and I promised that I would do everything possible to make his talent shine through.

"Just listen to me out there," I told him. "You'll be fine."

A few minutes later, we were facing off in the ring.

233

As we locked up, I didn't even think about the fact that this would be my last match. I was concentrating on Colt- whispering directions and making sure that everything went as planned. Because I had the size advantage, we planned a couple of spots where he back-flipped out of an armbar and then leapfrogged over me and landed a dropkick. The studio audience began to rally behind the rookie and a small "Colt" chant began.

I was smiling on the inside and snarling on the outside.

Eventually, I gained the advantage on my young opponent and backed him into a corner. There, I nailed Colt with the stiffest chops and slaps I could muster. He reeled in pain, and I kept striking him harder and harder. This was all part of breaking into pro wrestling- I cared about Colt, but if I went soft on him then he would have a false sense of security in his future matches. Pain will always be a part of pro wrestling and that's why Uncle Lenny didn't hold anything back.

I promise kid, you'll thank me for this one day.

By this point, the kids in the audience began screaming at their new hero to fight back. As the referee turned his back to check on Colt, I began kicking the mat with my right foot. The old school fans began to scream bloody murder because they knew The Grappler's boot was locked and loaded. I grabbed Colt by his hair and then whipped him into the ropes. When he bounced back, I lifted my leg to deliver the knockout blow.

But, just as we planned, Colt recovered in time to grab my boot in mid-air. He then spun me around, kicked me in the gut and latched on a front facelock. From there, Colt Toombs dropped The Grappler with- you guessed it- a DDT.

After the referee made the three count, I rolled out of the ring and on to the studio floor where I pretended to be seriously injured. In reality, I was swelling with pride. Our match had gone just as planned and Colt had done one hell of a job. I was thrilled to kickstart his career with a victory and go out like a professional. After the taping, we shared a hug.

"Thank you for *everything* Uncle Lenny," he said with a smile.

Gratitude like that is something that I have received a lot of in the past few years. Even people that have never heard of Lynn Denton have heard me praised by some legendary figures. In his WWE Hall of Fame acceptance speech, The Ultimate Warrior personally thanked me for contributing to his success. After that, I read an interview where Jake Roberts called me one of his "favorite guys to ever wrestle". Finally, I heard a podcast where Hall of Fame announcer Jim Ross called me one of "the most underutilized talents of the past several generations". In other words, I was a talented worker that made other wrestlers look good, but I could have achieved more individual success. I was a local star that should have been a superstar.

I don't know if I completely agree with that assessment: I did accomplish a lot of great things in the past 35 years. But, during my journey from Humble, Texas to the Heavyweight Championship, I also helped a lot of friends along the way. If that's how I'm remembered- as a talented worker who helped elevate some all-time legends- well, I'm thrilled. Sure, that kind of sentiment won't put me in the Hall of Fame, but it will definitely put a smile on my face.

With that thought, I'll wrap things up with a new take on an old promo:

They've got a name for you when you're a great wrestler that is always ready to help your brothers succeed! They don't call you a great wrestler... they call you The Grappler!

Beat me if you can!

ACKNOWLEDGMENTS

When we set out to write this book, we wanted to give a truthful and accurate account of professional wrestling's "territorial" era. That can be a tricky proposition when you are trying to remember matches and events from thirty years ago. It's twice as tricky when you have been DDT'd approximately one million times in the past three decades. This book represents my recollections of professional wrestling in the 1970s, 80s and 90s. We made every effort to corroborate those memories by reviewing old video clips, news accounts and match results. Unfortunately, many old professional wrestling programs have been lost to history, while others are locked up in a vault in Stamford, Connecticut. So, if you feel a few minor details are "off", that's probably because we were unable to find footage of a particular match or event. I promise that we are not trying to "work" anyone.

Having said that, we would like to thank all the wrestlers, fans and writers who are working to preserve the history of professional wrestling. In particular, we would like to thank our friend Rich Patterson who has preserved hundreds of hours of Portland Wrestling broadcasts that would have otherwise been lost. Rich was an invaluable source when it came to dates and results from the "House of Action". We also would like to thank the talented David Sherman for designing the cover for this book.

We must also thank our good friend Roddy Piper for writing the foreword, and generously sharing this book with his fans around the world. Often times, when you meet a childhood hero, they don't measure up to your lofty expectations. But Roddy Piper *exceeds* those expectations- he is a great performer and an even better person.

Of course, we must thank our wives and children for their love and support. After all, they may read this and if we leave them out, we'll never hear the end of it.

In all seriousness, we are two lucky men that have been blessed with wonderful families and incredible women. We couldn't have done any of this without you.

Finally, a sincere THANK YOU to pro wrestling fans everywhere. *You are the ones that make dreams come true.* Without your support and passion, we're just a bunch of guys rolling around in a ring.

ABOUT THE AUTHORS

Better known as "The Grappler", **Edward Lynn Denton** has worked in professional wrestling for over 35 years. He is currently the booker for the West Coast Wrestling Connection and lives in Portland with his wife Katie. He has two daughters and a granddaughter that he spoils rotten.

For the past 15 years, **Joe Vithayathil** has worked as a television news reporter. He lives in Beaverton, Oregon with his wife Jenny and two daughters.

CPSIA information can be obtained at www.ICGtesting.com
Printed in the USA
LVOW12s2005260515

439952LV00030B/801/P